THE COOKBOOK

THE COOKBOOK

{ CONTENTS }

Foreword by April Bloomfield   6
The Intro   8
Drinks   18
Snacks   58
Meats, Sauces & Rubs   102
Slaws & Sides   186
Sweet Stuff   244
Index   282
Acknowledgments   287

FOREWORD

BY

{ APRIL BLOOMFIELD }

· · · · · · · · · · · · ·

Perfecting barbecue (BBQ) is a slow process. It takes time to get it right. From smoking a whole hog to finding the perfect sweet-to-spicy ratio in a sauce, it can take years to reach satisfying results. In the American South, BBQ is something of a bragging right. Families hold decades-old secret recipes dear to their hearts. Considering the commitment and individuality of a truly great BBQ recipe, it is inspiring when a new restaurant introduces something distinctive and delicious. The undertaking is even more impressive when the restaurant isn't in the US, as most are, but in London.

Pitt Cue, by far, serves some of the most refined BBQ I have ever eaten. Simply put, the meat is cooked to perfection. The smoke is elegant and the meat is so juicy and tender that it melts off the bone with each bite. I appreciate the English charm that comes through in the manageable portions served on white-enameled trays with sides served in pickle jars. Delicate but packed with flavor.

I really appreciate Pitt Cue's take on BBQ. You can tell that they care. It is especially obvious in the way the hickory chips have been burnt off to just the right point. It's that moment when you see the thin blue line of smoke with its intoxicating aroma and all that's left is the sweet layered smoke that has gently laid itself over the copious amount of beef ribs, pork shoulders, and sausage. Pitt Cue makes one of the most amazing sausages, almost like cotechino; delicately smoked and lightly charred. And the spicy short ribs are something I often crave. They are cooked in a spicy-yet-sweet vinegary sauce with hints of overly blackened bell peppers that makes them irresistible and totally addictive.

There is no mistaking Pitt Cue's attention to detail. The pride they take in the food they produce is reflected in all the recipes they share with you here. This book will be loved again and again and the pages will undoubtedly be coated with the sweet, smoky residues of tenderly made BBQ. And who knows? Maybe some of the recipes will become family secrets of your own.

· · · · · · · · · · · · ·

THE | # INTRO

Before Pitt Cue

At some point in history our ancestors discovered that meat tastes better when cooked, and soon after they worked out that grilling is best done over the glowing coals of a dying fire. The evolution of man is intrinsically linked to cooking meat over fire. The manipulation of fire by Homo erectus provided early humans with warmth, protection, and a point of social contact, but most importantly brought with it a radical change in the way dinner was served. Our ancestors had the means to evolve only so far until they realized their ability to cook hunks of animal meat to make it digestible and, with this massive change in the way we could assimilate protein, our brains grew considerably. Barbecue is unequivocally the oldest form of cooking and is quite possibly the very thing that made us human!

Barbecue as we know it sprouted from the Caribbean in the form of barbacoa and was spread by Spanish explorers throughout the region. They also introduced the pig into the Americas, which in itself is a pretty awesome achievement, and the Native American People in turn introduced the Spanish to the concept of true slow cooking and preserving with smoke. Eventually this smoking went from a method of cooking or preserving food to a way of flavoring food when these Spanish colonists settled in South Carolina, and it was in that early American colony that Europeans first learned to prepare and to eat "real" barbecue. During this period, poverty in the Southern states meant that every part of the pig was eaten or saved for later including the extremities and variety meats, and because of the effort to rear and cook these hogs, pig slaughtering was a time for celebration and merriment, and the neighborhood would be invited to join in.

If only more of these gatherings were seen today. These feasts were called "pig pickin's" and traditional Southern barbecue continued to grow out of these gatherings.

Every part of the Southern states has its own particular variety of barbecue, particularly concerning the sauces, but also extending to the cuts, spice rubs, wood, and types of meat they use. But of course, barbecue is not solely a culture and cuisine of the US. It is a technique used all over the world, the very first technique to be mastered in fact! Almost every culture and country has their own form of barbecue, from the asador found in northern Spain, the asado in Argentina, the ocakbasi of Turkey, or robatayaki in Japan. All these forms of barbecue inspire and inform us and we are guilty of that very British tendency for mixing styles from wherever it is we feast and fatten ourselves.

Our First Year

In 2011 Tom and Jamie formed Pitt Cue, named after the small village where Tom grew up near Winchester. They started with very few expectations, and seemed destined for failure. Everything kept going wrong, and had they not developed an invaluable talent for "winging it" the history of Pitt Cue could have been a lot shorter. The smoker was stopped at customs (apparently they had to check no families or bombs were hiding inside) and arrived the day before they were due to open. Given the fact that our pork shoulders needed a solid 15 hours to cook, this was a significant setback. It was promptly housed under a DIY rickety lean-to in the back passage of a friend's deli.

KELSO
NUT-BROWN
LAGER.

COTTRELL
OLD·YANKEE
ALE

SIXPOINT
VIENNA
PALE

CAPTAIN
LAWRENCE
·LIQUID·
GOLD

WANDERING
·STAR·
MILD
HEART

CONEY
ISLAND
·PILS·

It was sod's law that the café across the road was a vegan stronghold with many of the surrounding residents members of the dark side. Those divine meaty smells that our smoker put out through the night were not so enticing apparently. It would be nice to think we converted some people with those smells. In reality, very few of them saw the light and we had weekly complaints. Even those residents of the meatier sensibility kicked up a stink as we kept them awake with middle of the night pork prep, dishwashing sessions, and Captain Beefheart stuck on repeat.

The used catering trailer was twice the size as expected, and our beat-up 4x4 compiled the already mounting problems when she gave up the ghost the night before opening. Fortunately, RAC roadside assistance took pity on us. About a week later than anticipated we opened the trailer's hatches for the first time on Friday 20th May; fortunately there had been enough group texts and emails to guarantee some custom.

Slowly but surely Pitt Cue gained a following on Twitter, which in turn solicited the attention of some influential London-based bloggers and then gradually the ladies and gentlemen of the press caught wind of our pig meddling. There were all-day parties, all-night parties, some terrible public dancing, daily sell-outs, an unhealthy amount of staff picklebacks, no sleep whatsoever, collaborations with some brilliant restaurants and people, and we even managed to stop the trains from Charing Cross to Waterloo after the billowing smoke from our half-drum jerk barbecues was seen through the railroad tracks. At the end of the summer, Pitt Cue had been reviewed in publications as diverse as the *Evening Standard* and *Eurostar*

magazine, and more importantly had amassed several thousand followers on Twitter, a loyal army who turned out regularly throughout one of the most miserable summers on record to eat pig, bosh picklebacks and Fernet Brancas, and listen to a some horrendously amateur busking on the South Bank (we were very close to throwing one particularly painful bag-piper into the Thames) while getting soaked under the most porous bridge in London. After that initial summer trading on the South Bank, we teamed up with a few of those regulars, Richard of Hawksmoor, and Simon and Andy of The Albion, to help us grow up a little and open a bricks-and-mortar restaurant in Soho in January 2012.

Pitt Cue is now barely a year old, very young to be writing a cookbook perhaps, but these recipes are just a little snapshot of some of our first year, combined with an articulation of our attitude toward food and farming, an attitude that seems to prevail today. The attitude of anything is possible and that rules are there to be broken, or at least bent a little, as long as the results are super tasty.

While researching for the restaurant, we traveled extensively throughout the Southern states in search of inspiration and lots of bourbon. We found barbecue to be localized, much the same as Italian food is regionalized, and were amazed at both the quality and variety of food to be found. Most significantly perhaps, our travels confirmed that trying to replicate US barbecue was exactly the route we did not want to go down. We just needed to carry on cooking food that we enjoyed eating, keeping it simple, and using the very best British produce to do so.

Barbecue is affected by many variables and this is what makes it such a challenge to nail, as well as what makes it interesting. Although our recipes suggest cooking times and temperatures, the reality is that these will soon become irrelevant, little more than rough guidelines, when you get going on your own barbecue and using the meat you have sourced yourself.

Your barbecue and your meat will be different from ours and this is just the first variable to consider. Our meat recipes should thus be taken as a guide to how to approach your barbecue. Barbecue is a technique, just as poaching, baking, and frying are techniques, and should be approached similarly. If you source the very best meat for your daily cooking, do the same when cooking with fire and smoke; if you buy the lesser cuts of meat for braising and long slow roasting, do not feel you have to change this habit on the barbecue. The practice of sourcing meat should not change for a new technique and this is perhaps the most important thing to take on board. When you combine grilling and smoking with stunning meat there is very little that needs to be done above and beyond to create a brilliant meal. We have eaten great barbecue all over the world but the best meals are repeatedly had at the tables of those who put the sourcing and the provenance of their produce up there with the skills they use to cook them.

Although our recipes are often simple, the real work started quite some time ago, on an expanse of beautiful green countryside or woodland where the animals are free to roam, root, and frolic. In this book you'll see our own animals that are reared in Pitt, in the woods (our "Pigtopia") running free to forage—Pitt Pigs if you will—and at the time of writing we have already taken many to their final destination and served them in the restaurant. The results of our labors have proved jaw dropping, as far removed from any pork we'd ever cooked as can be; a revelation.

By the time this book is published we will have a sizable herd of pigs, producing what we believe to be the best pork in the country. We hope to be rearing all our own pigs for the restaurant in the near future. It is, for us, the only way to guarantee that the very best pork goes into the restaurant each day: pork as it once tasted from pigs living the lives they deserve to live.

It takes time for an animal to grow, and although modern farming methods and breeds speed things up, this makes for the kind of flaccid, tasteless mush that can be found on the shelves of your local supermarket. We strongly encourage you to source the best possible meat you can and to engage with your local butcher. The future of small dedicated farmers really does hinge on us buying better meat.

Next

We have ambitions to rear and keep a herd of Highland Cattle: Pitt Beef. We also want to open more Pitt Cues, not identikit copies but restaurants with the same philosophy of sourcing and cooking style, each one very different but connected. Watch this space.

Tom, Jamie, Simon, and Richard
January 2013

DRINKS

DRINKS

· · · · · · · · · · · ·

ALL BOURBON IS WHISKEY
NOT ALL WHISKEY IS BOURBON
{ A VERY, VERY BRIEF HISTORY OF BOURBON }

· · · · · · · · · · · ·

Bourbon is an unsung hero in the UK, the underappreciated and undervalued stepchild of the spirits world, and Pitt Cue is out to change all that. It is the quintessential American liquor, with roots that go straight back to the men who shaped the country: George Washington made it, as did Abraham Lincoln's father—and it even provoked America's first civil war, the Whiskey Rebellion of 1791–4, sparked by a tax on distilled spirits levied to help pay for the War of Independence. Amazingly, it took George Washington more men to put down an army of whiskey distillers than to defeat the British: no wonder Americans have had a love affair with the spirit ever since.

In a strange twist of fate, it was the Scots and Irish, fleeing famine and religious persecution in the British Isles, who took distilling techniques to North America. But there, too, they faced an anti-Catholic society, so as soon as they could, many continued west. In what is now the modern state of Kentucky, these settlers were given land as part of a government incentive as long as they promised to grow corn. Naturally, they used this to make whiskey. For this reason, we have

one of the few remaining wholly corn whiskeys on our list at Pitt Cue.

The name "bourbon" derives from a county within what is now Kentucky. It takes its name from the French royal family, in recognition of the assistance the French gave the Americans during the War of Independence. Ah, the irony.

There are various people credited as being the first to distill bourbon— Elijah Craig and Evan Williams being favorites; however, no one really knows, and to name a single person is fanciful. What is true is that in Kentucky the settlers found a land flowing with pure, alkaline water from limestone deposits beneath the soil. The spirit that flows from the stills is clear and is known as "white dog mash" (a version of which we also stock behind the bar), so called because it is clear and has a bite like a dog. It was this that was drunk before the whole process of barrel aging was developed. Surplus whiskey distilled in Kentucky was placed in barrels to be sent south down the Mississippi River to places such as New Orleans. Legend has it that the barrels were stamped with the word

"Bourbon" to designate their origin... Whatever the truth of that is, the intense heat of the South—combined with the duration of the transit and presumably additional storage time— led people to discover the maturing and mellowing effects of keeping the spirit in barrels. Like many food and drink legends, whether champagne or roquefort cheese, the discovery was a happy mistake. Later, the practice of aging the whiskey in charred barrels became common and set us well on the way to modern bourbon.

It is claimed that the characteristic properties of aging spirit in charred oak were discovered at a time when the only barrels available to whiskey makers were those that had been previously used to store salted fish, and to get rid of the smell they charred the inside of the barrels. The longer the maturation in barrel, the more flavor and color is imparted to the bourbon. But there are two downsides: first, if left too long in a barrel, the bourbon can become overly woody and unpleasant tasting. Second, the longer bourbon remains in a barrel the more spirit is lost to evaporation and leakage. Typical maturation periods range from two years upward. Currently, we stock bourbons that have been aged for as many as ten, twelve, eighteen, or more years in barrel.

With the proliferation of distilleries came the growth of movements to put them out of business. The temperance movement whipped the churches into choruses of disapproval and led directly to the Prohibition Act in 1919, when the consumption of alcohol was almost universally banned in the United States: see *Boardwalk Empire* for details. Entrepreneurial man that he was, Jamie's grandfather resorted to making "bathtub gin," which might have contributed to his early death. During this time, most Americans who found a way to continue drinking had to rely on the lighter-flavored whiskey that was smuggled in from Canada, which meant that the more strongly flavored bourbons and ryes fell out of fashion when Prohibition was repealed in 1933.

From the beginning of Pitt Cue, bourbon has been a crucial part of our menu. Well before that, it's fair to say we've long been drawn to bars, and Jamie in particular has always felt their irresistible allure. As a child, he spent Christmas and Easter in the French Alps, always staying in the same hotel. Being the only child of a single mother, somewhat more used to the company of adults than his peers, the bartender let him stand behind the speed-rail and help out a little bit, while Jamie watched him ply his craft. Social services would have had a field day. On Jamie's twelfth birthday, his mother gave him a bartender's handbook, a cocktail shaker, a marble slab, and two cases of spirits—and told him to get on with it. The rest, as they say, is history.

SOME WHISKEY TERMS

BOURBON
A whiskey with a corn content of between 51–80% is classified as bourbon. The remainder of the formula can be made of rye, wheat, malted barley, or malted rye.

RYE
Rye is another form of American whiskey but must be made from at least 51% rye, the other ingredients of the mash being, typically, corn and barley.

SINGLE BARREL
A whiskey for which each bottle comes from an individual aging barrel instead of being created by blending together the contents of various barrels to provide a consistency of color and flavor.

SMALL BATCH
This rather unspecific term is meant to induce greater confidence in the consumer because the contents of a relatively small number of selected barrels are combined, but because there is no set parameter for the term it is pretty meaningless...

STRAIGHT WHISKEY
Any whiskey that has been aged for a minimum of two years in charred, new oak barrels is a straight whiskey. All of the bourbons served at Pitt Cue are straight whiskeys.

THIS TWO-SHOT DRINK DOESN'T
REALLY QUALIFY AS A COCKTAIL,
BUT IT IS SO INTEGRAL TO PITT
CUE THAT THERE IS NO WAY WE
CAN LEAVE IT OUT. IT BEGAN LIFE
IN NEW YORK, WHERE A SHOT OF
JAMESON'S IRISH WHISKEY WAS
"CHASED" WITH A SHOT OF PICKLE
JUICE. THE IDEA BEING THAT THE
SAVORINESS OF THE PICKLE JUICE
ACTS TO NEUTRALIZE THE EFFECTS
OF THE HARSHNESS OF THE WHISKEY
ON THE THROAT AND TASTE BUDS,
PREPPING YOU READY FOR ROUND
TWO AND BEYOND. WE OPENED THE
PITT CUE TRAILER WITH BOURBON
PICKLEBACKS AND THESE SHOTS
RAPIDLY BECAME SYNONYMOUS
WITH OUR BUSINESS.

THE PICKLEBACK

SERVES 1

bourbon	1¼ ounces
Our Pickle Brine *(see page 78)*	1 ounce

These two shots are to be taken in quick
succession, the whiskey first and then the
pickle juice. We prefer a smaller shot of
pickle juice … we also recommend trying the
juice from other types of pickles: pickled
beet juice looks splendid and pickled pear
juice is festive in the winter months.

THE BOILERMAKER

AGAIN, NOT STRICTLY A COCKTAIL, BUT
NO LESS DELICIOUS FOR THAT. THIS DRINK
EXPERIENCE COMBINES A GLASS OF BEER
AND A SHOT OF WHISKEY AND IS SAID TO
DATE BACK TO THE BARS THAT CLUSTERED
AROUND THE STEEL MILLS IN THE
HEYDAY OF THE INDUSTRIAL BOOM. THE
COMBINATION PROVIDED JUST THE RIGHT
BALANCE OF REFRESHMENT AND INTOXICATION
REQUIRED BY THE MEN WHO CAME OFF SHIFTS
IN THE SWELTERING FACTORIES.

SERVES 1

bourbon	1¼ ounces
draft beer	8 ounces

Some people pour the shot into the beer,
some even drop in the entire filled shot
glass, but we prefer to chase the shot with
the beer.

— MANHATTANS —

RATHER LIKE ALMOST EVERY CLASSIC COCKTAIL, THE ORIGINS OF THE MANHATTAN ARE LOST IN THE MISTS OF TIME, IN THIS CASE THE NINETEENTH CENTURY. ESSENTIALLY IT CONSISTS OF A SPIRIT AND RED VERMOUTH—THE ARCHETYPAL VERSION INVOLVES RYE WHISKEY, BECAUSE THE GREATER SPICINESS IS BETTER ABLE TO DO BATTLE WITH THE OTHERWISE POTENTIALLY OVERPOWERING VERMOUTH.

THE MANHATTAN

SHOULD THIS CONCOCTION SEEM A LITTLE TOO AUSTERE, ADD A SPOONFUL OR TWO OF THE SYRUP FROM A JAR OF MARASCHINO CHERRIES TO MAKE THE DRINK SWEETER, A SO-CALLED SWEET MANHATTAN. YOU CAN ALSO EXPERIMENT WITH DIFFERENT TYPES OF BITTERS—PART OF THE JOY OF MAKING COCKTAILS IS DISCOVERING WAYS TO FINE TUNE DRINKS TO MAKE THEM MORE TO YOUR OWN TASTE.

SERVES 1

rye whiskey	1¾ ounces
sweet vermouth	1 ounce
Angostura bitters	a dash

GARNISH

maraschino cherry or orange slice (or both)

Assemble all the ingredients in an ice-filled old-fashioned glass and stir to ensure that they are mixed and chilled.

Garnish with a maraschino cherry or a slice of orange (or both), and add two straws.

BIG MAC 'N' RYE

THIS IS POSSIBLY THE FIRST PITT CUE COCKTAIL—DEVELOPED ON THE TRAILER IN MAY 2011. INSPIRED BY THE DIRTY MARTINI, WHEREBY SOME OF THE LIQUOR FROM A JAR OF PICKLED ONIONS IS ADDED TO THE DRINK, OUR PICKLE JUICE IS ADDED TO A CLASSIC MANHATTAN. THE SAVORY SWEETNESS OF THE PICKLE JUICE CREATES A DRINK THAT WE BELIEVE COMPLEMENTS THE FOOD WE SERVE IN A MOST DELIGHTFUL WAY. SOMEONE WHO ONCE TRIED THE DRINK COMMENTED THAT IT TASTED SIMILAR TO THE SAUCE USED ON A BIG MAC, AND SO THE NAME WAS BORN.

SERVES 1

rye whiskey	1¾ ounces
red vermouth	1 ounce
Our Pickle Brine (see page 78)	a dash
Angostura bitters	a dash

GARNISH

orange zest or slice

Assemble all the ingredients in an ice-filled old-fashioned glass and stir to ensure that they are mixed and chilled.

Garnish with orange zest or a slice of orange, and add two straws.

THE J-DAWG

THIS RUM MANHATTAN WAS NAMED AFTER JAMIE BY COLIN GRANDFIELD, ONE OF THE BARTENDERS AT PITT CUE, A JOKE THAT STUCK ... WE USE A VERY DELICIOUS AND RICH DARK PANAMANIAN RUM, WHICH IS AGED IN USED BOURBON BARRELS (SEE THE THEME?) AND HAS A SWEETNESS THAT MAKES THE ADDITION OF MARASCHINO SYRUP OPTIONAL. HOWEVER, ALWAYS EXPERIMENT WITH THE FLAVORS AND, IF YOU THINK THAT THE DRINK COULD DO WITH AN INCREASE IN RICHNESS, FEEL FREE TO ADD SOME.

SERVES 1

dark rum	1¾ ounces
red vermouth	1 ounce
orange bitters	a dash
Angostura bitters	a dash

GARNISH

orange slice

Assemble all the ingredients in an ice-filled old-fashioned glass and stir to ensure that they are mixed and chilled.

Garnish with a slice of orange, and add two straws.

CUE JUMPER

THIS IS A DELICIOUS VARIANT ON A MANHATTAN, USING BOURBON (WHICH IS SLIGHTLY LIGHTER THAN RYE WHISKEY) AND POMEGRANATE PICKLE JUICE. IT STARTED OUT AS A PUN IN SEARCH OF A DRINK, BUT AFTER USING SOME LEFTOVERS FROM A BATCH OF PICKLED POMEGRANATE, IT ALL CAME TOGETHER. THE PICKLED POMEGRANATE JUICE IS LIGHTER AND LESS HEADY THAN OUR REGULAR PICKLE JUICE AND YET DOESN'T LOSE ANY RICHNESS. IT IS A MARVELOUS DRINK, WHICH, ALAS, WE SELDOM HAVE ON THE MENU BECAUSE THERE ISN'T MUCH CALL FOR PICKLED POMEGRANATES.

SERVES 1

bourbon	1¾ ounces
red vermouth	1 ounce
Pickled Pomegranate juice (see page 197)	1 ounce
Angostura bitters	a dash

GARNISH

orange or blood orange slice

Assemble all the ingredients in an ice-filled old-fashioned glass and stir to ensure that they are mixed and chilled.

Garnish with a slice of orange or blood orange, and add two straws.

RED RYE

THE RED RYE IS A CLASSIC MANHATTAN AUGMENTED BY THE ADDITION OF FERNET BRANCA. AH, FERNET … JAMIE IS ALWAYS IN SEARCH OF A WAY TO GET THIS AMAZING AMARO INTO COCKTAILS TO JUSTIFY ITS PRESENCE ON THE BACK BAR, WHERE IT NEEDS TO BE BECAUSE ITS REVIVING PROPERTIES ARE OFTEN CALLED UPON, IN THE FORM OF SHOTS, DURING THE COURSE OF THE DAY. THESE AND OTHER MEDICINAL PROPERTIES LED TO THE SALE OF FERNET REMAINING LEGAL DURING THE ERA OF PROHIBITION.

SERVES 1

rye whiskey	1¾ ounces
red vermouth	1 ounce
Fernet Branca	½ ounce
Angostura bitters	a dash

GARNISH

lemon slice

Assemble all the ingredients in an ice-filled old-fashioned glass and stir to ensure that they are mixed and chilled.

Garnish with a slice of lemon, and add two straws.

SOURS

POSSIBLY THE MOST POPULAR STYLE OF COCKTAIL AT PITT CUE,
SOURS COME IN A WIDE VARIETY OF GUISES. BUT LET'S START
AT THE BEGINNING.

WHISKEY SOUR

ONCE THE SWEETNESS, OR OTHERWISE, OF THE LEMON JUICE IS TAKEN INTO ACCOUNT,
THE AMOUNT OF SUGAR SYRUP YOU ADD IS ALL A MATTER OF TASTE. BUT WE FEEL
THAT BOTH SOUR AND SWEET SHOULD PLAY AN EQUAL PART AND NEITHER ONE SHOULD
DOMINATE THE OTHER. THE ANGOSTURA BITTERS ADD A DELICIOUS, ALMOST NUTMEGGY
RICHNESS TO THE DRINK. THE TRICK IS TO SHAKE THE COCKTAIL FIERCELY TO DEVELOP
FROTH ON TOP WHEN IT IS POURED INTO A GLASS.

SERVES 1

bourbon	1¾ ounces
lemon juice	1¾ ounces
Sugar Syrup *(see page 56)*	a dash
Angostura bitters	a dash
free-range egg white	¼

GARNISH

lemon slice

Shake all the ingredients hard in a Boston
shaker with ice, then strain over ice in
an old-fashioned glass.

Garnish with a slice of lemon, and add
two straws.

NEW YORK SOUR

THE NEW YORK SOUR WAS THE ONLY COCKTAIL FRAN ASTBURY, OUR BAR MANAGER, INSISTED THAT WE HAVE ON OUR DRINKS MENU WHEN WE OPENED IN JANUARY 2012. VISUALLY IT IS A DELIGHT, BECAUSE THE RED WINE BLEEDS INTO THE CREAMY SOUR BELOW. THE TRICK HERE IS TO POUR THE WINE SLOWLY DOWN THE LONG TWISTED HANDLE OF A BAR SPOON. THE DIFFERENCES IN THE SPECIFIC GRAVITIES OF THE WINE AND THE SOUR ARE SUFFICIENT TO SUPPORT THE WINE ON TOP. CAREFUL EXPERIMENTATION WITH THE SWEETNESS OF THE SOUR IS REQUIRED, BUT THE DILEMMA IS THAT THE ONLY WAY TO ENSURE THE WINE FLOATS IS TO MAKE THE SOUR OVERLY SWEET. IN THE END THE DRINK WILL PROBABLY BE MIXED TOGETHER, SO THE RESULTS OF ALL YOUR EFFORTS WILL BE, AS EVER, TRANSITORY.

SERVES 1

bourbon	1¼ ounces
lemon juice	1¼ ounces
Sugar Syrup (see page 56)	a dash
Angostura bitters	a dash
red wine	1¾ ounces

Shake everything except the red wine in a Boston shaker with ice, then strain over ice in an old-fashioned glass.

Float an inch or so of red wine on top by pouring it down a spiral-handled bar spoon. Add two straws.

NEW PORT SOUR

THIS IS A MORE PUNCHY VERSION OF A NEW YORK SOUR. THE ADDED KICK COMING FROM THE PORT PRESENTS MORE OF A CHALLENGE TO THOSE WISHING TO KEEP THE TWO LAYERS DISTINCT—IT IS ALMOST IMPOSSIBLE, BUT THEN SO LONG AS ONE HAS WILLING DRINKERS THERE SHOULD BE NO WASTAGE!

SERVES 1

bourbon	1¼ ounces
lemon juice	1¼ ounces
Sugar Syrup (see page 56)	a dash
Angostura bitters	a dash
late-bottled vintage (LBV) port	1¾ ounces

Shake everything except the port in a Boston shaker with ice, then strain over ice in an old-fashioned glass.

Float an inch or so of the port on top by pouring it down a spiral-handled bar spoon. Add two straws.

SOHO SOUR

THIS COCKTAIL STARTED THE TREND AT PITT CUE OF NAMING COCKTAILS TOPOGRAPHICALLY AND BEGAN LIFE AS ONE OF OUR FAVORITE DRINKS, THE AMARETTO SOUR (1¾ OUNCES AMARETTO, 1¾ OUNCES LEMON JUICE, A DASH OF EGG WHITE, A DASH OF ANGOSTURA BITTERS), FROM WHICH WE REMOVED THE EGG WHITE AND SUBSTITUTED BOURBON. THE RATIO OF AMARETTO HAS BEEN REDUCED TO ACCOMMODATE THE BOURBON, SO SOME SUGAR SYRUP IS NEEDED, BUT BE CAREFUL WITH THE QUANTITY TO AVOID MAKING IT OVERLY SWEET. HOWEVER, WITH A LITTLE EXPERIMENTATION IT ISN'T HARD TO MAINTAIN A BALANCE WITH THE SOURNESS OF THE LEMON JUICE.

SERVES 1

bourbon	1¾ ounces
amaretto	1 ounce
lemon juice	1 ounce
Sugar Syrup (see page 56)	a dash
Angostura bitters	a dash

GARNISH

maraschino or bourbon-soaked chery

Shake all the ingredients in a Boston shaker with ice, then strain over ice in an old-fashioned glass.

Garnish with a maraschino or bourbon-soaked cherry, and add two straws.

CIDER SOUR

WE ARE VERY LUCKY TO HAVE ACCESS TO
THE MOST DELICIOUS FARMHOUSE CIDER,
FROM CORNISH ORCHARDS, AND IT SEEMED
ONLY LOGICAL TO INCORPORATE IT INTO
A COCKTAIL AS WELL. FRAN CAME UP
WITH THIS WONDERFUL CONCOCTION,
PAIRING IT WITH OUR HOUSE BOURBON.
THE SWEETNESS COMES NOT ONLY FROM
THE CIDER BUT ALSO FROM OUR OWN
GINGER SYRUP, WHICH IS EASILY MADE
AND KEEPS VERY WELL. THE RESULT IS
A VERY REFRESHING DRINK THAT QUICKLY
FOUND ITS WAY TO A PERMANENT PLACE
ON OUR COCKTAIL MENU.

SERVES 1

bourbon	1¼ ounces
still cider	1¼ ounces
lemon juice	1 ounce
Ginger Syrup *(see page 56)*	1 ounce

GARNISH

green apple slice

Shake all the ingredients in a Boston shaker
with ice, then strain over ice in an old-
fashioned glass.

Garnish with a slice of green apple, and
add two straws.

THE GANTON

PARTLY INSPIRED BY THE SIDE TRUCK AND INFLUENCED BY SOURS, THE GANTON TAKES ITS NAME FROM THE STREET ON THE CORNER WHERE PITT CUE IS LOCATED IN SOHO. WE TRIED TO DO SOME RESEARCH TO DISCOVER THE PROVENANCE OF THE NAME, BUT AS FAR AS WE CAN TELL THE REFERENCE IS TO A TOWN IN NORTH YORKSHIRE WITH A FAMOUS GOLF COURSE.

SERVES 1

rye whiskey	1¾ ounces
Cointreau	1 ounce
lemon juice	1 ounce
free-range egg white	¼
orange bitters	a dash

GARNISH

orange slice

Shake all the ingredients hard in a Boston shaker with ice, then strain over ice in an old-fashioned glass.

Garnish with a slice of orange, and add two straws.

BUZZ CUT

THIS COCKTAIL USES WHITE DOG MASH, WHICH IS SOMETHING THAT HAS ONLY RECENTLY COME ON TO THE MARKET EVEN THOUGH IT HAS BEEN AVAILABLE FOR CENTURIES. IT IS THE RAW SPIRIT THAT COMES OFF A STILL BEFORE IT IS PLACED INTO A CHARRED OAK BARREL FOR AGING—IN EFFECT IT IS MOONSHINE. DESPITE ITS STRENGTH (THE ABV IS SOMEWHERE IN THE REGION OF 63.5%) IT HAS A NOTICEABLE CORN FLAVOR AND WE KEEP IT ON THE BACK BAR MAINLY AS A CONVERSATION PIECE FOR JAMIE TO START A DISCUSSION ON THE MANUFACTURE OF BOURBON. THIS COCKTAIL WAS NAMED AFTER COLIN GRANDFIELD ON THE OCCASION OF A RATHER DRASTIC HAIRCUT, FOR WHICH REASON IT IS ALSO SERVED WITHOUT A GARNISH.

SERVES 1

applejack (American apple brandy)	1¾ ounces
White Dog Mash	½ ounce
lemon juice	1 ounce
Sugar Syrup (see page 56)	a dash
free-range egg white	¼

Shake all the ingredients hard in a Boston shaker with ice, then strain over ice in an old-fashioned glass. No garnish, but add two straws.

FRENCH TOAST

BOURBON OBVIOUSLY, BUT THIS
COCKTAIL ALSO RELIES ON CHAMBORD, A
FRENCH BLACK RASPBERRY LIQUEUR THAT
COMES IN THE MOST HILARIOUS BOTTLE,
PACKAGED LIKE AN ORB AND SAID TO
DATE BACK TO THE DAYS OF LOUIS XIV.

TO MAKE THIS DRINK, YOU MUST USE
PROPER CLOUDY APPLE JUICE, THE
NICER THE BETTER; THE CLEAR STUFF
JUST WON'T DO. IT IS A DRINK
THAT WE OFTEN GIVE TO THOSE WHO
CLAIM NOT TO LIKE DRINKS MADE
WITH BOURBON … AND IT HAS
NEVER FAILED YET.

SERVES 1

bourbon	1¾ ounces
Chambord	1 ounce
apple juice	1 ounce
cherry bitters	a dash

GARNISH

apple slice

Shake all the ingredients in a Boston
shaker with ice, then strain over ice in
an old-fashioned.

Garnish with a slice of apple, and add
two straws.

INDIAN SUMMER

THIS IS ONE THAT WE MAKE FOR CUSTOMERS
WHO CLAIM NOT TO LIKE WHISKEY.

SERVES 1

rye whiskey	1¼ ounces
Cointreau	1 ounce
lemon juice	⅔ ounce
Sugar Syrup *(see page 56)*	a dash
ginger ale	1¾ ounces

GARNISH

thin cucumber slices	3

Shake the whiskey, Cointreau, lemon juice,
and sugar syrup in a Boston shaker with ice,
then strain over ice in an old-fashioned
glass. Top off the glass with the ginger ale.

Garnish with the thin slices of cucumber,
and add two straws.

MAPPLE

THIS DRINK COMBINES JAMIE'S
MEMORIES FROM ALL OVER AMERICA:
THE MAPLE SYRUP CONJURES UP NEW
ENGLAND, THE BOURBON THE SOUTHERN
STATES, AND THE ORANGE FLORIDA,
WHERE HIS GRANDPARENTS LIVED WHEN
HE WAS GROWING UP. THE COMBINATION
IS AUTUMNAL, BUT DON'T LET IT BE
LIMITED TO SERVING AT THAT TIME
OF THE YEAR.

SERVES 1

bourbon	1 ounce
applejack	1¼ ounces
still cider	1 ounce
maple syrup	½ ounce
orange bitters	a dash
orange wedge	1

GARNISH

orange slice

Add all the liquid ingredients with ice to a Boston shaker, squeeze in the juice from the orange wedge then drop in the wedge as well. Shake, then strain over ice in an old-fashioned glass.

Garnish with a slice of orange, and add two straws.

THE SIDE TRUCK

THIS COCKTAIL IS INCLUDED ON OUR
MENU IN HOMAGE TO THE SIDECAR,
WHICH FAMILY LEGEND HAS IT WAS
INVENTED BY JAMIE'S MOTHER'S
GODFATHER, WHO WAS AN AIDE TO
GENERAL "BLACK JACK" PERSHING
DURING THE FIRST WORLD WAR
AND SPENT MOST OF THE WAR IN
A MOTORCYCLE SIDECAR NEVER FAR
FROM HIS TRUSTY COCKTAIL SHAKER.
IN ADAPTING IT FOR PITT CUE, WE
REPLACED THE BRANDY WITH BOURBON,
AND ADDED SOME BITTERS AND SUGAR
SYRUP TO ROUND OFF THE FLAVORS.

SERVES 1

bourbon	1¼ ounces
Cointreau	1 ounce
lemon juice	1 ounce
orange bitters	a dash
Sugar Syrup (see page 56)	a dash

GARNISH

orange slice

Shake all the ingredients in a Boston shaker with ice, and strain over ice in an old-fashioned glass.

Garnish with a slice of orange, and add two straws.

3 CAMPARI-BASED COCKTAILS

THIS COLLECTION IS ROOTED IN JAMIE'S LOVE OF CAMPARI AND ALL THINGS BITTER.

CAMP AMERICA

THIS COCKTAIL CAME ABOUT AS A RESULT OF BEING PRESENTED WITH A QUANTITY OF BITTER SEVILLE MARMALADE, AND HAS THE ADDED BONUS OF GENERATING CONFUSED LOOKS ON FACES WHEN WE SPOON JAM INTO A COCKTAIL SHAKER. THE TRICK HERE IS TO SHAKE IT WELL TO RELEASE ALL THE DELICIOUS FLAVOR FROM THE THICK-CUT SEVILLE ORANGE RINDS, THEN STRAIN IT SO THAT NONE OF THE RIND GETS INTO THE GLASS. THE LEMON JUICE BALANCES THE SWEETNESS AND LENDS A WONDERFUL COLOR TO THE FINISHED DRINK.

SERVES 1

bourbon	1¾ ounces
Campari	1 ounce
thick-cut bitter seville marmalade	2 teaspoons
lemon juice	a dash

GARNISH

orange or blood orange slice

Shake all the ingredients hard in a Boston shaker with ice, then strain over ice in an old-fashioned glass. Garnish with a slice of blood orange, and add two straws.

BOURBORONI

THIS IS A RIFF ON THE NEGRONI, REPLACING THE GIN WITH BOURBON; ITS ACTUAL NAME IS THE BOULEVARDIER, BUT WE THINK THAT BOURBORONI IS MORE FUN AND CERTAINLY GIVES A GREATER HINT AS TO WHAT'S TO FOLLOW. USE THE BEST RED VERMOUTH YOU CAN FIND—THE MOST DELICIOUS WE'VE EVER TRIED IS THE CARPANO ANTICA FORMULA, THE COST OF WHICH WE PRETEND TO JUSTIFY BECAUSE IT COMES IN 34-OUNCE BOTTLES.

SERVES 1

Campari	1¼ ounces
bourbon	1¼ ounces
sweet vermouth	1¼ ounces

GARNISH

orange slice

Assemble all the ingredients in an ice-filled old-fashioned glass and stir to ensure that they are mixed and chilled. Garnish with a slice of orange, no straws.

LBC

THIS COCKTAIL STARTED LIFE AS A STAFF DRINK—IT WAS SERVED IN RED SOLO PARTY CUPS THAT WE HAD SHIPPED FROM AMERICA. THE FIRST LBC WE EVER SOLD WAS TO A YOUNG WOMAN WHO, WHEN ASKED WHAT SHE WANTED TO DRINK, SPOKE OF HER LOVE OF CAMPARI. IT IS LIGHT AND REFRESHING; ANOTHER PERFECT SUMMER DRINK.

SERVES 1

bourbon	1¾ ounces
Campari	1 ounce
lemon juice	½ ounce
lime, quartered	1

GARNISH

lime slice

Add all the liquid ingredients with ice to a Boston shaker, squeeze in the juice of the lime quarters, then drop the lime quarters in as well. Shake, then strain over ice in an old-fashioned glass.

Garnish with a slice of lime, and add two straws.

HARD LEMONADE I

THIS WAS THE BEST-SELLING DRINK AT
THE PITT CUE TRAILER IN SUMMER.
AT THE RESTAURANT, THE HARD LEMONADE
EVOLVED INTO THE HARD LEMONADE II
(SEE NEXT RECIPE).

SERVES 1

gin	1¾ ounces
elderflower cordial	a dash
homemade lemonade, to top off (see below)	

GARNISH

lemon slices

Assemble all the ingredients in an
ice-filled old-fashioned glass and stir to
ensure that they are mixed and chilled.
Garnish with slices of lemon, and add a straw.

HARD LEMONADE II

THIS IS A PUNCHIER DRINK THAN
ITS ELDER COUSIN, WITH A GREATER
RICHNESS AND COMPLEXITY ACHIEVED
BY REPLACING GIN WITH BOURBON
AND COINTREAU.

SERVES 1

bourbon	1¾ ounces
Cointreau	1 ounce
homemade lemonade, to top off (see below)	

GARNISH

lemon slices

Assemble all the ingredients in an
ice-filled old-fashioned glass and stir to
ensure that they are mixed and chilled.
Garnish with slices of lemon, and add a straw.

LEMONADE SYRUP

MAKES ABOUT 2 CUPS

unwaxed lemons	10
sugar (we use soft light brown)	2 cups
water	1½ cups

Zest the lemons, then juice them, placing
all the zest and juice in a pan. Add the
sugar and the water and heat slowly,
stirring all the time, until the sugar
has dissolved. The liquid should approach
boiling point, but not boil.

Pass the liquid through a sieve to strain
off the zest and lemon seeds.

Bottle, while still warm, in sterilized
bottles (see page 78). The syrup can be kept
in the fridge for several weeks.

For homemade lemonade, dilute to taste:
3 or 4 parts water to 1 part syrup.

For a more unusual syrup, you can also try
adding a tiny amount of fresh chile.

MEAN SHANDY

THE NAME IS A NOD NOT ONLY TO THE
MEANTIME BREWERY, WHICH PRODUCED
THE DRAFT BEER THAT THIS COCKTAIL
WAS FIRST MADE WITH, BUT ALSO TO
THE FACT THAT, WITH THE ADDITION
OF BOURBON, IT IS FAR STRONGER AND
TOUGHER THAN THE AVERAGE LAGER SHANDY
THE BRITISH ARE FAMILIAR WITH.
SHAKING CARBONATED LIQUIDS IN ANY
QUANTITY PRESENTS POSSIBLE HAZARDS,
SO MAKE SURE THE SHAKER IS TIGHTLY
SEALED. OPEN CAREFULLY ONCE SHAKEN.

SERVES 1

bourbon	1¾ ounces
Lemonade Syrup *(see page 42)*	1 ounce
bottled beer	1⅓ ounces

GARNISH

lemon slice

Shake all the ingredients in a Boston
shaker with ice, then strain over ice
in an old-fashioned glass. Garnish with a
slice of lemon, and add two straws.

KENTUCKY LIBRE

THIS IS OUR VERSION OF THE CLASSIC
RUM AND COKE DRINK, THE CUBA LIBRE—
SPANISH FOR "FREE CUBA." AGAIN THE
ORIGINS OF THE NAME ARE UNCERTAIN,
BUT ONE THEORY DATES IT BACK TO
THE SPANISH-AMERICAN WAR OF 1898,
AND THIS IS THE ONE THAT APPEALS
TO JAMIE, BECAUSE HIS GREAT-
GRANDFATHER, ROBERT H. BECKHAM,
FOUGHT IN THAT WAR, TAKING PART IN
THE FAMOUS ACTION ON SAN JUAN HILL.

SERVES 1

bourbon	1¾ ounces
homemade cola, to top off *(see page 56)*	

GARNISH

lime wedge

Assemble all the ingredients in an
ice-filled old-fashioned glass and stir to
ensure that they are mixed and chilled.

Garnish with a wedge of lime, and add
one long straw.

CHERRY COLA

ANOTHER COLA-BASED COCKTAIL, THE CHERRY COLA SELLS INCREDIBLY WELL, BUT THEN AGAIN THE DELICIOUS COMBINATION OF CHERRY AND COLA HAS LONG BEEN UNDERSTOOD. THIS COCKTAIL INSPIRED A SIMPLER VERSION THAT WE SERVE ON THE TRAILER—THE TRASH (SEE RECIPE BELOW).

SERVES 1

bourbon	1¾ ounces
Cherry Heering	1 ounce
lemon juice	1 ounce
Cola Syrup *(see page 56)*	⅔ ounce

GARNISH

maraschino cherry

Shake all the ingredients in a Boston shaker with ice, then strain over ice in an old-fashioned glass.

Garnish with a maraschino cherry, and add two straws.

TRASH

OUR CREATION HERE IS TRYING TO MATCH THE FLAVOR PROFILE OF THAT STABLE OF THE 1980S, CHERRY-FLAVORED COLA—THE FIRST OF THAT RATHER DUBIOUS FAMILY OF "FLAVORED COKES" TO SEE THE LIGHT OF DAY. WE WANTED SOMETHING BOOZY YET DECADENT; THAT WOULD TASTE SLIGHTLY "WRONG" AS IT WERE, BUT IN A CHEERFUL WAY.

SERVES 1

bourbon	1¼ ounces
Cherry Heering	1 ounce
cherry bitters	a dash
cola, to top off	

GARNISH

maraschino cherry

Add all the ingredients to a highball glass and stir well.

Garnish with a maraschino cherry, and add two straws.

BOOM TOWN

THIS COCKTAIL USES OUR OWN COLA
SYRUP. UNLIKE THE FORMULA FOR
COCA COLA™, WHICH SINCE ITS CREATION
IN 1886 HAS BEEN JEALOUSLY GUARDED,
OURS IS AVAILABLE ON PAGE 56.
LIME JUICE IS USED TO CUT THROUGH
THE SWEETNESS OF THE COLA SYRUP.
WE RECOMMEND PLACING THE SQUEEZED
WEDGES IN THE SHAKER AND SHAKING
THEM TOGETHER WITH THE LIQUID
TO INCREASE THE INTENSITY OF
THE FLAVOR, BECAUSE MORE WILL BE
EXTRACTED FROM THE RIND DURING
THE SHAKING PROCESS.

SERVES 1

bourbon	1¼ ounces
Cola Syrup *(see page 56)*	1¼ ounces
draft beer	1¼ ounces
lime wedges, squeezed	4

GARNISH

lime wedge

Shake all the ingredients including the
squeezed lime wedges in a Boston shaker
with ice, then strain over ice in a
highball glass.

Garnish with a wedge of lime, and add one
long straw.

PITT PONY

THIS DRINK WENT THROUGH A COUPLE
OF NAME CHANGES: IT STARTED OUT
AS A KENTUCKY MULE, IN RECOGNITION
OF ITS DEBT TO THE MOSCOW MULE.
BUT NO ONE ORDERED IT WHEN IT
FIRST WENT ON THE SPECIALS BOARD,
SO THE PITT PONY WAS BORN.
IT IS, OF COURSE, POSSIBLE TO USE
STORE-BOUGHT GINGER BEER (THOUGH IT
ISN'T QUITE AS MUCH FUN AS MAKING
YOUR OWN), BUT IN THAT CASE THE
RESULT WILL BE MUCH SWEETER.

SERVES 1

lime wedges	3
bourbon	1¾ ounces
Angostura bitters	a dash
ginger beer (preferably homemade), to top off	

Squeeze the juice of the lime wedges into
an 8-ounce glass and drop in the squeezed
wedges as well. Then pour over the bourbon and add the bitters before stirring the
whole mixture together with ginger beer.

Garnish with the squeezed lime wedges, and
add one long straw.

HAIR OF THE HOG

BACON VODKA IS DEVILISHLY EASY TO MAKE. SIMPLY FRY SOME SMOKED BACON SLICES IN A PAN UNTIL CRISP, THEN DEGLAZE THE PAN WITH SOME VODKA. PLACE THE BACON, ALL THE JUICES, AND THE REST OF THE VODKA IN A SEALED CONTAINER TO STEEP, THEN FREEZE IT BEFORE STRAINING THE CONTENTS TO PRODUCE BACON VODKA. THE CHEAPER THE BACON, THE MORE INTENSE THE VODKA. THE SPICIER THE DRINK, THE BETTER IN OUR OPINION, BUT MAKE SURE THERE AREN'T TOO MANY BITS IN THE SPICE MIX, BECAUSE THEY ALL END UP AT THE BOTTOM OF YOUR GLASS.

SERVES 1

bacon-infused vodka	1¾ ounces
tomato juice	2½ ounces
Spice Mix *(see page 57)*	1 teaspoon (or to taste)

Assemble all the ingredients over ice in a shaker, stir, then strain into an old-fashioned glass, no ice.

Add two straws and serve with Fennel-Cured Scratchings (see page 62).

PINK PIG

IF YOU'VE MADE IT THIS FAR LOOKING FOR A COCKTAIL WITHOUT BOURBON IN IT AND NOT BEEN IMPRESSED WITH THE TWO ALREADY ON OFFER, LET US INTRODUCE THE PINK PIG: MADE WITH RHUBARB SYRUP, OR AT LEAST THE LIQUOR LEFT OVER WHEN STEWING RHUBARB, IT IS ALSO A SEASONAL COCKTAIL. LIGHT AND REFRESHING, THE LEMON MAKES SURE THERE IS SOME RESIDUAL TARTNESS.

SERVES 1

gin	1¾ ounces
rhubarb syrup	1 ounce
lemon juice	a dash
Sugar Syrup *(see page 56)*	a dash

GARNISH

lemon slice

Shake all the ingredients in a Boston shaker with ice, then strain over ice in an old-fashioned glass.

Garnish with a slice of lemon, and add two straws.

BOURBON HOT TODDY

THIS TODDY IS PERFECT FOR A COLD DAY, AND WHILE ITS CURATIVE POWERS IN DEALING WITH A COLD MAY BE IN DOUBT MEDICALLY, THERE IS LITTLE DOUBT THAT PSYCHOLOGICALLY THE PATIENT IS BETTER OFF FOR DRINKING ONE. PLACE THE CLOVE-STUDDED LEMON SLICE IN THE BOTTOM OF THE GLASS AND ADD SOME OF THE BOILING WATER IMMEDIATELY TO RELEASE NOT ONLY THE FLAVOR OF THE LEMON BUT ALSO THE INTENSITY OF THE CLOVE ESSENCE. THE OVERALL EFFECT SURE TAKES THE STING OUT OF BEING LAID UP WITH THE FLU.

SERVES 1

bourbon	1¾ ounces
lemon juice	1 ounce
Honey Syrup *(see page 56)*	a dash
Ginger Syrup *(see page 56)*	a dash
orange bitters	a dash
boiling water, to top off	

GARNISH

lemon slice, studded with cloves

Asssemble all the ingredients in an 8-ounce glass and stir. Garnish with a lemon slice studded with cloves, no straw.

GODFATHER

WHILE ON THE SUBJECT OF GODFATHERS, THIS SEEMS A GOOD PLACE TO PUT THIS COCKTAIL, WHICH JAMIE MADE SURE WAS ON THE MENU AT HIS GODSON JACKSON BOXER'S BAR, AT BRUNSWICK HOUSE IN LONDON, AND THAT MAKES OCCASIONAL APPEARANCES AS A SPECIAL COCKTAIL AT PITT CUE. THOUGH SURPRISINGLY DRINKABLE, THE LACK OF ANY MIXER MAKES IT NOT FOR THE FAINT-HEARTED; THE BITTERS BALANCE THE SWEETNESS OF THE AMARETTO.

SERVES 1

bourbon	1¾ ounces
amaretto	1¼ ounces
orange bitters	a dash

GARNISH

orange slice

Assemble all the ingredients in an ice-filled old-fashioned glass and stir to ensure that they are mixed and chilled.

Garnish with a slice of orange, and add two straws.

GODFATHER PART II

RUNNING WITH THE GODFATHER THEME, HERE THE AMARETTO IS REPLACED BY TUACA, AN ITALIAN VANILLA AND CITRUS LIQUEUR.

SERVES 1

bourbon	1¾ ounces
Tuaca	1¼ ounces
chocolate bitters	a dash

GARNISH

candied orange peel

Assemble all the ingredients in an ice-filled old-fashioned glass and stir to ensure that they are mixed and chilled.

Garnish with a piece of candied orange peel, and add two straws.

SYRUPS

SYRUPS KEEP FOR UP TO 2 WEEKS OR A MONTH IN THE FRIDGE, AND CAN BE USED FOR COCKTAILS AND OTHER DRINKS, SUCH AS COFFEE AND ICED TEA.

SUGAR SYRUP

MAKES APPROXIMATELY 1½ PINTS

boiling water	2 cups
superfine sugar	2½ cups

Pour freshly boiling water onto the sugar and stir until it dissolves.

Let cool, then pour into sterilized bottles (see page 78) and store in the fridge for up to a month.

GINGER SYRUP

MAKES APPROXIMATELY 1½ CUPS

boiling water	scant 1 cup
superfine sugar	¾ cup
fresh ginger, peeled and finely grated (preferably using a microplane)	5½ ounces

Pour freshly boiling water onto the sugar and ginger and gently stir until the sugar dissolves.

Allow to steep, then strain and pour into sterilized bottles (see page 78). Store in the fridge for up to a month.

Dilute to taste: about 3 or 4 parts water to 1 part syrup.

COLA SYRUP

MAKES APPROXIMATELY 1¼ CUPS

water	scant 1 cup
superfine sugar	1¼ cups
zest of 1 lime, 1 lemon, and ½ an orange	
star anise	1
ground ginger	½ teaspoon
ground cinnamon	½ teaspoon
grated nutmeg	a pinch
turbinado sugar	1 tablespoon

Pour the water into a pan and add the superfine sugar, citrus zests, and spices. Simmer over low heat for 1 hour, then strain through a sieve lined with two layers of cheesecloth.

Add the turbinado sugar, stirring until it dissolves (this adds color to the syrup). Dilute to taste: about 3 or 4 parts water to 1 part syrup. Store in sterilized bottles in the fridge for up to 2 weeks.

HONEY SYRUP

MAKES APPROXIMATELY 1½ CUPS

boiling water	scant 1 cup
honey	¾ cup

Pour the boiling water onto the honey and stir until the honey has dissolved. Store in sterilized bottles in the fridge for up to 2 weeks.

SPICE MIX

MAKES APPROXIMATELY 1½ PINTS

BASE

lemon juice	1 cup + 2 tablespoons
cider vinegar	¾ cup
Worcestershire sauce	scant 1 cup

SPICES

dried red pepper flakes	¼ cup
cayenne pepper	3 tablespoons
paprika	2 tablespoons
dried celery flakes	¾ cup
fennel seeds	2½ tablespoons
freshly ground black pepper	1½ tablespoons
garlic powder	2 teaspoons
ground cumin	1 tablespoon
brown sugar	2½ tablespoons
salt	1 teaspoon

Mix the base ingredients together and stir in the spices, sugar, and salt. Let steep overnight, then strain to yield a devilishly spicy hot sauce. Use in Hair of the Hog (see page 50) and other restorative drinks. It should keep for a week stored in a sealed container in the icebox.

SNACKS

SNACKS

· · · · · · · · · · · ·

During the first summer of doing business from the trailer we came up close and personal with the realities of cooking outdoors in a British summer. When summer did show its face there were few things more pleasant, and late balmy evenings by the Thames often became debauched bourbon- and barbecue-fueled parties that went long into the night and the following morning. However, when the summer sun was not so willing, the gray and wet afternoons were all about snacking, occasionally a "mystery cocktail hour," or a nap on the floor by the oven, and constant development in the search for the perfect "scooby snack" to keep any boredom at bay. It was, in fact, a disguised blessing that it rained most of the time, with bourbon intake and partying largely relative to sunny hours by the river, and by the start of September when we closed the trailer for the summer our new waistlines were testament to all the rainy days spent gorging on the fruits of our snacky pursuits.

Our first menus on the trailer were really snack-heavy, based on what we felt like cooking that day and what we found at the market each morning. Such was our approach to most things when we started the trailer, so overexuberant and unbelieving were we that we were actually doing our own thing, most snacks (and drinks, in fact) were rarely sold on the menu but handed out gratis to whichever customers seemed most willing to try them. While we did not exactly run the trailer like the well-oiled machine the accountant might have hoped for, giving away, eating, and drinking as much bourbon, beer, and food as we sold, it was such an exciting time to cook and provided the blueprint for the restaurant and its menu. Those early days in the trailer really began our love affair with good snacking and proved their worth. With an onsetting panic hunger, whether standing at the bar having a drink or sitting at the table waiting for the main event to arrive, or even just well oiled, there are very few times when a solid snack will not be welcome and steadying. These trials and errors in the trailer unsurprisingly led to the restaurant menu having its own designated "snack" section for whatever we are in the mood to serve. With this section playing such a fundamental role in the restaurant, it seems only right to dedicate a little part of this book to a few of those snacks that have the ability to fill a hole when it most needs filling.

We have, unfortunately, had to leave out a great number of those snacks that have featured on the menu at various times, and also those which have never been on an actual printed menu but were made and served nonetheless when we opened the trailer.

· · · · · · · · · · · ·

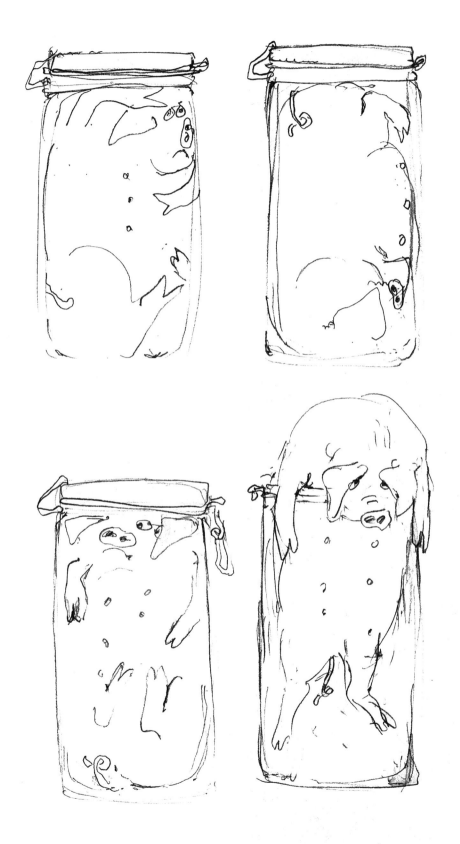

FENNEL-CURED
SCRATCHINGS

THIS RECIPE WAS BORN FROM THE LIMITATIONS OF OUR SOHO KITCHEN.
WHEN THE TRAILER FIRST OPENED WE HAD ACCESS TO A PIZZA OVEN THAT
WAS BRILLIANT FOR MAKING CRISPY PIGS' SKIN, BUT IN THE SMALL HOBBIT DEN
IN SOHO WE HAVE NO SUCH LUXURY. SO, ALTHOUGH IT MAY SEEM A TOUCH
LABORIOUS TO BE CURING, ROLLING, POACHING, AND FRYING SKIN, ALL THIS
LABOR IS REWARDED WITH THESE VERY TASTY BITS OF CRISPY PIG.

WE DO NOT WASH THE SKINS AFTER CURING, PREFERRING A SCRATCHING THAT IS FULLY
SEASONED OUT OF THE FRYER AND COATED IN HOT AROMATS. A PERFECT BEER BUDDY.

SERVES 4

pork skin, from a whole skinned pork neck end *(see page 135)*	9 ounces
Dry Cure *(see page 119)*, made without the molasses sugar	1 tablespoon
oil, for deep-frying	

Sprinkle both sides of the skin with the dry cure, then roll up the skin into a sausage shape so that the fat side remains on the inside. Place the sausage on a long piece of plastic wrap and roll it up very tightly. Tie up each end so that the roll is watertight and leave in the fridge for at least 24 hours.

Bring a medium pan of water to a gentle simmer and add the roll of skin. Weigh it down with a heatproof plate and simmer over low heat for 1 hour, or until the roll is soft to the touch. Remove from the pan and let cool, then refrigerate until you are ready to cook.

Unwrap the plastic wrap from the skin and slice the roll of skin into ¼-inch rings. Heat the oil to 355°F in a deep-fat fryer or large saucepan and fry the rings for 4 to 5 minutes, or until golden and crispy. The scratchings should not need seasoning.

—— HABANERO PIGS' EARS ——

CRISPY PIGS' EARS FIRST MADE AN APPEARANCE IN THE RESTAURANT AS A SIMPLE ACCESSORY FOR OUR SMOKED PIG'S HEAD. THE EARS DEVELOP A LEATHERY QUALITY WHEN SMOKED FOR A LONG PERIOD OF TIME, SO THEY ARE REMOVED WHEN SMOKING THE HEADS. THIS GIVES US THE EARS TO PLAY AROUND WITH AND THERE IS NO DOUBT THEY ARE BEST WHEN CRISPY. IT IS WORTH NOTING THAT NOT ALL PIGS HAVE EARS THAT ARE BEST MEANT FOR THE POT. OUR MIDDLE WHITE PIGS ON THE FARM IN PITT, FOR INSTANCE, HAVE SMALL BATLIKE EARS THAT ARE DELICIOUS, BUT WHEN COMPARED TO A GLOUCESTER OLD SPOT, CORNISH LOP, OR LARGE BLACK, WHICH ARE ALL BLESSED WITH EARS THAT COVER MOST OF THEIR FACE, THEY SEEM SLIGHTLY LESS POT-WORTHY.

SERVES 2

large pigs' ears, shaved, and ready for cooking	4
mixture of peeled and minced vegetables (onion, carrot, celery, leek, garlic)	1 cup
black peppercorns	10
bundle of herbs (thyme, rosemary, bay, 3 dried chiles)	1
oil, for deep-frying	
Habanero Rub *(see below)*, to taste	

HABANERO RUB

granulated sugar	1½ tablepoons
Maldon sea salt	3 tablespoons
fennel seeds, toasted	1½ tablespoons
coriander seeds, toasted	2 tablespoons
dried red pepper flakes	1 teaspoon
dried habanero chiles	1 teaspoon
black peppercorns	2 teaspoons
finely grated zest of 1 lime	

Put all the ingredients for the habanero rub into a blender and blitz to a rough powder. Place in an airtight container until needed.

Fill a medium saucepan with cold water, add the pigs' ears, and bring to a boil. Drain, discarding the water, then fill the pan with fresh cold water. Add the vegetables, peppercorns, and the bundle of herbs. Bring to a low simmer and cook the pigs' ears for 1½–2 hours, or until gelatinous and giving, continually skimming the surface of the pan and making sure the liquid never boils. Carefully remove the ears to a platter and refrigerate overnight until firm and dry.

The next day, heat the oil to 355°F in a deep-fryer or large saucepan.

Slice the ears into long thin strips (they should be roughly 3 inches long and ¼ inch wide). Then, working in small batches, drop the strips into the fryer. If you add too many at once they will stick together and you will get a misshapen "ear cake," by no means a hardship to eat, but not what we are looking for. Check after 3 to 4 minutes—the strips should be golden and crisp.

Remove them from the fryer and place on paper towels. Season with a liberal shaking of the habanero rub. Serve with a helping of either Kimchi (see page 214), Nduja Mayonnaise (see page 232), or aioli, and definitely a cold beer.

CRUMBED HOG JOWLS

HOG JOWLS (THE CHEEKS) ARE ONE OF THE BEST PARTS OF THE ANIMAL. AS A MUSCLE THEY HAVE BEEN WELL WORKED, DUE TO THOSE LITTLE CHAPS CONSTANTLY EATING, AND CONTAIN LOTS OF COLLAGEN THAT MELTS INTO BEAUTIFULLY GELATINOUS LOVELINESS! THIS JUST MEANS THEY NEED TO BE COOKED FOR LONGER TO BREAK THE MUSCLES RIGHT DOWN. THIS IS A REALLY SIMPLE RECIPE WHICH PRODUCES A SUPER EPIC SNACK. IN THE RESTAURANT WE USE THE JOWL MUSCLE ITSELF, ABOUT THE SIZE OF A FLATTENED GOLF BALL IF SUCH A THING EVEN EXISTS. SERVE THEM WITH SOME APPLE KETCHUP, AND YOU'RE WINNING.

MAKES 10

hog jowls, inner muscle only	10
dark soy sauce	⅓ cup
honey	heaping ¼ cup
pigs' feet stock or pork stock	scant 1 cup
smoked dripping	½ cup
mirin	1 tablespoon
star anise	4
all-purpose flour	heaping ¾ cup
free-range eggs	4
milk	2 tablespoons
Japanese panko breadcrumbs	1¼ cups
vegetable oil, for deep-frying	

Heat your oven to 300°F.

Heat a Dutch oven on the stove. Drizzle in some oil, add the hog jowls, and lightly brown on both sides. Add the soy sauce, honey, stock, dripping, mirin, and star anise, and bring to a simmer. Cover, and braise in the oven for about 3 hours, or until the jowls are tender and juicy.

Remove the jowls from the sauce and set aside to cool. In a separate pan reduce the cooking liquid over high heat until it is a sticky sauce, then remove from the heat and keep warm.

Time to crumb your jowls. Get ready three shallow bowls. In the first put the flour. In the second, beat the eggs with the milk, and put the panko breadcrumbs into the third.

Coat the jowls first in flour, dusting off any excess. Next dip into the eggs and milk, then lastly coat in panko breadcrumbs.

Heat the oil to 375°F in a deep-fat fryer and fry the jowls for 1 minute, or until golden. Drain well, then serve with the reserved cooking sauce on the side and some Apple Ketchup (see page 126). Very cheeky.

—— BUFFALO PIGS' TAILS ——

MOST GOOD BUTCHERS WILL BE ABLE TO FIND YOU SOME TAILS IF YOU ASK IN ADVANCE. YOU MAY FEEL SLIGHTLY WEIRD ASKING FOR A BAG OF TAILS—IT IS NOT EXACTLY A STAPLE IN THE WEEKLY GROCERIES—BUT THEY ARE A WORTHY PART OF THE PIG AND SHOULD BE USED FOR MORE THAN JUST A GOOD STOCK. IF THEY ARE A TOUCH HAIRY, FIND A RAZOR AND GIVE THEM A GOOD SHAVE.

THE TAILS NEED TO COME OUT OF THE BRAISING LIQUID VERY TENDER—YOUR FINGERNAIL SHOULD PIERCE THE SKIN WITHOUT ANY EFFORT AFTER BRAISING. TAILS REQUIRE THE SAME HANDS-ON APPROACH AS A CHICKEN WING, AND BENEFIT THOSE PEOPLE PARTIAL TO GNAWING AT THE BONE.

SERVES 4

pigs' tails	4
chicken stock	2 cups
Hot Sauce (see page 124)	scant 1 cup
unsalted butter	1 stick
cider vinegar	scant ½ cup
all-purpose flour	heaping ¾ cup
Pork Rub (see page 118)	⅓ cup
free-range eggs	4
milk	2 tablespoons
Japanese panko bread crumbs	2½ cups
oil, for deep-frying	

STILTON SAUCE

sour cream	scant ½ cup
mayonnaise	scant ½ cup
Stilton cheese (we use Colston Bassett or Stichelton, which is technically not a Stilton)	4¼ ounces

Heat your oven to 300°F.

Put the tails in a Dutch oven, cover with water, and bring to a boil. Once boiled, remove from the heat and drain the tails, discarding the water. Return the tails to the Dutch oven and cover with the chicken stock, then place uncovered in the oven for 6 hours, or overnight, until tender. When cooked, remove the tails from the stock and let cool.

To make the Stilton Sauce: put the sour cream and mayonnaise into a blender with 3½ ounces of the Stilton and blitz until smooth. Pour into a bowl and crumble the remaining Stilton evenly over the mixture. Set aside.

Put the hot sauce, butter, and cider vinegar into a pan and warm gently, whisking until emulsified. Keep warm.

Get ready three shallow bowls. In the first, mix the flour with the pork rub. In the second, beat the eggs with the milk, and put the panko bread crumbs into the third. Lightly coat the tails with flour, then dip them into the egg and milk mixture, and finally roll them gently in the panko bread crumbs. Heat the oil to 355°F in a deep-fat fryer and deep-fry the tails for 2 to 3 minutes, or until golden and crispy.

Dip the crispy pigs' tails into the warm sauce and serve with the Stilton Sauce and Pickled Celery (see page 194).

OXTAIL & OGLESHIELD NUGGETS

THE CHICKEN NUGGET WAS INVENTED, BELIEVE IT OR NOT, BY A PROFESSOR AT CORNELL UNIVERSITY IN THE 1950S, INTENT, AS ONE IS, ON REFORMING CHICKEN INTO A VARIETY OF UNNATURAL SHAPES. HE DID THIS THROUGH THE RATHER UNSAVORY CREATION OF "MEAT SLURRY" OR "MALLEABLE MEAT," WHEREBY MEAT AND MUSCLES ARE BROKEN DOWN AND EMULSIFIED TO FACILITATE RESHAPING INTO SOMETHING SMALL, BONELESS, AND UNNATURAL. IT HAS ALWAYS BAFFLED US AS TO WHY PEOPLE WOULD TAKE A CHICKEN, BLITZ, PURÉE, CRUSH, AND RECONSTITUTE IT BACK INTO THE SAME DRUMSTICK FORM FROM WHENCE IT CAME. PEOPLE CANNOT BE THAT AFRAID OF BONES, SURELY? BUT THE PROFESSOR AT CORNELL GOES UNDER THE RADAR, FOR IT WAS FAST FOOD THAT GAVE THE NUGGET CENTER STAGE AND IS RESPONSIBLE FOR OUR GUILTY APPRECIATION OF THE EMULSIFIED "CHICKEN" NUGGET. WE, OF COURSE, AVOID THE RECONSTITUTED CHICKEN ROUTE AND INSTEAD MANIFEST OUR LOVE OF A MEATY BITE-SIZED SNACK IN OXTAIL FORM. THE PICKED MEAT, PACKED FULL OF GELATIN, LENDS ITSELF VERY WELL TO BECOMING A NUGGET, AND THE CHUNKS OF CHEESE DOTTED THROUGHOUT ARE A GOOEY NO-BRAINER.

IF YOU CANNOT FIND THE WONDERFUL OGLESHIELD CHEESE OR CHEDDAR CHEESE CURDS, THEN A SWISS RACLETTE-STYLE CHEESE OR DECENT CHEDDAR WILL SUFFICE.

SERVES 4

oxtail, chopped into 1-bone sections	2¼ pounds
House Rub (see page 119)	¾ cup
Mother Sauce (see page 120)	⅓ cup
Ogleshield cheese or Cheddar cheese curds, cut into ½-inch dice	3½ ounces
Japanese panko bread crumbs	1¼ cups
all-purpose flour, sifted	heaping ¾ cups
free-range eggs	5
oil, for deep-frying	
Maldon sea salt	
freshly ground black pepper	

Prepare a barbecue for smoking (see The Setup on pages 114-15) and set the temperature to 230°F.

Coat the oxtail evenly with a heaping ½ cup of the house rub. Put the oxtail on the barbecue and smoke for 8 hours, or until the meat pulls away from the bones with little effort. The internal temperature should be around 190°F.

Pick all the oxtail meat from the bones and mix it with the Mother Sauce, the remaining rub, and the diced cheese. Season with salt and pepper to taste. Place the mixture on a long piece of plastic wrap and roll it into a tight sausage about 2 inches wide. Tie up the ends and refrigerate to firm up overnight.

Next day, remove the plastic wrap and cut the sausage into disks ½ inch thick. Get ready three shallow bowls. In the first put the sifted flour, in the second beat the eggs, and in the third put the panko bread crumbs. Lightly coat the nuggets with flour, then dip them into the eggs, and finally roll them gently in the panko bread crumbs.

Heat the oil to 355°F in a deep-fryer or large saucepan and deep-fry the nuggets in batches for 2 minutes, or until golden. Drain on paper towels, then serve with Kimchi Hot Sauce (see page 124).

SMOKED LIVERS

POULTRY VARIETY MEATS ARE UNDOUBTEDLY THE MOST ACCESSIBLE OF ALL VARIETY MEATS AND THE STARTING POINT FOR ANYONE SLIGHTLY SQUEAMISH ABOUT EATING THE "OTHER BITS" OF THE ANIMAL. LIVERS AND HEARTS ARE INCREDIBLY GOOD VALUE, PERHAPS THE CHEAPEST OF ALL MEAT OFFERINGS AND HAVE THE ABILITY TO BE TRANSFORMED INTO THE MOST DELICIOUS.

THOUGH NOT EASY TO FIND, THERE ARE A FEW GOOSE FARMERS WHO REMAIN HELL-BENT ON PRODUCING FOIE GRAS JUST AS THOSE GLUTTONOUS ROMANS DID WHEN THEY FIRST DISCOVERED THAT A GOOSE TAKES TO FATTENING AND GORGING ITSELF BEFORE ITS ANNUAL MIGRATION. SUCH FREE-RANGE GEESE LIVE UP TO 9 MONTHS WITHOUT ANY FORCE-FEEDING, UNLIKE MUCH FOIE GRAS THAT HITS THE SHELVES AT A STAGGERING 6 WEEKS OF AGE.

THIS RECIPE IS BASED ON A CLASSIC PARFAIT WITH THE LIVERS SMOKED FOR JUST A FEW MINUTES BEFORE BEING TREATED AS YOU WOULD IN A NORMAL RECIPE. THE FOIE GRAS REALLY DOES ADD SOMETHING EXTRA SEXY TO THE RECIPE, BUT IT CAN BE REPLACED WITH MORE DUCK LIVERS IF GOOD ETHICAL FOIE GRAS PROVES HARD TO OBTAIN. SIMILARLY, CHICKEN LIVERS MAKE A PERFECTLY LOVELY SUBSTITUTE FOR THE DUCK LIVERS. IF YOUR BUTCHER HAS DUCK HEARTS ON SHOW WHEN YOU BUY YOUR LIVERS, SNATCH THEM UP WITHOUT A THOUGHT, THEN BROIL THEM QUICKLY AND SPREAD THEM ON THE TOAST.

SERVES 4

duck livers	3½ ounces
fresh foie gras	3½ ounces
small free-range eggs	2
unsalted butter, melted	1¾ sticks

REDUCTION

bourbon	1 tablespoon
maple syrup	1 tablespoon
shallots, finely chopped	2
black peppercorns, toasted	½ teaspoon
fennel seeds, toasted	½ teaspoon
generous sprig of thyme	1
smoked Maldon sea salt	1 teaspoon

Prepare a barbecue for smoking (see The Setup on pages 114-15) and set the temperature to 195°F.

Put the duck livers and foie gras into a shallow pan or dish and smoke in the barbecue for 5 minutes. Very little smoke is required—too much can quickly overpower the livers.

Meanwhile, heat the oven to 320°F. Put all the ingredients for the reduction into a pan and simmer until reduced by half.

Put the smoked livers into a blender with the warm reduction. Add the eggs and blitz until smooth, then continue to blend while pouring in the melted butter in a slow, steady stream until everything is combined.

Pass the mixture through a fine sieve into 4 ramekins and cover with foil. Stand the ramekins in a roasting pan and pour in water to come halfway up the sides, then bake in the oven for 1 hour. Remove from the oven and let cool before refrigerating. Serve with toast and pickles.

SMOKED OX CHEEK
— ON TOAST WITH PICKLED WALNUTS —

OX CHEEKS ARE GREAT FRESHLY SMOKED, BUT WHEN CHILLED THEY SET VERY WELL FOR SLICING, AND BECAUSE THE CHEEK IS SUCH A DENSE MUSCLE, IT PAN-FRIES BEAUTIFULLY. THIS IS VERY GOOD TO KNOW IF, HEAVEN FORBID, YOU HAVE ANY LEFTOVERS FROM YOUR DINNER. THE TOAST ACTS JUST LIKE A TRENCHER IN THIS RECIPE (SEE PAGE 166), ONLY CHEEK-SIZED.

WHILE WE PICKLE ALMOST ANYTHING AND EVERYTHING IN THE RESTAURANT, YOU REALLY CANNOT BEAT A JAR OF OPIES PICKLED WALNUTS.

MAKES 4 SMALL SERVINGS

ox cheek	1, weighing about 1 pound 2 ounces
House Rub (see page 119)	¼ cup
slices of sourdough bread, 1cm thick	4
butter or Whipped Bone Marrow (see page 228), for spreading	
Barbecue Sauce (see page 122)	scant ½ cup
pickled walnuts, cut into ¼-inch slices (we use Opies)	1 x 13-ounce jar
fresh horseradish, peeled (or use horseradish sauce)	1

Prepare a barbecue for smoking (see The Setup on pages 114-15) and set the temperature to 230°F.

Rub the ox cheek all over with the house rub and smoke for 7 to 8 hours. The cheek will shrink and the internal temperature should be about 186° to 190°F°. It should be slightly soft and gelatinous to the touch when cooked, and long tendrils of gelatin may well be hanging from the underside. When ready, remove the cheek, wrap in foil, and let rest for 10 minutes.

Toast the sourdough well on both sides, then butter or spread with whipped bone marrow on one side. Cut the ox cheek into ½-inch slices. Grill or pan-fry the cheek slices over high heat until caramelized on both sides. Once caramelized, begin to brush with the barbecue sauce.

Top each piece of toast with a slice of cheek, and finish with several slices of pickled walnut and a liberal grating of fresh horseradish.

SMOKED LAMB MARROW
WITH ANCHOVY

> LAMB MARROWS HAVE ALL THE UNCTUOUSNESS OF BEEF MARROW BUT WITH LOVELY LAMB FLAVORS COMING THROUGH—ASK YOUR BUTCHER FOR THE EQUIVALENT OF BEEF MARROWBONES, BUT FROM LAMB.
>
> SHOOTING PICKLE BRINE AFTER EATING THESE IS OPTIONAL, BUT HAS GREAT RESTORATIVE BALANCING POWERS AFTER CONSUMING THE RICH AND FATTY MARROW.

SERVES 4

lamb marrow bones, split	4
smoked anchovy fillets	8
parsley, chopped	3 tablespoons
shallot, chopped	1
garlic clove, crushed	1
sourdough bread crumbs	¼ cup
finely grated zest of 1 lemon	
slices of sourdough bread, ½-inch thick	8
smoked Maldon sea salt	
freshly ground black pepper	

TO SERVE

4 large shots of chilled pickle juice from Bread & Butter Pickles *(see page 191)*

Prepare a barbecue for direct grilling (see pages 112–15) and set the temperature to 355°F.

Carefully cut the bone marrow into ¼-inch dice and put into a bowl. Dice half the anchovies and mix with the parsley, shallot, garlic, bread crumbs, and lemon zest, and season with smoked salt and pepper. Carefully combine with the diced bone marrow and put the mixture into the 4 split marrow bones.

Place the marrow bones, filled-side up, on the barbecue and grill with the lid closed for 6 minutes. Place on paper towels to drain away any excess fat, then arrange on a serving plate.

Lay half a smoked anchovy fillet on top of each bone and serve with toasted sourdough slices. Once consumed, shoot the chilled pickle juice with haste.

SMOKED FOIE GRAS
— ON TOAST WITH PICKLED CHERRIES —

WHILE FORCE-FEEDING IS REQUIRED
TO MEET THE FRENCH DEFINITION
OF FOIE GRAS, THERE ARE
PRODUCERS IN SPAIN AND ITALY
THAT DO NOT FORCE-FEED BIRDS
IN ORDER TO PRODUCE FATTENED
LIVERS, ALLOWING THEM TO EAT
FREELY. INTEREST IN ALTERNATIVE
PRODUCTION METHODS HAS GROWN,
DUE TO ETHICAL CONCERNS, AND
SUCH LIVERS ARE CALLED FATTY
GOOSE LIVER OR ETHICAL FOIE
GRAS. THIS METHOD INVOLVES
TIMING THE SLAUGHTER TO COINCIDE
WITH THE WINTER MIGRATION, WHEN
LIVERS ARE NATURALLY FATTENED.

SERVES 6

fresh foie gras	1 lobe, weighing about 1¼ pounds
Duck Rub *(see page 118)*	⅓ cup
slices of sourdough bread, ½-inch thick	6
Pickled Cherries *(see page 197)*	12

Prepare a barbecue for smoking (see The Setup on pages 114-15). Set the temperature to 355°F and put a small ovenproof pan directly over the coals to heat.

Coat the foie gras with half of the duck rub—it should form a crust. Place it in the pan and cook in the barbecue for 5 minutes on each side. It should be well caramelized and slightly soft to touch, and the internal temperature should reach 120°F. Remove the pan from the heat and let the foie gras rest for 5 minutes.

Meanwhile, toast the sourdough slices. Cut the foie gras at an angle into ½-inch slices and lay them on the toast. Season with more duck rub and eat at once, with the pickled cherries.

OUR PICKLE
— BRINE —

> THIS PICKLE BRINE IS VERY BASIC,
> A STARTING POINT. MAKE IT, TRY IT,
> THEN GO FROM THERE WITH DIFFERENT
> AROMATICS, VINEGARS, AND SUGARS TO
> MAKE MORE INTERESTING PICKLES. THE
> BRINE REFRIGERATES WELL, SO IT IS
> WORTH MAKING A GOOD AMOUNT IF YOU
> PLAN ON DOING A LOT OF PICKLING,
> THOUGH YOU CAN EASILY SCALE IT DOWN
> SIMPLY BY HALVING THE AMOUNTS.

MAKES 5¼ PINTS

water	3¼ pints
cider vinegar	2 pints
superfine or turbinado sugar	3½ cups
sea salt	2½ tablespoons

optional aromats (peppercorns, bay leaves,
fennel seeds, coriander seeds, mustard seeds,
star anise, cardamom pods, garlic, licorice root)

Put all the ingredients into a large pan and
bring to a boil, stirring occasionally until
the sugar and salt are dissolved.

Prepare whatever fruit or vegetables you
want to pickle and drop them into the
hot brine. Let cool, then refrigerate in
sterilized jars for 3 to 5 days.

This pickle brine works especially well
for carrots, celery, beets, fennel bulbs,
cauliflower, kohlrabi, peas, and chiles.

· To sterilize jars, thoroughly wash and dry your jars and
lids. Place the jars in a cold oven and heat to 320°F. After
20 minutes, turn the oven off and let the jars cool slightly.
Pour in your pickles while the jars are still hot, then seal
and let cool completely.

— PICKLED SEAFOOD —

PICKLED ANCHOVIES

SERVES 10

Maldon sea salt	2 tablespoons
superfine sugar	2 tablespoons
fresh anchovy fillets, pinboned and scaled	40
carrot, peeled and thinly sliced	1
banana shallot, thinly sliced	1
stick of celery, thinly sliced	1
garlic clove, peeled and thinly sliced	1
Our Pickle Brine (see page 78)	1 cup
interesting vinegar	
(we like white malt vinegar)	1½ tablespoons

Mix together the salt and sugar in a bowl. Layer the anchovy fillets in a plastic container, distributing the salt and sugar between the layers. Refrigerate for 3 hours.

Meanwhile, put the sliced vegetables into a bowl. Bring the pickle brine to a boil and pour over the vegetables, then let cool.

Wash the anchovy fillets and arrange them in layers in a sterilized 9-ounce glass jar (see page 78), alternating with the pickled vegetable mixture, making sure to spread the ingredients evenly.

Cover with the lid, put into the fridge overnight, then eat, sprinkled with interesting vinegar.

PICKLED MACKEREL

SERVES 10

black peppercorns, crushed	2 teaspoons
mustard seeds, crushed	1½ teaspoons
coriander seeds, crushed	1 tablespoon
zest and juice of 1 orange,	
1 lemon, and 1 lime	
Maldon sea salt	2 tablespoons
superfine sugar	2 tablespoons
extremely fresh mackerel fillets, pinboned	10
carrot, peeled and thinly sliced	1
banana shallot, thinly sliced	1
stick of celery, peeled and thinly sliced	1
fresh horseradish, peeled and	
thinly sliced	¾-inch piece
lemon, thinly sliced	½
Our Pickle Brine (see page 78)	1 cup
interesting vinegar	
(we like white malt vinegar)	1½ tablespoons

Mix together the spices, citrus zests, salt, and sugar in a bowl. Layer the mackerel fillets in a plastic container, distributing the spice mix between the layers. Refrigerate for 3 hours.

Meanwhile, put the vegetables and sliced lemon into a bowl. Bring the pickle brine and citrus juices to a boil and pour over the vegetables, then let cool.

Rinse the mackerel fillets and arrange them in layers in a sterilized 1-pint glass jar (see page 78), alternating with the vegetable mixture, making sure to spread the ingredients evenly.

Cover, put into the fridge for 2 or 3 days, then eat, sprinkled with interesting vinegar.

PICKLED SHRIMP

SERVES 10

jumbo raw shell-on shrimp	2¼ pounds
Our Pickle Brine (see page 78)	2 pints
banana shallot, thinly sliced	1
carrot, peeled and thinly sliced	1
small leek, thinly sliced	1
stick of celery, peeled and thinly sliced	1
garlic cloves, thinly sliced	2
capers, with brine	heaping ⅓ cup
mixed herbs (parsley, tarragon, thyme, bay, cilantro)	small bunch
unwaxed lemon, thinly sliced	1
white peppercorns	4
pink peppercorns	4
black peppercorns	4
star anise	1
Maldon sea salt	2 teaspoons
red chile, thinly sliced	1

Peel and devein the shrimp, reserving the flesh until needed. Place the heads and shells in a large pan with the pickle brine and bring to a gentle simmer. Skim any impurities and continue to simmer gently for 8 minutes to make a stock.

Place all the vegetables and lemon slices in a separate pan with the reserved shrimp, capers, herbs, spices, salt, and chile. Pass the hot shrimp stock through a fine sieve into the pan, then bring back to a gentle simmer and remove from the heat immediately.

Mix well, then transfer to a sterilized 2-pint glass jar (see page 78) and let cool. Seal the jar, and refrigerate for a minimum of 12 hours and up to 36 hours before serving. Serve as an appetizer, with cocktail sauce or mayonnaise.

PICKLED SCALLOPS

SERVES 4

scallops, in their shells	12
Our Pickle Brine (see page 78)	2 pints
banana shallot, thinly sliced	1
carrot, peeled and thinly sliced	1
stick of celery, peeled and thinly sliced	1
garlic clove, thinly sliced	1
unwaxed lemon, thinly sliced	½
white peppercorns	4
pink peppercorns	4
black peppercorns	4
star anise	1
red chile, thinly sliced	1
capers, with brine	2 teaspoons
Maldon sea salt	1 teaspoon
mixed herbs (parsley, tarragon, thyme, bay, cilantro)	small bunch

Shuck the scallops, reserving the meat and scallop skirt. Put the scallop meat into a bowl and set aside. Remove the dark grit sack from the scallop skirt and discard, then rinse the skirt under cold running water until clean.

Place the scallop skirt in a pan with the pickle brine and bring up to a gentle simmer. Continue to simmer for 6 minutes to make a stock, skimming off any impurities. Put the reserved scallop meat into a separate pan with all the remaining ingredients, then pass the scallop stock through a fine sieve into the pan. Bring back to a gentle simmer, then skim any impurities again, and remove from the heat.

Mix well, then transfer to a sterilized 2-pint glass jar (see page 78) and let cool. Seal the jar, and refrigerate for a minimum of 12 hours and up to 36 hours before serving.

PICKLED OYSTERS

SERVES 8

unwaxed lemon, thinly sliced	½
red chile, thinly sliced	1
banana shallot, peeled and thinly sliced	1
black peppercorns, crushed	4
Our Pickle Brine *(see page 78)*	1 cup
small rock oysters, in their shells	24
small cucumber, peeled and sliced	½

Put the lemon slices into a large heatproof bowl with the sliced chile and shallot.

Add the peppercorns and pickle brine to a pan and bring it to a boil, then remove from the heat and pour over the lemon, chile, and shallot and let cool.

Shuck the oysters and rinse in cold water, reserving the meat until needed—the cold water stops the oysters from forming a cloudy goo in the pickle.

When the pickle brine mix has cooled down, toss in the oysters and cucumber slices, mix well, then transfer to a sterilized 2-pint glass jar (see page 78). Seal the jar and refrigerate for a minimum of 12 and up to 48 hours. Serve with Saltine Crackers (see page 96).

PICKLED WIENERS

PICKLED SAUSAGES ARE POPULAR IN EASTERN EUROPE, BUT WE FIRST CAME ACROSS PICKLED WIENERS IN TEXAS. EATEN COLD WITH A BEER THEY ARE HIGHLY ADDICTIVE. OUR VERSION USES WIENERS MADE FOR US BY OUR "SAUSAGE GURU" STANKOV IN LONDON, BUT YOU CAN PICKLE ANY GOOD-QUALITY COOKED SAUSAGE.

MAKES 2 x 2-PINT JARS

Our Pickle Brine *(see page 78)*	2 pints
hot dog wieners or Polish sausage,	
such as Keilbasa	2¼ pounds
chiles	3
garlic cloves	4
sprigs of thyme	3

Put the pickle brine into a pan and bring to a boil.

Stack the wieners neatly in 2 large sterilized glass jars (see page 78), with the chiles, garlic, and thyme spread evenly throughout the jars.

Add the hot pickling liquid and seal the jars. Let cool, then refrigerate for 1 week before eating.

BEET-
PICKLED EGGS

NOT JUST FOR PRESENTATION, PICKLING IN BEET JUICE IMPARTS AN EARTHY
FLAVOR TO THE EGGS THAT MARRIES WELL WITH THE DEVILED PREPARATION ON
PAGE 98. THE EGGS WILL DARKEN IN COLOR AS THEY PICKLE AND TAKE ON MORE
OF THE BEET FLAVOR THE LONGER THEY ARE IN THE JAR.

MAKES 12

small free-range eggs	12
Our Pickle Brine *(see page 78)*	3 cups
beet juice (concentrated)	1¼ cups

Boil the eggs for 6 minutes, then turn off
the heat. Remove the eggs from the pan
and roll them lightly on a work surface to
give a cracked mosaic look to the shells.

Place the pickle brine and beet juice in
a large bowl, add the eggs, and let cool
in the liquid. Refrigerate in a sterilized
glass jar (see page 78) and let pickle for
2 days and up to 2 weeks.

To serve, remove the eggs from the liquid,
peel off the shells, and either eat as they
are or serve in salads.

DEVILED BEET-PICKLED EGGS

THE BEET-PICKLED EGGS ABOVE
CAN ALSO BE TURNED INTO VERY
SEXY DEVILED EGGS. THE RECIPE
HERE IS JUST ONE IDEA, BUT
FEEL FREE TO GET CREATIVE.

Halve the beet-pickled eggs lengthwise.
Scoop out the yolks and place them in a
mixing bowl.

Beat the yolks with the goat cheese,
olive oil, and plenty of black pepper,
then pass through a fine sieve to make a
smooth paste.

MAKES 12

Beet-pickled Eggs (see above)	6
creamy goat cheese	1¾ ounces
extra virgin olive oil	3 tablespoons
plenty of freshly ground black pepper	

Place the yolk mixture in a pastry bag
with a plain tip and pipe neatly into
the egg cavities.

Refrigerate for at least 20 minutes
before serving.

PICKLED SHIITAKE

WE WERE BLOWN AWAY BY THE PICKLES AT MOMOFUKU IN NEW YORK, ESPECIALLY THE SHIITAKE. THIS RECIPE IS BASED ON THOSE SAME PICKLES, WITH JUST A FEW CHANGES TO MAKE THEM STAND OUT A BIT MORE WHEN DEEP-FRIED. DRIED SHIITAKE CAN BE FOUND IN MOST ORIENTAL SUPERMARKETS. THEY CAN BE VERY SMALL AND MOSTLY STALK, SO FIND THE BIGGEST YOU CAN, OTHERWISE THE PICKLE WILL NOT BE PLEASANT. THESE PICKLED MUSHROOMS KEEP WELL AND IMPROVE WITH TIME.

MAKES 2 PINTS

dried shiitake mushrooms	7 ounces
boiling water	4¼ pints
superfine sugar	1 cup
soy sauce	scant 1¼ cups
cider vinegar	scant 1¼ cups
ginger, peeled	¾-inch piece
licorice root	½ stick
star anise	½

Put the mushrooms into a container and add the boiling water. Place a small pan lid or plate on top of the mushrooms to keep them submerged and let stand to fully rehydrate for 5 to 6 hours.

Remove the mushrooms from the water and discard the stalks. Cut the caps in half. Reserve 2 cups of the steeping liquid and strain it to remove any debris. Any remaining liquid can be used for stocks and sauces.

Put the mushrooms into a pan with the reserved steeping liquid and all the other ingredients. Bring to a gentle simmer, stirring occasionally and making sure the mushrooms are submerged, and cook for 30 minutes. Discard the ginger, licorice, and star anise. Let cool, then transfer to a sterilized jar (see page 78) and refrigerate. The pickled shiitake will be ready in 3 days, but will be better after a week.

CRISPY PICKLED SHIITAKE

SERVES 4 TO 6

all-purpose flour	heaping ½ cup
free-range eggs	3
whole milk	3 tablespoons
Japanese panko bread crumbs	1½ cups
Pickled Shiitake (see above), drained	14 ounces
oil, for deep-frying	

Get ready three shallow bowls. In the first, add the flour, in the second beat the eggs with the milk, and in the third put the panko bread crumbs. Lightly coat the pickled shiitake in flour, then dip them into the egg and milk mixture, and finally toss them carefully in the panko bread crumbs. The shiitake should be uniformly coated. Work neatly and in small batches so that the crumbs do not become wet and clumpy. Place the mushrooms on a sheet of waxed paper. They freeze very well like this.

Heat the oil to 375°F in a deep-fryer and fry the shiitake for 2 minutes, until golden and crisp. Drain on paper towels and serve.

HOT WINGS

SERVES 4

3-joint free-range chicken wings	2¼ pounds
Master Chicken Brine (see below)	2 pints
House Rub (see page 119)	scant ½ cup
unsalted butter	½ stick
cider vinegar	3 tablespoons
Hot Sauce or B****** Hot Sauce (see pages 124 and 125)	3 tablespoons

MASTER CHICKEN BRINE

water	8½ pints
Maldon sea salt	1½ cups + 2 tablespoons
interesting sugar (Muscovado or maple, for instance)	scant 1 cup
spice bag (dried chiles, small licorice stick, peppercorns, star anise, cloves, cumin seeds, coriander seeds)	1
mixed herbs (thyme, bay, rosemary)	1 bunch

HOW HOT YOU MAKE THESE WINGS IS UP TO YOU. THIS RECIPE IS DEFINITELY HOT ENOUGH FOR US AND REQUIRES THE COOLING EFFECT OF A GOOD COWS' CURD AND SOME PICKLED CELERY.
WE STUMBLED ACROSS A HOT SAUCE IN THE RESTAURANT THAT CAME WITH A SAFETY NOTICE AND LOOKED LIKE SATAN'S BLOOD. OUR MILK STOCKS WERE UNUSUALLY LOW THE NEXT DAY. THESE WINGS SHOULD NOT HAVE THAT EFFECT. USE THE HOT SAUCE TO TASTE. TOO HOT AND IT IS A WASTE OF GOOD CHICKEN. YOU CAN ALWAYS ADD MORE.

IF YOU ARE PARTICULAR ABOUT YOUR WINGS, REMOVE THE FIRST JOINT AND COOK IT SEPARATELY— IT MAKES FOR A MORE CIVILIZED WING AFFAIR.

To make the master chicken brine, add all the ingredients to a large pan and bring to a boil, then let cool. Load the wings into the brine and refrigerate for 2 hours.

Prepare a barbecue for smoking (see The Setup on pages 114-15) and set the temperature to 220°F.

Remove the wings from the brine and dry thoroughly on paper towels. Rub them all over with the house rub. Smoke the wings in the barbecue for 1 hour 30 minutes, checking after 30 to 45 minutes and turning them over. They need to reach an internal temperature of at least 160°F on your meat probe. Once smoked, remove them from the barbecue.

Meanwhile, put the butter, vinegar, and hot sauce into a large pan and bring to a boil. Whisk until the mixture has emulsified.

When ready to cook, adjust the barbecue for direct grilling—you may need to add more charcoal and adjust the vents to get the temperature just hot enough to char the wings. Grill the wings until they are crispy and slightly charred, about 2 minutes each side.

Toss the wings in the hot sauce, then serve with Pickled Celery (see page 194), pickled chiles, and a side of cows' curd.

· Fresh cows' curd and goats' curd work fantastically well with hot food, so don't be afraid to use them with Buffalo Pigs' Tails (see page 66) or even on top of Chipotle & Confit Garlic Slaw (see page 198). Curd is much more widely available now than a few years back, and for good reason.

KIMCHI HOT WINGS

SERVES 4

3-joint free-range chicken wings	2¼ pounds
Master Chicken Brine *(see page 90)*	8½ pints
House Rub *(see page 119)*	scant ½ cup
Kimchi Hot Sauce *(see page 124)*	scant 1 cup
oil, for deep-frying	

Load the wings into the master chicken brine and refrigerate for 2 hours.

Remove the wings from the brine and dry thoroughly with paper towels. Rub them all over with the house rub.

Prepare a barbecue for smoking (see The Setup on pages 114–15) and set the temperature to 220°F. Smoke the wings in the barbecue for 1 hour 30 minutes, checking after 30 to 45 minutes and turning them over. They need to reach an internal temperature of 160°F. Once smoked, these wings can be chilled, ready for deep-frying when you are ready. If deep-frying is not your thing, a good grilling would also work well.

Put the kimchi hot sauce into a large mixing bowl. Heat the oil to 375°F in a deep-fat fryer or large saucepan and deep-fry the wings for 2 minutes, or until golden and crispy. When cooked, toss the wings in the kimchi hot sauce.

Serve with Pickled Celery (see page 194) and a side of curd. Or, if you are feeling industrious, you can pull all the meat off of the bones after dressing, roll it up in lettuce leaves, dunk them in Anchovy Hollandaise (see page 174), and feel very good about yourself.

APRICOT & GREEN CHILI WINGS

SERVES 4

3-joint free-range chicken wings	2¼ pounds
Master Chicken Brine *(see page 90)*	2 pints
House Rub *(see page 119)*	scant ½ cup
oil, for deep-frying	
juice of 5 limes	
green chile, thinly sliced	1
cilantro stalks and leaves, chopped	small bunch

GLAZE

apricot jam	½ cup
light soy sauce	3 tablespoons
cider vinegar	1 tablespoon
Tabasco or Frank's Red Hot Sauce	1 tablespoon
green chiles, chopped into rounds	2

Load the wings into the master chicken brine and refrigerate for 2 hours.

Remove the wings from the brine and dry thoroughly with paper towels. Rub them all over with the house rub.

Prepare a barbecue for smoking (see The Setup on pages 114–15) and set the temperature to 220°F. Smoke the wings in the barbecue for 1 hour 30 minutes, checking after 45 minutes and turning them over. They need to reach an internal temperature of 160°F. Once smoked, remove from the barbecue, cover, and chill until needed.

Combine the ingredients for the glaze in a pan over low heat and stir until the jam has dissolved. Set aside and keep warm.

Heat the oil to 375°F in a deep-fat fryer or large saucepan and deep-fry the wings for 2 minutes, or until golden and crispy. When cooked, toss the wings in the warm glaze to coat, then drench in the lime juice. Garnish with the green chile slices and chopped cilantro and serve.

CHIPOTLE & MAPLE WINGS

SERVES 4

3-joint free-range chicken wings	2¼ pounds
Master Chicken Brine (see page 90)	2 pints

MARINADE

fennel seeds, toasted	heaping ⅓ cup
cumin seeds, toasted	1½ tablespoons
coriander seeds, toasted	3 tablespoons
black peppercorns	heaping ⅓ cup
onion, peeled and grated	1
roasted garlic paste	1¾ ounces
vegetable oil	scant ½ cup
apple juice	1½ cups
chipotle in adobo, puréed	2½ ounces
House Rub (see page 119)	scant ⅓ cup
maple syrup	⅓ cup
blackstrap molasses	½ cup
apricot preserve	½ cup
tomato ketchup	1 cup
English mustard	scant ½ cup
smoked Maldon sea salt	2 teaspoons
Granny Smith apple, grated	1

Load the wings into the master chicken brine and refrigerate for 1½ hours. Meanwhile, grind the toasted seeds and peppercorns to a powder.

In a saucepan, sweat the onion and garlic paste in the oil over high heat for 5 minutes. Add 1 cup of apple juice and cook until it has reduced and evaporated. Pour the reduced mixture into a large bowl, then add all the remaining ingredients except the grated apple. Stir well to combine, then fold in the grated apple and the remaining apple juice.

Remove the wings from the brine and dry with paper towels. Drop the wings into the marinade and let stand for 1 hour.

Prepare a barbecue for smoking (see The Setup on pages 114–15) and set the temperature to 220°F. Smoke the wings for 1 hour 30 minutes, checking after 45 minutes and turning them over. They need to reach an internal temperature of 160°F. Remove the wings and adjust the barbecue for direct grilling. Grill the wings until crisp and slightly charred, about 1 to 2 minutes each side, basting with any excess marinade as they cook. Serve with pickles.

BUTTER CONFIT TURKEY WINGS

SERVES 4

3-joint free-range turkey wings	2¼ pounds
Master Chicken Brine (see page 90)	2 pints
House Rub (see page 119)	scant ½ cup
butter	2¼ pounds
garlic cloves, separated	2 bulbs
sprigs of thyme	5

Load the wings into the master chicken brine and refrigerate for 2 hours. Remove the wings from the brine and dry thoroughly with paper towels. Rub them all over with the house rub.

Place in a roasting pan that fits inside your barbecue, and add the butter, garlic, and thyme.

Prepare a barbecue for smoking (see The Setup on pages 114–15) and set the temperature to 220°F. Confit the wings by smoking them in the barbecue for 3 hours, or until they are soft to the touch. Remove the wings from the barbecue and let drain on paper towels.

When ready to cook, adjust the barbecue for direct grilling—not super-hot but just hot enough to char the wings. Grill the wings until they are crispy and slightly charred, about 2 minutes each side. Serve with Hot Sauce (see page 124) and a side of curd.

BURNT TOMATOES
— & SHALLOTS ON TOAST —

WE ARE NOT SURE IF THIS IS A
SIDE DISH, AN APPETIZER, OR
JUST A LITTLE SCOOBY SNACK
FOR WHEN HUNGER BITES—MAYBE
ALL OF THE ABOVE. IT IS
ALSO VEGETARIAN, WHICH IS A
BIT OF A SURPRISE. TOMATOES
ARE THE STAR OF THE SHOW,
AND USING GREAT TOMATOES IS
THE LAW HERE. ALSO, NEVER
REFRIGERATE TOMATOES—IT IS
A SLAP IN THE FACE OF THE
TOMATO. REALLY GOOD HOME-
GROWN TOMATOES ARE AROUND
FOR SUCH A SHORT TIME IN THE
SUMMER, SO TREAT THEM WELL
AND YOU WILL BE REWARDED.

SERVES 4

ripe tomatoes, at room temperature	4
banana shallots	4
lemon juice	good squeeze
extra virgin olive oil	1 tablespoon
large slices of sourdough bread, toasted	2
garlic clove, cut in half	1
Maldon sea salt	
freshly ground black pepper	

GARNISH

mint tips	1 tablespoon
chive tips	1 tablespoon
flat-leaf parsley, leaves picked	1 tablespoon

Heat a barbecue or cast-iron ridged grill
pan until smoking hot.

While the grill is heating up, cut the
tomatoes in half lengthwise. Peel the
shallots and halve them lengthwise, keeping
the root intact. Toss the shallots in a bowl
with the tomatoes, lemon juice, olive oil,
salt, and pepper, then set aside at room
temperature until the grill is hot.

Place the tomatoes and shallots, cut-side
down, on the grill or pan and leave for a
few minutes—if you move them you will break
the seal and they will leak their juice.
When slightly burnt, remove the tomatoes and
turn the shallots over to color the other
side. Keep turning the shallots for about
6 or 7 minutes, or until cooked all the
way through.

Meanwhile, toast the sourdough, rub with the
cut sides of the garlic clove, and pour over
any remaining marinade from the bowl. Place
the shallots and tomatoes on top, garnish
with the herbs, and serve immediately.

SALTINE CRACKERS

IN KREUZ MARKET, JUST OUTSIDE AUSTIN, TEXAS, WE DISCOVERED THEY SERVED THEIR BARBECUE WITH SAUERKRAUT, SALSA, AVOCADOS, AND THESE SALTINE CRACKERS. GENIUS. THIS IS ABOUT AS DREAMY A MOUTHFUL AS YOU WILL EVER FIND.

MAKES SHED LOADS

all-purpose flour	2 cups
salt	1 teaspoon
baking soda	½ teaspoon
butter, chilled	2 tablespoons
milk	⅔ cup
Maldon sea salt	

Heat the oven to 400°F.

Put the flour, salt, and baking soda into a bowl, and grate in the chilled butter. Rub the butter into the flour using your fingertips until the mixture resembles bread crumbs, then stir in the milk and knead lightly.

Roll out thinly, about ⅛ inch thick, and place on a nonstick cookie sheet. Prick with a fork around the edge, sprinkle with sea salt, and cut into squares. Bake in the oven for 10 minutes, or until golden.

Serve warm topped with a slice of fresh tomato, avocado, a couple of onion rings, and a slice of smoked tri-tip roast or beef brisket.

DEVILED EGGS WITH
ROAST CHICKEN SKIN

DEVILED EGGS ORIGINATE FROM ROME AND WERE FIRST FOUND ALL OVER CENTRAL EUROPE IN THE NINETEENTH CENTURY. TOPPINGS WOULD VARY, DEPENDING ON THE CUISINE AND PRODUCE OF THE COUNTRY: THE RUSSIANS TOPPED A MAYONNAISE AND EGG MIXTURE WITH CAVIAR AND POTATO, THE SWEDISH USED PICKLED HERRING AND DILL, AND SO ON. WE BELIEVE THAT DEVILED EGGS ARE GREAT IN MANY GUISES—THIS IS OUR FAVORITE, AND MAKES FOR SOME DEVILISHLY GOOD EGGS. THIS RECIPE MAKES MORE CHICKEN SKIN THAN YOU WILL NEED—EVERYONE NEEDS EXTRA CHICKEN SKIN.

MAKES 12, ENOUGH FOR 4

large free-range hen's eggs	6
Anchovy Salad Cream *(see page 205)*	3 tablespoons
Kimchi Hot Sauce *(see page 124)*	3 tablespoons

ROAST CHICKEN SKIN

sprigs of thyme	3
chicken skins	9 ounces
chicken stock	3 tablespoons
Maldon sea salt, to taste	

First, make the roast chicken skin. Heat the oven to 340°F.

Put the sprigs of thyme into a medium-sized roasting pan and lay the chicken skins on top. Add the chicken stock, then put the pan into the oven and cook, uncovered, for 40 minutes, stirring every 10 minutes.

When the 40 minutes are up, drain off the fat and return the pan to the oven for a further 20 minutes to crisp up. The skins will not have the crunch of pork scratchings but will be like roast chicken skin. Season to taste.

Next, make the deviled eggs. Fill a pan large enough for 6 eggs with water and bring to a boil. Gently lower the eggs into the water and cook for 8 minutes. Remove the eggs, refresh under cold running water, and peel off the shells.

Halve the eggs lengthwise and transfer the yolks to a bowl. Mix the yolks with the anchovy salad cream and pass through a fine sieve.

Arrange the halved eggs on a serving dish. Put ½ teaspoon of kimchi hot sauce into the cavity of each egg, then place the yolk mixture in a pastry bag and pipe neatly into the egg cavities, on top of the sauce. Refrigerate for at least 20 minutes, then crumble the crispy chicken skin on top and serve.

HOT RIB TIPS

SERVES 2

pork rib tips (trimmed section from spare ribs)	1 pound 2 ounces
House Rub (see page 119)	scant ½ cup
Barbecue Sauce (see page 122)	3 tablespoons
Hot Sauce (see page 124)	3 tablespoons
oil, for deep-frying	

Prepare a barbecue for smoking (see The Setup on pages 114–15) and set the temperature to 230°F.

Sprinkle the rib tips with the rub.

Smoke the rib tips in the barbecue for 4 to 5 hours, or until they have a dark bark and are soft. Slightly overcooked is best here, because when deep-fried it is the crust that contrasts so well with the very soft meat.

Once smoked, remove the rib tips and refrigerate overnight until chilled and firm. Portion them individually (usually 3 to 4 from each section), then cut these in half again. The result will be about eight 2 x 1-inch sections from each whole offcut.

Put the barbecue sauce and hot sauce into a pan and cook over medium heat for 5 minutes, whisking to combine.

Heat the oil to 375°F in a deep-fryer or large saucepan. Add the little pieces of rib in batches and deep-fry until dark and crispy, about 2 minutes. Toss in the hot sauce and serve.

NOT EXACTLY "TIPS," BUT THE LAST 3 TO 4 SMALL RIBS FROM THE BACK END OF THE RIBCAGE. WE READ ABOUT PLACES IN CHICAGO SMOKING IT SEPARATELY AS LITTLE BAR SNACKS. RIBS AND BAR SNACK IN THE SAME BREATH CAN ONLY BRING HAPPINESS, RIGHT? WE TRIED THIS, BUT ALTHOUGH IT HAD SATISFYING BONE-GNAWING QUALITIES, IT WAS NOT MENU-WORTHY. AND IT REMAINED THAT WAY UNTIL ONE DAY THE LITTLE SMOKED RIBS WERE THROWN INTO THE FRYER AND TOSSED IN HOT SAUCE.

MEATS, SAUCES {&} RUBS

MEAT SOURCING

It is for good reason that provenance —the source and origin of food—is now an integral part of good cooking and good eating. It has become fashionable to buy food from responsible sources, to know breed from breed, to know the feed and the farmer, and all this information is of huge importance when searching for the best meat to buy and cook.

We do not source meat from some of the most dedicated farmers in the country to gloat about it. It is something that drives us, fascinates us, and fulfills us, and ultimately it is the meat we want to be cooking and serving to our customers. Awesome meat starts well before it gets to the butcher or the chef—it starts with the farmer, and the conscientious cook should want to know what it is they are buying and cooking. We receive the kill tag of every carcass, forequarter, and rib that comes into the restaurant, with the farmer's name, kill date, age of cow, and slaughterhouse used. For us, the importance of knowing all these things cannot be overstated. It may not interest the customers the way it interests us, but they can rest easy that we know and have full confidence in the farms

and farmers that produce the food they eat. If this same approach is taken at home when sourcing your own meat, there is no doubt that over time you will have great satisfaction from eating and cooking with meat that you are proud to have purchased. This information provides not only some assurances but also fascinating information that shows just how variable meat can be.

Variances can be attributed to many things: breed; different periods of dry-aging; the time of year that the animal was slaughtered, from when the grass is rich and lush in spring, summer, and fall, to when it suffers in the lean winter months; to the cows that spend all year up on the moors or those in the wetter lowlands. Pork is also different throughout the year, with pigs laying down more fat in the winter to protect themselves from the cold. The difference is staggering, and is another point of endless fascination when carefully

sourcing your meat. We now farm our own rare-breed pigs in the village of Pitt, and it is our duty and our joy to provide them with proper husbandry and care. We are confident that our pigs could not be happier, roaming around in a huge woodland rooting and eating all the good things a big old woodland has to offer, and with a daily back-scratch and belly-rub for good measure. It is only right to buy from farms and farmers who have a similar approach to animal welfare and husbandry. Although it sounds contradictory, it is only through buying meat butchered from heritage breeds from dedicated farmers that the American heritage-breed industry will grow and these passionate farmers can continue their great work.

Look for heritage breeds that have been grown slowly and naturally, fed without the aid of hormones and not pumped full of grain to fuel fast growth. Good meat comes down to four main factors: genetics or breed, feed, husbandry, and slaughter. The quality of the meat will be compromised when any one of these factors is neglected and, unsurprisingly, the best meat will come from those farmers who value the importance of each one.

· · · · · · · · · · · · ·

GENETICS

Different breeds produce different meat. Some are lean, some fat, some dark, some pale; the loins in some are long and in others they are short. Commercial pig farmers selectively cross-breed lean pigs with fast-growing pigs,

to produce large litters and large carcasses in 16 to 20 weeks that satisfy the supermarkets' need for lean protein. Taste is secondary to profit in such circumstances. Similarly, in commercial beef farming in the UK, lean, muscle-heavy continental breeds such as Limousin and Charolais are often crossed with dairy cows and are hard-fed hormone-rich, high-protein feeds to produce a commercially viable animal for the supermarket in 15 months. The resulting beef is devoid of fat, flavor, and any characteristics that may make it an enjoyable dinner prospect. This beef is simply not comparable to the slow-maturing native British breeds that are left to develop fat and muscle over 30 months and beyond. More importantly, commercial animals reared in such a way are not going to lead a happy life.

Heritage-breed pigs mature and grow much more slowly than leaner commercial breeds. The natural ability to develop fat has not been bred out of them, and by the time they reach maturity they may have developed a thick layer of back fat with a prolific marbling of fat throughout the eye of the loin and into the shoulder. This is something to admire, to become giddy with excitement about, and even slightly emotional over. When we picked up our first Middle White carcass from the slaughterhouse and saw a thick, glistening layer of back fat beneath the skin, it was an amazing sight; confirmation of the inherent qualities of such pigs and justification of the sourcing of them to breed and rear. Not all heritage-breed pigs are the same, however, each breed having its own particular qualities

and characteristics that become apparent when you eat the meat. There are, of course, other factors to consider than just fat development as a sign of tasty meat. Of the native British breeds, we keep Middle White and Tamworth, and have kept Berkshire in the past. All of them are beautiful pigs and have produced some of the best pork we have ever eaten. Alongside these we have focused specifically on Mangalitza, a very rare Hungarian breed introduced to the UK in 2006. While finding specific breeds of pig is an important issue when searching for the best pork, a high-quality rare-breed pig can only fulfill its genetic potential with the right feed, husbandry, and slaughter. Only when all four things combine will you begin to eat pork as it can and really should be eaten.

Unlike pork, where we are particular in the breeds we use, we use a number of slow-maturing British breeds of beef in the restaurant and again remain perpetually fascinated by the individual characteristics and flavor profiles of each breed, raised on different types of land. Dexter, Longhorn, Shorthorn, Red Poll, Hereford, White Park, Highland, North Devon, and Belted Galloway all come through the restaurant on a regular basis from a variety of farmers, and are sound bets to provide you with great beef if fed, kept, and aged properly.

. . . .

——— FEED ———

It was an unforgettable moment when we tasted the first of the Mangalitza pigs we had reared. We had previously cooked with and eaten a lot of Mangalitza, and that was the main reason we chose to rear these beautifully furry pigs. What we produced, however, was unlike any other pork we had ever eaten—the meat was soft and dark with a thick web of marbling throughout, and had a 2-inch layer of hard, bright white back fat that was far sweeter, cleaner, and nuttier than usual. It was the most deliciously satisfying confirmation of the importance of feed and husbandry in pig farming. The pigs had been fed cobnuts from the hazel copse in which they lived, whey from the local cheese producer, pea shoots that we sowed in the late spring, and piles of old peaches and nectarines from the local vegetable market.

For us, the best beef comes from animals that have matured slowly, been allowed to eat the grass from the rich pastures on which they live, and fed only with grains in the last month or so of their life to help build the decent covering of fat needed for the dry-aging process that will shortly follow. The very best British beef is grass-fed and finished in such a way. Commercial beef, on the other hand, follows an altogether unnatural feeding process, in which the cows are fed high-protein feeds that are also high in growth hormones, antibiotics, and unnatural amounts of grain, which allow the cows to develop a desirable carcass weight within a short period of time. The poor and unnatural feed compounds the poor genetics to produce very poor beef.

OUR PIGS

Middle White

Mangalitza

Tamworth

. . . .

HUSBANDRY

The unnatural feeding process of some farmers, which results in animals being taken to slaughter at half the age of our animals, is an enterprise that brings fast profit and turnover, but one that produces animals of poor quality and those that can never be happy. Husbandry, the care of the animals, is a duty that the farmer must take seriously both for the welfare and happiness of the animal and the by-product of such welfare: brilliant meat.

Eat pork from free-range animals that live beyond 6 months, eat beef from cows that live beyond 25 months, and eat lamb from sheep that are allowed to develop fat and flavor at 6 to 7 months of age.

We actually prefer mutton in the restaurant that comes from sheep that are fully mature and two years of age. As with pork and beef, the flavor from older, mature animals is far more developed, though the meat is slightly tougher. In all cases, try and buy from butchers who source from individual farmers. These are the people who need to be supported.

. . . .

SLAUGHTER

A farmer's hard work, good husbandry, and passion can be undone with a poorly executed slaughter. Again, the need for a stress-free and humane slaughter is twofold. The well-being of the animal is paramount. Animals deserve to be killed in such a way that they feel no stress, but the stress that a badly run slaughterhouse can produce in the animal also affects the quality of the meat. Stress releases hormones into the muscles of the animal, namely adrenalin, preparing it to either fight or run. If an animal is killed while it is stressed, the meat may become acidic, pale, pappy in texture, and develop an unnatural sheen and dark blood-red spots throughout from blood capillaries that burst in the stressful moments before and during slaughter.

As pigkeepers we could think of nothing worse than a stressful slaughter of an animal that has lived such a fulfilling life. It is simply in nobody's interest to have a stressed animal. We are very fortunate to have Laverstoke Park slaughterhouse for our Pitt pigs, which is just a few miles up the road from us. The slaughterhouse was designed by Temple Grundin, specifically with the animals' sensibilities in mind and consistently produces excellent carcasses for us. There are only natural curves with no artificial light or shiny surfaces in the building, and classical music plays throughout the process. The refrigeration is also exceptional. The carcass is not simply taken to a giant walk-in fridge after slaughter for rapid chilling, which can create something called cold shortening whereby the muscles contract to produce dry and tough meat, but is taken through a slow, gradual chilling process whereby the carcass takes 24 hours to chill fully. It is unlikely you will be able to know these things when buying from your butcher, but do look for the signs of stress in the meat and avoid it when you find them.

DRY-AGING

Aging is vital for both maximizing flavor and texture in meat, most noticeably in beef and lamb. Pork should be hung for anything up to two weeks in order to dry the carcass, but does not benefit from long periods of aging and is best enjoyed fresh. Beef, on the other hand, benefits immeasurably from aging and should not be eaten fresh or if it has been wet-aged, which means it has been vacuum-packed after butchery and left in the bag for a period of time. Wet-aged beef sits in its own blood and produces dry and unpleasant results. Dry-aging is undoubtedly superior, but is a costly practice and is only enjoyed by few people as a result.

After slaughter, the cow is split in two and hung in a large fridge through which air circulates quickly and freely. During the first 16 to 20 days of the dry-aging process, enzymes in the meat begin to dismantle the muscle fibers, making it more tender. The meat is essentially undergoing a controlled deterioration. This tenderization then ceases, but during this subsequent period, and as the meat is hung longer, moisture loss in the meat intensifies the flavor. The slow loss of moisture, as in salami or air-dried ham production, concentrates the sweet sugars and umami-rich proteins in the meat and also allows it to retain more moisture during cooking. These concentrated molecules, and the oxidization of fat that occurs during the process, boost the "meatiness" and umami in the meats and contribute to the spellbinding Maillard flavors (see page 108) during cooking. Meat that has been dry-aged for 25 days and beyond will have a distinctively sweet and nutty "funk" to it, one that is entirely pleasant and very addictive. In the restaurant we put a pack of salted peanuts next to a dry-aged rib of beef and the blind sniff test was very close. The moisture loss and the time taken for it to occur are the costly factors involved, but are also the factors that produce the flavor and texture in the meat. This is why commercial operations prefer wet-aging—there is no moisture and weight loss in the meat, and all meat is sold by weight.

We have found that dry-aged beef also produces the best low and slow barbecue for us. Wet beef ribs tend to curl up like a double helix and dry out when smoked for long periods of time and the flavor of heavily dry-aged beef straight out of the smoker is something that cannot be replicated with inferior wet-aged beef. We like the flavor of the meat to be the dominant force in our barbecue with smoke and sauce following after, so dry-aging has become a significant part of the restaurant. All our beef ribs are from carcasses hung for 35 days, after which the rib racks are removed and left to dry on racking for a further week or two. Our chuck is taken even further, often to 40 to 50 days, and we have found that this helps shorten the "stall" (see page 116) during cooking and produces exactly the brisket we want to be eating and serving. The featherblade, which sits on the blade bone of the shoulder, we hang alongside our brisket to intensify the flavor.

When buying dry-aged beef, speak to your butcher and ask for beef that has been hung for at least 28 days. Start with 28 days and see how you like it and how it cooks. When you return, try some beef hung for 35 days and compare the two flavors. Tri-tip of beef can hang for up to 70 days and we enjoy our ribs of beef around 45 days depending on the breed and fat content in the animal.

• • • • • • • • • • • •

PORK FAT

The value of pork fat cannot be overstated; its uses are endless and the need for it in the cooking of pork is clear. When buying pork, be sure that there is both a hard thick layer of fat on top of the loin and shoulder, and a good amount of fat running through the muscle. Even if you do not intend to eat all the fat, it will aid the cooking, basting the meat as it begins to render, and producing better-flavored pork. When you bite into meat and break the muscle tissue, the fat that is embedded in the muscle, in the connective tissue, fills your mouth and this is what helps produce a juicy mouthful. This is only possible with proper fatty pork.

Fat is also a vital source of aroma and flavor in cooked meat, with the feed of the animal particularly affecting the flavor of the fat.

Our decision to start breeding Mangalitza was largely influenced by the quality of the fat and its special composition—its fat is more mono-unsaturated than any other pork fat, and higher in oleic acid than any other breed. The breed was once so highly prized for its ability to produce sweet, light, and clean-tasting fat that it was traded on the Vienna stock exchange. It is interesting to note that our Mangalitza pigs benefit from 2 to 3 weeks hanging and it is their

special fat composition that allows this. It is an extreme lard-type pig that takes up to 20 months to mature (four times longer than most breeds), and as such produces joints of meat very high in fat that are of intense flavor and incredibly juicy. The very slow growth and high fat renders the Mangalitza about as undesirable as a pig could be for commercial pig farming and, consequently, it was in severe danger of extinction in the 1970s. The Mangalitza is the perfect example of the value of fat in pork, and while you may not want to eat pure fat, when buying pork remember that fat will be playing the key role in the final enjoyment of a pork dish.

COLLAGEN

Different cuts of meat have varying degrees of tenderness and this can largely be attributed to the collagen in each muscle. Collagen is made of naturally occurring proteins and is the main component of connective tissue in muscle. The strength of the collagen varies in different cuts of meat and is also dependent on the age, breed, and sex of the animal. Those muscles that do very little work have weak collagen. Cuts such as fillet, rib-eye roast, sirloin, and rump all contain weak collagens and are all relatively tender.

Understanding collagen is an important part of understanding low and slow cooking. In order to turn a tough collagen-rich cut such as brisket, shank, or shoulder into something delicious, juicy, and tender, the muscle must be cooked with a low and even heat for a long period of time so that the collagen molecules unravel, break down, and dissolve into soft gelatin that bastes and moistens the meat. This is why much barbecue requires low and slow cooking.

MAILLARD & DRIPPINGS

Maillard is the chemical reaction that occurs when meat is browned and is one of the main reasons why roasted meat tastes so delicious. While understanding the processes involved in Maillard is not necessary, understanding that it exists certainly is. Knowing that a grill needs to be hot for it to happen, and sensing when the time is right to season your steak and get it on the grill, is far more important than understanding how sugars and

amino acids in meat combine in the face of high heat to produce reactions and new flavor compounds of high awesomeness.

The reason why the flavor of grilled meat is so unique and addictive is not only down to the complex Maillard reactions that occur when meat hits a hot grill—it is, in fact, the drippings from the cooking meat and not the charcoal itself that produce the flavor

in grilled meat. When the fats, the sugar, and protein-rich juices from the meat fall down onto the hot charcoal, they combust into smoke and flame and rise to coat the cooking meat in a multitude of unique and aromatic flavor compounds. So when you are weighing up whether to use a ridged grill pan or light the barbecue, know that only one will really satisfy your need for grilled meat.

{ PIG CUTS }

1	JOWL
2+3	SHOULDER/
	BOSTON BUTT
4	HAND/PICNIC
	SHOULDER
5	FOREFOOT
6	HINDFOOT
7	BEST/BLADE END
8	LOIN/RIB END
9	T BONE/
	CENTER LOIN
	(TENDERLOIN)
10	RUMP
11	RIB BACON
12	BELLY BACON
13	HAM (BUTT END)

HOW IT GETS USED

LOW 'N' SLOW	GRILL
HEAD	SHOULDER/BOSTON BUTT
JOWL	LOIN/RIB END
NECK	LOIN/RIB END CHOPS
SHOULDER	RUMP
PICNIC	SHOULDER BUTTERFLIED
SHOULDER	SHOULDER CHOPS
HOCKS	BEST/BLADE END
BELLY	RIBS
RIBS	LEG STEAKS
	HEART
	LIVER
	KIDNEYS

{ SHEEP CUTS }

1. NECK
2. SHOULDER
3. FORESHANK
4. RIB OR RACK
5. LOIN
6. RUMP
7. LEG
8. HINDSHANK
9. FLANK
10. BREAST

HOW IT GETS USED

LOW 'N' SLOW	GRILL
NECK	SHOULDER (SQUARE CUT)
SHOULDER	RACK (RIB CHOPS,
SHANK	FRENCHED RIB CHOPS)
HEAD	LEG (AMERICAN LEG)
BREAST	LOIN (LOIN CHOPS)
LEG	

{ COW CUTS }

#	Cut
1	TONGUE
2	CHEEK
3	NECK
4	BRISKET
5	SHIN
6	PLATE (SHORT RIBS)
7	FLANK
8	LEG
9	ROUND (SILVERSIDE)
10	CHUCK
11	RIB
12	SIRLOIN
13	T-BONE & PORTERHOUSE
14	RUMP
15	OXTAIL

HOW IT GETS USED

LOW 'N' SLOW	GRILL
CHEEKS	STEAKS (DENVER,
TONGUE	BOXEATER, FLAT IRON,
NECK	UNDERBLADE FILLET)
FEATHERBLADE	RIB-EYE
BRISKET	PORTERHOUSE
RIBS	SIRLOIN
TAIL	FILLET
FLANK	RUMP CAP
PLATE (SHORT	HANGER
RIBS)	HEART
SHINS	
OXTAIL	

SMOKING

{ DIRECT AND INDIRECT }

WHAT DIRECT MEANS

In the UK, direct grilling is what most people think of when we say barbecue. When you have watched your old man nuking sausages, burgers, and piles of helpless chicken wings, he will have been using a direct heat source, a barbecue set up for grilling. The heat from the charcoal or gas directly impacts the meat with high surface temperatures. The heat is not deflected or absorbed by anything during the cooking process and does not affect the meat solely through the convection currents in the barbecue, as it does with indirect cooking, when the barbecue is used like an oven. Direct heat should not be synonymous with burning, however, and with a little bit of skill it is one of the most exciting and important methods of cooking. Cooking over fire, whether it be direct grilling or indirect smoking, boils down to the ability to control temperature, and while it is possible to guide someone as to how this happens, it is really only something that can be learned through time spent in the loving company of your barbecue.

When we first opened the trailer, all we had was a smoker and a grill. Both were vital cooking sources for us, used all day, every day, and represent the value in cooking directly as well as indirectly. While at the restaurant we have a charcoal grill and smokers to satisfy our need to grill and smoke simultaneously, at home this is not necessary. You can, however, put yourself in a similar position in going from cooking low and slow (indirect) to quickly finishing your meat over direct heat. We believe you get the most flavor from cooking this way, and almost all the main meat recipes following in this chapter call for finishing over direct high heat.

The majority of barbecue books we have read (apart from those of Adam Perry Lang) skim over, or at least pay very little attention to, the importance of direct grilling over charcoal or wood. It is an essential cooking technique, and without it our menu would be half as long and our lives half as exciting. There is no way we could ever cook a pork chop in a pan on our induction stove; it just wouldn't be right. It would be boring to cook, pretty boring to eat, and a bit of a turn-off.

We appreciate and enjoy the decadence of old-school French meat cookery—a côte de boeuf roasted and basted in a pint of nutty foaming butter with garlic, shallots, and thyme is a very attractive thing, and we could happily work our way through a plate of it—but it just doesn't excite in the same way that cooking directly over charcoal does and it is not the way we like to do things. While a pork shoulder smoked for 15 hours using indirect heat can be the zenith of barbecue, so can a pork chop cooked in 10 minutes. Both are barbecue and both methods deserve to be learned and practiced. Being able to cook both ways will undoubtedly make you a better person, a happier person, a sexier person, and a fatter person.

We have cooked directly over charcoal every day since Pitt Cue began, and while we have all been obsessed with it for as long as we have been cooking, we still know relatively little about it and learn constantly from mistakes and from those people around us who share the passion. We are in perpetual awe of the Turkish chefs who master the raging ocakbasi, barely sweating as they feed entire restaurants from the single long grills they sit behind. We have been stopped in our tracks each time we've visited a small restaurant outside San Sebastián, where everything is cooked to perfection on handmade grills. These are people who have dedicated their lives to cooking in such a way and have become successful only through years of making mistakes and learning from them.

So, while we can give you our recipe for cooking a pork chop and advise you on how to set up a grill, all it really boils down to is practice. Just keep lighting your barbecue and cooking on it, and you will begin to understand the hot spots and cool spots on the grill; how long it takes for the coals to burn down for the optimum grilling temperature (we light the charcoal at 5 PM in the restaurant for service to begin at 6 PM, though arguably the best stuff comes off the grill later in the night); which brand of charcoal cooks for longest and which brand cooks at a higher temperature; and how long a full load of charcoal lasts you.

WHAT WE GRILL

There are many cuts of meat that benefit from time spent on the grill, but only a few can be covered in this book.

PIG	SHEEP	COW
shoulder	butterflied shoulder	chuck
butterflied shoulder	shoulder joint	Denver cut
shoulder chops	chops	rib-eye
best/blade end	rump	porterhouse
rib end chops	lamb ribs	sirloin
T bones	leg	fillet
leg steaks	heart	tri-tip
rump	liver	cap steak
heart	kidneys	hanger steak
liver		flat iron
kidneys		underblade
		heart

WHAT INDIRECT MEANS

Indirect cooking is how we cook low and slow. The heat source and radiant heat is never in direct reach of the meat. In the case of a ceramic barbecue, it is diffused through a thick ceramic plate. In an offset smoker, the fire pit is completely separate from where the meat is. In a kettle barbecue, a good setup diffuses radiant heat through water trays, with the meat positioned as far away from the burning coals as possible so as to only be affected by the indirect convection currents flowing through the barbecue.

The cooking in all three types of common home barbecue works the same way a convection oven does, with the heat being diffused throughout the cooking chamber so that it flows evenly around the meat while it's cooking. The cooking is therefore much more even than over direct heat. Direct heat requires constant flipping, turning, and attention in order to cook evenly, while indirect heat requires a well thought-out setup, and then beer and patience in equal measure.

WHAT WE SMOKE

Traditional barbecue would suggest that the lesser, collagen-rich cuts such as shoulder, belly, brisket, head, shank, and hocks would all be best suited to indirect cooking and smoking, where the low, even heat is able to break down the collagens into gelatin without the whole cut overcooking. They all certainly favor this form of cooking and would not be pleasant if cooked quickly over direct heat. This is how we cook these cuts, but we also like to cook many primal cuts using indirect heat for the beginning of their journey.

Cooking sections of pork loin, rump, ribs of beef, and rolled shoulder to medium-rare and rare using indirect techniques before finishing them over direct heat has changed the way our menu works at the restaurant, and is perhaps the best way of using indirect heat to really benefit carefully sourced meat. So, while indirect cooking has become synonymous with pulled pork, ribs, and brisket, do not be limited to those.

LOW AND SLOW

PIG

head, jowls, neck, shoulder, foot, hock, belly, ribs

SHEEP

head, leg, shoulder, breast, belly

COW

cheeks, neck, brisket, ribs, featherblade, tail, flank, shank, chuck

INDIRECT TO MEDIUM-RARE

PIG

shoulder joint, loin, rump, chops

SHEEP

boned shoulder, saddle, rump, butterflied leg

COW

chuck, Denver cut, shoulder chops, flat iron, hanger, côte de boeuf, rump,

HEAT SOURCE

Barbecue at its most basic is the alchemy of wood, smoke, and meat. Awesome barbecue can come from both wood and charcoal, but there is no doubt that the quality of the fuel used can dramatically affect the flavor of your final offering. It is fair to say that the best hardwood will create the best barbecue. Hardwood cells contain large amounts of lignin, which is the main reason smoked food tastes so good. When hardwood is heated, this lignin breaks down, producing new volatile chemicals that are responsible for the aromatic smoke you find in great barbecue joints, and the sweet and aromatic flavors that this smoke imparts to the meat. Hardwoods, such as mesquite, oak, and hickory are all high in lignin and are unsurprisingly the most common woods used in American barbecue, whereas softer woods, such as pine, contain low amounts of lignin and produce a bitter and acrid smoke. The huge stacks of drying hickory and white oak outside many of the best barbecue joints in Texas are testament to this fact.

At home, your best bet is to use hardwood lump charcoal, made from good-quality hardwoods with none of the added chemicals that help lesser charcoals burn sufficiently well. This charcoal will become the backbone of your barbecue, the fuel that keeps the whole operation running. To this base different types and different quantities of hardwood chunks can be added, depending on the flavor profile you are looking for.

We have used apple, mesquite, hickory, and oak, and we have also dabbled with cherry wood chunks at home and in the restaurant. We like smoke to aid the flavor of the meat. The sourcing of awesome meat has always been the essence of the restaurant, and we dislike super intense and smoky barbecue where there is excessive use of mesquite or soaked wood chips. There are a load of places to find good wood chunks so try as many types of wood as possible, settling on whichever wood gives you the flavor profile you most enjoy.

THE SETUP

There are many ways to skin a pig, and while at home we cook on both ceramic and classic kettle barbecues, it is pretty safe to say that the majority of people who want to try barbecuing will be able get their hands on a kettle barbecue, such as a Weber, a basic offset smoker, or a ceramic barbecue, such as a Big Green Egg. These are what we cook on most, too, so it

made sense to gear the recipes in this book toward these types of barbecues. Nearly all these pieces of kit come with their own instructions, but the following methods are what have worked best for us and are widely used by the most avid home cooks. Good barbecuing is all about being able to control the heat on the barbecue you are using, understanding what is happening at different temperatures and knowing the benefits of cooking at those temperatures. This comes naturally the more you cook, but setting up a two-zone barbecue will stand you in good stead.

The setup is very simple, and basically means that one side of your grill is hot, producing direct heat that allows for fast grilling and for the important Maillard reactions to happen, while the other side of the grill produces none of its own heat but relies on the convection heat currents in the barbecue to create indirect heat and the kind of temperatures that are ideal for smoking. By controlling the temperature of your barbecue using the air vents, you will be able to begin implementing the techniques that we use in the restaurant for both the primal cuts that are taken to medium-rare and the lesser cuts that come out of the smoker low and slow. This setup also provides a safety net if you have a super-fatty piece of meat and do not want to suffer the mega flareups that could ruin something so special. Being able to moderate the cooking using two different zones is particularly helpful if this is the case. Our robata grill in the restaurant works in a similar way. If the grill is getting a bit angry and beautiful things are at risk of burning, we just set them on the top level of the grill, right at the back, where they can rest and take stock until the grill begins to behave again.

The aim with your two-zone setup is to have two very different temperatures at either side of your grill. Ideally, the indirect zone will hover at around 220° to 265°F and the direct zone will sit at around 340° to 375°F. Keeping the temperature at

225° to 230°F, the magical temperatures for much great low and slow cooking, is most definitely not essential, but keeping the temperature as constant as possible within these basic guidelines will definitely help, and will allow you to begin to get an idea of how long different cuts are going to take to cook next time you try them again. We have tasted some unbelievable meat at various barbecue competitions where smokers were being set to 265°F and upward, but these people were militant in their checking and had honed their recipes over many years. Stick to 220° to 260°F and you cannot go too far wrong.

To achieve this you need to fill up a chimney starter with charcoal, light the charcoal, and wait until ready to use (watch for white, ash-covered coals, which are the best sign of readiness) before pushing all the lit coals to one side of the bottom ash grate in the barbecue. Place an aluminum tray filled with hot water next to the coals on the other side of the barbecue, then put the grill grate on and place another aluminum water-filled tray on the grill grate directly above the coals. You can now cook indirectly on the other side of the grill grate, next to the top water tray. The two water trays will help moderate the heat from the coals and also provide an important source of moisture when cooking. The right humidity in the barbecue is very important. Cooking large volumes in one smoker creates a very humid cooking atmosphere, and often produces a moister and faster-cooked product. The water trays are there to help this when cooking only one or two things for a long period of time at home. You are now ready to cook indirectly. Add a few wood chunks over the lit coals in order to begin smoking.

CONTROL

Keeping the temperature constant is the biggest challenge when smoking at home. The vents at the bottom of the barbecue are the key and should be used to effect oxygen intake, which in turn dictates how fast and how hot the coals burn. Opening the bottom vents in the barbecue will increase the air flow, or draft, sucking more oxygen-rich air into the fire and causing it to burn fiercer and faster. Closing the bottom vents will reduce the draft and the oxygen that reaches the fire, causing it to cool and burn more slowly. The ability to control the temperature through the manipulation of draft and oxygen is the goal.

In the search for complete temperature control, the top vents are less significant and do not provide the same control as the bottom vents. The top vents do affect the draft, however, and how easy it is for the smoke and air to leave the barbecue. The top vents should remain half open to allow for draft, and to avoid excessive buildup of smoke in the barbecue, which creates acrid, sooty deposits and could ruin your hard work. Start with the bottom vents fully open to allow the coals to get going. You will see the temperature begin to rise, and as

you begin to reach 210°F, close the vents by half. This should halt the rise in temperature, and from here it is a case of making fine adjustments to get to your desired temperature for low and slow. The top vents need not be played with too much, but positioning the meat directly above the vents will force the smoke over the meat, and also allow you to poke a thermometer through the vents to where the meat is cooking so that you can work out exactly what temperature the most important part of the barbecue is at.

For larger cuts, like brisket, shoulder, and most definitely suckling pig, you will have to be prepared to light the chimney starter on numerous occasions to maintain the lit charcoal in the barbecue. The general rule of thumb is to add six chunks of lit coal every hour. This should help maintain a constant temperature. Adding unlit coals is fine—it just prolongs any dip in temperature. This is where a ceramic barbecue becomes very useful, with one load of charcoal lasting longer than you will ever really need to cook a single large roast.

SMOKING

GRILLING

WHEN IS IT READY?

This is one of the most important questions. While cooking something for half a day at a low temperature provides the cook with greater margin for error, removing the meat from your barbecue at the right time is crucial. There are so many variables in cooking outdoors. The insulation of your barbecue, the weather, the fuel, and the genetics of the animal all play a key role in how a piece of meat is going to cook. Timings for our recipes are approximate in the loosest sense, and need to be taken with a fistful of salt. This may sound stupid for a cookbook, and maybe it is, but barbecue is far from an exact science and that's just the way it is. As long as you have a meat probe thermometer handy, use the timings as a guide, and use "the force," you will be just dandy.

Probe thermometers are invaluable tools, but touch should not be forgotten, especially when cooking over direct heat. This is something that becomes apparent purely through experience, although using touch and a probe alongside each other will allow you to train your touch without too many botch-ups. There is no shame at all in using a meat probe, and it is really the only way to produce consistent barbecue straight away. If possible, buy a remote meat probe that allows you to read the internal temperature without lifting the lid of the barbecue. Lifting the lid releases all the moisture from the cooking chamber and drops the temperature. Our friend David calls this "peeking," and is convinced that it is the root of all evil. The more moisture that is retained inside your barbecue, the better, so a remote probe is a great tool to have.

One time where "peeking" usually becomes rife is when the meat "stalls" or "plateaus." When the meat reaches an internal temperature of roughly 160°F, it stops and may not rise a degree in temperature for an hour or so. This is when people sweat a little and start to panic. The barbecue is then opened, the meat is checked, and the vents are opened to try to force the temperature up. These are all bad moves. The stall in temperature is standard and occurs when the collagen begins to break down into gelatin. The reaction absorbs energy and forces moisture to the surface of the meat, which cools it. These panic reactions lose more moisture and temperature in the cooking chamber and only contribute to a longer stall. Some people "crutch" when this occurs, which means wrapping the meat in foil, often with some fruit juice, butter, and stock, and returning it to the smoker to speed through the stall. Some people believe this creates a moister end result, which is no surprise because it is essentially a braise, but it prevents a decent bark from forming. It is up to you. We do not bother with it.

DIRECT INTERNAL TEMPERATURES

115° F—BLEU
120° F—RARE
130° F—MEDIUM-RARE
140° F—MEDIUM
340° F—WHERE MAILLARD BEGINS

INDIRECT TEMPERATURES

160° F—THE STALL
185 to 195° F—TIME TO REMOVE THE MEAT FROM THE SMOKER
230° F—IDEAL COOKING TEMPERATURE

PITT CUE MISE-EN-PLACE

There really is no set armory for barbecue. In its purest form, fire and something with which to support the meat over the fire is all that is really needed. But we have evolved from caveman dining (sort of), and the modern-day cook seeks comfort and assurance when setting out to make dinner, so there are a few things that will help you get started and ensure that mistakes are few and far between. A lot of barbecue is winging it, and this seems to have worked for us so far, but beyond experience there are a few key tools to push you forward:

ESSENTIALS

A SOLID BARBECUE—A decent barbecue is a pretty essential starting point. Whether you go ceramic (Big Green Egg), kettle (Weber), gas, offset, or feel like building yourself a pit, just make sure you are not setting yourself up for a fall before you even begin—you do not have to remortgage your house to cook solid barbecue.

CHARCOAL—Natural hardwood lump charcoal.

HARDWOOD—Not a euphemism. Look for chunks of good hardwood (i.e. oak, hickory).

HEAVY CAST-IRON GRILL GRATE—For direct grilling, a good surface is essential, because it retains heat better and aids in the all-important quest for Maillard.

CHIMNEY STARTER—If you are cooking on a Weber-style barbecue, this is essential. Unsurprisingly, Weber themselves make the best one. Clever chaps.

INSTANT-READ MEAT PROBE THERMOMETER—Meat probe thermometers will save you a huge number of headaches in the long run. We smoke a lot of bigger cuts to medium-rare or rare in the restaurant smokers, and having a meat probe can be a real lifesaver. The following recipes are all written with a meat probe in mind, so unless "the force" is super strong you may struggle.

ALUMINUM WATER TRAYS—Look for the the 12 x 6-inch containers.

YOUR HANDS—The more you cook, the more important touch becomes. With time you will be able to know through touch when a steak is rare and when a brisket is reaching perfection. Never underestimate your hands.

SQUEEZE BOTTLES

TONGS

DISH CLOTH

APRON

AWESOME KNIFE

RUBS

THESE RUBS ARE ESSENTIAL TO BARBECUE AND ARE BASED ON WHAT MEAT YOU PLAN TO SMOKE, BUT THEY CAN AND SHOULD BE ADJUSTED TO SUIT YOUR TASTE AND INTRIGUE.

BEEF RUB

MAKES 12¼ OUNCES

Maldon sea salt	scant 1 cup
maple sugar or soft light brown sugar	½ cup
English mustard powder	heaping ¼ cup
hot smoked paprika	3½ tablespoons
freshly ground black pepper	¼ cup

Blitz all the ingredients in a blender. Store in an airtight container for up to 1 week.

PORK RUB

MAKES 12¼ OUNCES

Maldon sea salt	scant 1 cup
maple sugar or soft light brown sugar	1 cup
fennel seeds, toasted	¼ cup
freshly ground black pepper	¼ cup
sage leaves	heaping ¼ cup
rosemary leaves	2½ tablespoons
garlic cloves	3 tablespoons (about 10 cloves)

Blitz all the ingredients in a blender and spread on a clean baking pan to dry. Blitz again, then store in an airtight container. Keeps for up to 1 week.

LAMB RUB

MAKES 12¼ OUNCES

Maldon sea salt	scant 1 cup
maple sugar or soft light brown sugar	½ cup
English mustard powder	heaping ¼ cup
fennel seeds, toasted	¼ cup
garlic cloves	3 tablespoons (about 10 cloves)
rosemary leaves	2½ tablespoons
thyme leaves	3½ tablespoons
zest of 1 lemon	

Blitz all the ingredients in a blender. Store in an airtight container for up to 1 week.

DUCK RUB

MAKES 11½ OUNCES

Maldon sea salt	scant 1 cup
maple sugar or soft light brown sugar	½ cup
black peppercorns	3½ tablespoons
fennel seeds, toasted	1½ tablespoons
star anise	10
5-inch cinnamon stick	1
zest of 1 orange	

Blitz all the ingredients in a blender. Store in an airtight container for up to 1 week.

HOUSE RUB

MAKES 10½ OUNCES

fennel seeds	1½ tablespoons
cumin seeds	1 teaspoon
black peppercorns	1 teaspoon
coriander seeds	1 teaspoon
soft dark brown sugar	½ cup packed
granulated sugar	¼ cup
garlic powder	1 tablespoon
fine salt	heaping ⅓ cup
smoked paprika	2 tablespoons
paprika	¼ cup
dried oregano	1 teaspoon
cayenne	1 teaspoon

Toast the fennel seeds, cumin seeds, peppercorns, and coriander seeds in a dry pan over medium heat for a few minutes, shaking the pan, until the spices release an aroma. Tip into a bowl and let cool.

Blitz the toasted spices in a blender to a rough powder. Combine with the remaining ingredients and mix thoroughly. Keep in a sealed container for up to 1 week.

PENNY BUN RUB

MAKES 10½ OUNCES

dried ceps (or shiitake if not available)	3½ ounces
Maldon sea salt	scant ½ cup
light Muscovado sugar	½ cup
smoked paprika	1 teaspoon
freshly ground black pepper	1 teaspoon

Blitz the dried mushrooms to a powder (a coffee grinder will work best). Mix with all the other ingredients and store in an airtight container. Rub it on beef or use as a seasoning.

SMOKED BACON RUB

MAKES 14 OUNCES

smoked bacon	7 ounces
smoked Maldon sea salt	scant ½ cup
maple sugar or soft light brown sugar	½ cup packed
freshly ground black pepper	pinch
hot smoked paprika	pinch
freshly ground anise seed	pinch

Heat the oven to 350°F. Get two heavy metal baking pans and two sheets of waxed paper ready.

Sandwich the bacon between the waxed paper sheets and the two pans and bake in the oven for 30 minutes, or until brown and crispy. Remove from the oven and lay the bacon on paper towels to cool and dry out.

Use a mortar and pestle to grind the dry bacon to a fine powder with the remaining ingredients. Spread out on a clean baking pan to dry further. When completely dry, grind once more and put into airtight jars. Once a jar has been opened, use within 1 week.

DRY CURE

MAKES 2¾ POUNDS

salt (a 50:50 mix of Maldon sea salt and smoked Maldon sea salt is a winner)	2¼ pounds
molasses sugar	¾ cup
cracked black pepper	1½ tablespoons
star anise, finely ground	1
fennel seeds, toasted and crushed	1½ tablespoons

Mix all the ingredients in a bowl until they are thoroughly combined.

SAUCES

MOTHER SAUCE

MAKES 5¼ PINTS

dry-aged beef trim, diced	1 pound 2 ounces
beef stock	2 pints
pork stock	2 pints
shallots, finely diced	5
butter	½ stick
sweet Madeira	scant 1 cup
tomato ketchup	scant 1 cup
French's mustard	¼ cup
cider vinegar	1 tablespoon
Worcestershire sauce	2 tablespoons
Tabasco	1 teaspoon
cloudy apple juice	scant ½ cup
blackstrap molasses	3½ tablespoons
pork dripping	3½ ounces

WE HAVE A MOTHER SAUCE AT THE RESTAURANT. THE AIM OF THIS WAS TO PRODUCE THE MEATIEST OF ALL SAUCES. NOT SWEET OR ACIDIC, LIKE A BARBECUE SAUCE, BUT A SAUCE SO PACKED WITH UMAMI AND SMOKY MEATINESS THAT YOU WOULD TASTE IT HOURS LATER.

Brown the dry-aged beef trim in a large pan over high heat until well browned. Add both stocks and deglaze the pan, then lower the heat and simmer, skimming the surface continuously, until the liquid has reduced by two-thirds.

Meanwhile, in another pan, sweat the shallots in the butter for about 5 to 8 minutes, or until soft. Add the Madeira, bring to a simmer, and reduce the liquid by half.

Add the Madeira mixture to the reduced stock and simmer to reduce the liquid by a further one-quarter, skimming continuously.

Mix together all the remaining ingredients, except the pork dripping, and add to the pan. Finally, whisk in the pork dripping until combined.

Pass the mixture through a fine sieve before using to baste meat before serving.

BARBECUE JELLY

MAKES APPROXIMATELY 14 OUNCES

black peppercorns	2 teaspoons
fennel seeds	2 teaspoons
mustard seeds	2 teaspoons
red bell peppers, seeded	2
chipotle chiles, split	2
ripe tomatoes	2
apples, peeled and cored	2
maple syrup	scant ½ cup
cider vinegar	scant ½ cup
smoked Maldon sea salt	2 teaspoons
pectin	1 sachet (¼ ounce)

Toast the peppercorns, fennel seeds, and mustard seeds in a dry skillet over medium heat for a few minutes, shaking the pan, until the spices release an aroma. Remove from the heat and crush with a mortar and pestle.

Chop the bell peppers, chiles, tomatoes, and apples roughly and place in a stainless steel canning pot or stockpot, along with the maple syrup, vinegar, and salt.

Bring to a boil, then reduce the heat and simmer for 1 hour. Pour into a jelly bag and hang over a bowl overnight.

Put the resulting clear juice with the pectin into the canning pot or stockpot and boil, skimming as you go, until the mixture reaches a setting point of 220°F on a candy thermometer.

Decant into a sterilized 1-pint jar (see page 78) and cover the exposed surface at the top of the jar with a disk of waxed paper. This jelly makes a great accompaniment for all types of cooked meat.

PITT CUE BARBECUE SAUCE

THANKS TO BIG CONGLOMERATE BURGER JOINTS, BARBECUE SAUCE IS PERHAPS MORE WELL KNOWN AND RECOGNIZED THAN THE CUISINE, AND THE TECHNIQUES OF THAT CUISINE, FROM WHICH IT COMES. THIS IS NOT A FAIR REPRESENTATION OF BARBECUE SAUCE OR THE MANY VARIATIONS IN WHICH IT IS FOUND IN EACH OF THE BARBECUE REGIONS OF AMERICA. CLASSIFYING BARBECUE INTO DISTINCT REGIONS IS PROBLEMATIC. YOU CAN SAFELY SAY, HOWEVER, THAT THE SAUCES IN THE CAROLINAS WILL VARY FROM THOSE IN TENNESSEE, KANSAS, AND TEXAS, BUT WHAT IS PERHAPS MOST NOTICEABLE FROM TRAVELING AROUND THE SOUTHERN STATES IS THAT EVERYONE MAKES THEIR OWN SAUCE, STAMPING IT WITH THEIR OWN IDENTITY AND PERSONALITY. THIS IS PART OF THE INTRIGUE OF VISITING DIFFERENT PLACES. THE BASE OF THE SAUCE MAY BE SIMILAR ACROSS ONE REGION BUT THE FINAL PRODUCTS IN EACH BARBECUE JOINT ARE WORLDS APART. THIS IS OUR SAUCE, BASED ON NO REGION IN PARTICULAR.

MAKES 2 PINTS

vegetable oil	2 tablespoons
white onion, peeled and grated	1
garlic clove, peeled and grated	1
Spice Mix (see below)	1½ tablespoons
apple juice	½ cup
cider vinegar	½ cup
maple syrup	generous ½ cup
French's mustard	½ cup
blackstrap molasses	½ cup
apricot preserve	heaping ⅓ cup
Chipotle Ketchup (see page 125)	2 cups
smoked Maldon sea salt	2 tablespoons

SPICE MIX

fennel seeds	2 teaspoons
cumin seeds	2½ teaspoons
coriander seeds	1 tablespoon
celery seeds	2 teaspoons
mustard seeds	1½ teaspoons
black peppercorns	2 teaspoons

To make the spice mix, toast all the spices in a dry pan over medium heat for a few minutes, shaking the pan until golden. Tip into a bowl and let cool. Blitz the toasted spices in a blender to a rough powder.

Heat the vegetable oil in a pan over medium heat. Add the onion, garlic, and spice mix, and cook gently for 10 minutes, or until the onions are cooked through. This is important because undercooked onions will taint the final sauce with an unpleasant raw onion flavor. Add the apple juice and cider vinegar and simmer until reduced by one-third.

Add the remaining ingredients, bring to a simmer, and continue to simmer for 5 minutes.

Blitz the sauce with an immersion blender, then pass it through a fine sieve. Pour into a sterilized 2-pint bottle (see page 78). Once cool, store in the refrigerator and use within 2 weeks.

HOT SAUCE

MAKES APPROXIMATELY 1 PINT

red bell peppers	2¼ pounds
red chiles	9 ounces
Maldon sea salt	1 teaspoon
cider vinegar	1½ tablespoons
maple syrup	1½ tablespoons
garlic cloves	3 tablespoons (about 10 cloves)

Prepare a barbecue for smoking (see The Setup on pages 114–15) and set the temperature to 250°F.

Smoke the bell peppers in the barbecue for 2 hours, or until soft. Discard the skins and as many seeds as possible, then put the flesh into a saucepan.

Adjust the barbecue for direct grilling or heat a ridged grill pan on the stove until smoking hot, and grill the chiles until blackened. Remove the stalks, then add the whole chiles, skins and all, to the peppers. Add the rest of the ingredients to the pan, bring to a simmer, and cook over low heat for 30 minutes.

Put the mixture into a blender and blitz until well mixed but still a little chunky. Decant into a sterilized 1-pint jar or bottle (see page 78) and refrigerate. The sauce will keep for 1 week in the fridge.

KIMCHI HOT SAUCE

MAKES 2 PINTS

superfine sugar	½ cup
garlic cloves, peeled	¾ cup (about 3½ ounces)
scallions, white parts only	3½ ounces
carrots, peeled and roughly chopped	¾ cup
fresh ginger, peeled and roughly chopped	3½ ounces
Korean chili powder	1 cup
anchovy fillets	3½ ounces
light soy sauce	scant ½ cup
Tay Ninh salt chili shrimp	3½ ounces
water	scant 1 cup

Put all the ingredients into a blender and process to a smooth purée. Pass through a fine sieve and pour into a sterilized 2-pint bottle (see page 78).

This sauce will naturally ferment over time, so keep it in the fridge and use within 2 weeks. This sauce also acts as a base for other things: kimchi hollandaise is particularly awesome.

B****** HOT SAUCE

MAKES APPROXIMATELY 2 CUPS

red bell peppers	2¼ pounds
Scotch bonnet chiles	9 ounces
Maldon sea salt	1 teaspoon
cider vinegar	1½ tablespoons
maple syrup	1½ tablespoons
garlic cloves	3 tablespoons (about 10 cloves)

Prepare a barbecue for smoking (see The Setup on pages 114–15) and set the temperature to 250°F.

Smoke the bell peppers in the barbecue for 3 to 4 hours, or until soft. Remove the skins and as many seeds as possible and put the flesh into a bowl.

Adjust the barbecue for direct grilling or heat a ridged grill pan on the stove until smoking hot, and grill the Scotch bonnet chiles until blackened. Remove the green stalks, then add the whole chiles, skins and all, to the bell peppers. Add the rest of the ingredients.

Put the mixture into a blender and blitz until well mixed but still a little chunky. Decant into a sterilized 1-pint jar or bottle and refrigerate. The sauce will keep for 1 week in the fridge.

CHIPOTLE KETCHUP

MAKES APPROXIMATELY 2 PINTS

ripe tomatoes, chopped	2¼ pounds
peeled and chopped onions	1½ cups
peeled, cored, and chopped apples	2 cups
chipotle peppers	9 ounces
cider vinegar	1 cup
smoked Maldon sea salt	2 tablespoons
hot smoked paprika	3½ tablespoons
light Muscovado sugar	1¼ cups

Place all the ingredients except the Muscovado sugar in a stainless steel pan and bring to a gentle simmer. Continue to cook at a simmer for 2 hours, then pass through a stainless steel vegetable mill.

Return the mixture to the pan with the Muscovado sugar and continue cooking for around 30 minutes, or until thickened, stirring regularly to stop it from sticking to the bottom of the pan.

Decant into sterilized bottles or jars (see page 78) and seal. When cool, refrigerate for a few days before using. Use within 2 weeks.

FRUIT KETCHUPS

APPLE KETCHUP

MAKES APPROXIMATELY 1¾ CUPS

Granny Smith apples, peeled, cored, and very thinly sliced	¾ pound
superfine sugar	¾ pound
cider vinegar	scant ⅔ cup
vanilla bean	½
lemon juice	2 teaspoons

Put the apples, sugar, vinegar, and vanilla bean into a stainless steel pan and bring to a boil. Cook for approximately 10 minutes, or until the apples are very soft.

Drain the apples, reserving the liquid, and remove the vanilla bean. Put the fruit into a blender and blitz to a thick purée, adding the lemon juice and enough of the reserved hot pickling liquid to get the correct apple sauce consistency. It should be a smooth purée that holds its shape when on a plate.

Pass the sauce through a sieve and refrigerate until needed.

WHITE PEACH KETCHUP

MAKES APPROXIMATELY 1¾ CUPS

white peaches, peeled, stoned, and very thinly sliced	¾ pound
superfine sugar	heaping ⅓ cup
cider vinegar	scant ⅔ cup
lemon juice	2 teaspoons

Put the peaches, sugar, and vinegar into a stainless steel pan and bring to a boil, then continue to cook for roughly 10 minutes, or until the peaches are very soft.

Drain the peaches, reserving the liquid. Put the fruit into a blender and blitz to a thick purée, adding the lemon juice and enough of the reserved hot pickling liquid to get the correct consistency. It should be a smooth purée that holds its shape when on a plate.

Pass the sauce through a sieve and refrigerate until needed.

PEAR & MEAD KETCHUP

MAKES APPROXIMATELY 1¾ CUPS

pears, peeled, cored, and very thinly sliced	¾ pound
superfine sugar	scant ¾ cups
cider vinegar	scant ⅔ cup
lemon juice	2 teaspoons
mead	1 generous tablespoon

Put the pears, sugar, and vinegar into a stainless steel pan and bring to a boil, then continue to cook for roughly 10 minutes, or until the pears are very soft.

Drain the pears and reserve the liquid. Put the fruit into a blender and blitz to a thick purée, adding the lemon juice, the mead, and enough of the reserved hot pickling liquid to get the correct consistency. It should be a smooth purée that holds its shape when on a plate.

Pass the sauce through a sieve and refrigerate until needed.

PINEAPPLE & CHILE KETCHUP

MAKES APPROXIMATELY 1¾ CUPS

pineapple flesh, very thinly sliced	2 cups (about 10½ ounces)
superfine sugar	½ cup
cider vinegar	¾ cup
lemon juice	2 teaspoons
red chile, very finely diced	½

Put the pineapple, sugar, and vinegar into a stainless steel pan and bring to a boil, then continue to cook for roughly 10 minutes, or until the pineapple is very soft.

Drain the pineapple, reserving the liquid. Put the fruit into a blender and blitz to a thick purée, adding the lemon juice and enough of the reserved hot pickling liquid to get the correct consistency, then fold in the diced chile. It should be a smooth purée with flecks of chile that holds its shape when on a plate.

Pass the sauce through a sieve and refrigerate until needed.

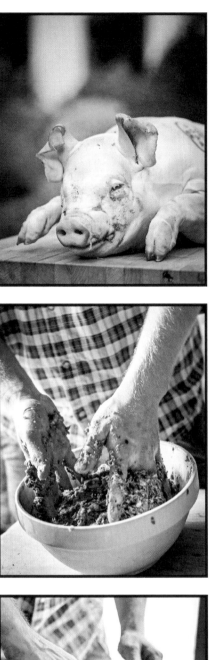
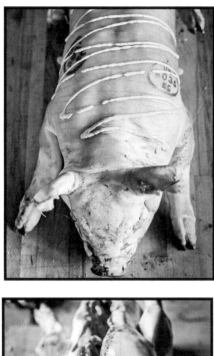

PIG DIP
—— (WHOLE LOW 'N' SLOW SMOKED SUCKLING PIG) ——

SERVES 15 HUNGRY INDIVIDUALS

pork dripping	½ cup
onions, peeled and sliced	4
garlic cloves, crushed	2
kidneys from the suckling pig, chopped	2
loaf of bread, cut into ¾-inch cubes	½
apple, grated	1
Devil Dip Gravy *(see page 130)*	
Porger Sausage meat, uncooked	
(see page 155)	2¼ pounds
whole suckling pig, gutted, cleaned,	
singed, and shaved	1, weighing about 22 pounds
smooth mustard of choice	scant ½ cup
House Rub *(see page 119)*	scant 1¼ cups

TO SERVE

Potato Rolls *(see page 240)*
Kimchi *(see page 214)*
slaw of choice *(see pages 198-203)*
Pitt Cue Barbecue Sauce *(see page 122)*
Baked Beans *(see page 239)*
Boston Bibb Lettuce & Herb Salad *(see page 209)*

FOR US, A BARBECUED SUCKLING PIG IS RIGHT UP THERE ON THE AWESOME SCALE. BIG FEASTING DISHES ARE A GREAT WAY TO ENJOY AN EVENING, AND THEY GIVE YOU THE GUILT-FREE OBLIGATION OF PUTTING TOGETHER AS MANY SIDE DISHES, SAUCES, AND PICKLES AS HUMANLY POSSIBLE TO SET ALONGSIDE THE FINE BEAST IN THE CENTER OF THE TABLE. SUCKLING PIGS ARE EASILY AVAILABLE FROM GOOD BUTCHERS, WILL JUST ABOUT FIT INSIDE YOUR BARBECUE, AND ARE INCREDIBLY EASY TO COOK. SMOKING THE SUCKLING PIG WILL NOT GIVE TEXTBOOK CRACKLING, BUT IT HAS VERY ENJOYABLE SMOKY, CHEWY QUALITIES OF ITS OWN.

Melt the pork dripping in a large pan and cook the onions and garlic over medium heat until soft. Add the chopped kidneys, the cubed bread, and the grated apple, and a ladle of devil dip gravy to moisten the mix, then set aside to cool.

Put the sausage meat into a bowl and add the cooled kidney mixture. Stuff into the cavity of the pig and sew the belly together using a large needle and cooking twine.

Score the skin of the pig and rub with mustard, then rub from head to toe with the house rub.

Prepare a barbecue for smoking (see The Setup on pages 114–15) and set the temperature to 300°F.

Place the pig in the barbecue belly down and with the legs tucked underneath. A 22-pound pig will take around 8 to 10 hours to smoke, and should reach an internal temperature at the shoulder of around 186°F when cooked. Some of the skin around the rump of the pig may begin to tear and pull away. If you gently poke the exposed flesh, you will gain a good idea of whether the pig is cooked through—it should be soft to the touch, similar to a pulled pork shoulder.

Transfer the pig to a large wooden board and let rest for 30 to 45 minutes. Then pull it apart and make sandwiches of the pork with the potato rolls, kimchi, slaw, and barbecue sauce, dipping them into the devil dip gravy as you eat. Serve alongside the baked beans and a fresh Boston Bibb lettuce salad. Depending on the efficiency of your dipping technique, this feast may require several yards of napkins.

DEVIL DIP GRAVY

THIS IS THE MOTHER OF ALL GRAVIES, THE GRAVY TO WHICH ALL OTHER GRAVIES MUST BOW DOWN. IT PROVIDES A GREAT DIP FOR ALMOST ANY BUN OR HOT DOG. JUST BE SURE YOU MAKE A LOT.

SERVES 8 TO 10

chicken wings, chopped	7 ounces
chicken skin, chopped	7 ounces
vegetable oil	2 teaspoons
shallots, chopped	4
garlic clove	1
button mushrooms, chopped	3½ ounces
sprig of thyme	1
small bay leaf	1
mixed peppercorns, crushed	1½ tablespoons
chipotle paste or Chipotle Ketchup (see page 125)	½ tablespoon
Madeira	scant ½ cup
white wine vinegar	scant ½ cup
chicken gravy	2 cups
beef gravy	2 cups

TO FINISH

mustard	scant ½ cup
butter	1 stick

Heat the oven to 340°F. Put the chopped chicken wings and chicken skin on a baking pan and roast for 30 minutes, or until golden.

Heat the oil in a large pan and sauté the shallots and garlic. Add the roast chicken wings and skin, the mushrooms, thyme, bay leaf, crushed peppercorns, and chipotle paste, and continue to cook until caramelized.

Add the Madeira and vinegar, then simmer to reduce by half before adding the chicken and beef gravies. Simmer for 30 minutes, then pass through a fine sieve and set aside.

Blend the mustard with the butter. When ready to serve, reheat the gravy and whisk in the mustard butter to taste.

PULLED PIG'S
—— HEAD CRUBEENS ——

PULLED PIG'S HEAD IS VERY SIMILAR TO PULLED PORK, JUST A TOUCH MORE
FATTY, DEPENDING ON HOW BIG YOUR HOG JOWLS ARE. THE CRUBEEN WAS A CLEAR
PROGRESSION FROM THE PULLED PIG'S HEAD AND FULFILLED OUR NUGGET LOVE.
THIS IS BEST SERVED WITH KIMCHI IN A BUN—KIMCHI IS A GREAT COMPANION TO
THE FATTY SMOKINESS OF THE CRUBEEN.

SERVES 4

fresh pig's head, shaved, singed, split, and well rinsed	1
Pork Rub (see page 118) plus extra to season	½ cup + 1 tablespoon
Deviled Pigs' Feet (see page 145)	7 ounces
parsley leaves, finely chopped	handful
oil, for deep-frying	
all-purpose flour, sifted	heaping ¾ cup
large free-range eggs	2
whole milk	2 tablespoons
Japanese panko bread crumbs	2½ cups
salt and pepper	

Prepare a barbecue for smoking (see The Setup on pages 114–15) and set the temperature to 220 to 230°F.

Take your pig's head and, depending on the size of the head, remove the skin from the jowls and score the cheeks. Remove the ears and reserve them for making crispy Habanero Pigs' Ears (see page 64). Apply the pork rub all over, then place the head in your barbecue to smoke. It can take 10 to 12 hours to smoke, but is very forgiving. It is better to wait longer than to rush and remove the head early. The meat needs to be meltingly soft for the crubeens. Alternatively, roast in the oven at 275°F for 6 to 8 hours.

Remove the head when the deepest part of the cheek reaches an internal temperature of 195°F. Let the cheek cool slightly so it can be pulled apart. Discard the tough, hard skin and remove all the meat from behind the eyes and cheekbones, along with the jowl and any scraps of meat and fat you can find, putting it all into a bowl. Mix the deviled pigs' feet through the head meat, add the parsley, and season with the remaining pork rub to taste.

Spread three layers of plastic wrap on a work surface and place the meat mixture on top. Mold it into a long sausage, then roll the plastic wrap over it. Roll tightly from each end of the plastic wrap until firm. Chill in a container of water in the refrigerator for several hours. Cut into ½-inch disks, then remove the plastic wrap. Alternatively, for a pig's head bun, as in the photograph opposite, roll into a sausage the width of your buns, chill as above, and slice into ¾-inch disks.

Get ready three shallow bowls. In the first put the flour, in the second beat the egg with the milk, and in the third put the panko bread crumbs. Roll the disks first in flour, then coat with the egg mixture, then lightly coat in the panko crumbs—the disks should be evenly coated. Heat the oil to 375°F in a deep-fryer or a large saucepan. Carefully drop them into the oil in batches and deep-fry for 2 to 3 minutes, or until golden. Drain on paper towels, then serve, either on their own as a snack or in Potato Rolls or London Bath Buns (see page 240) with Kimchi (see page 214) and Hot Sauce (see page 124).

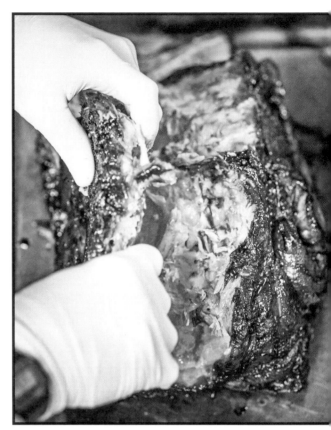

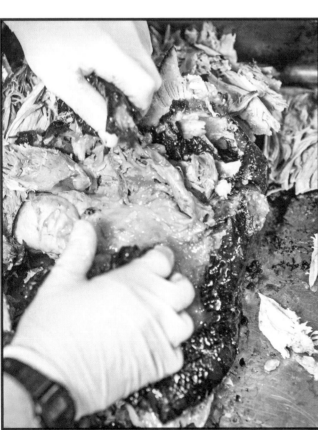

— PULLED PORK SHOULDER —

MAKES ENOUGH FOR 16 SANDWICHES

pork neck end shoulder	1, weighing 8¾ to 11 pounds
House Rub *(see page 119)*	1½ cups
Mother Sauce *(see page 120)*	scant 1 cup
Maldon sea salt	
freshly ground black pepper	

Skin the pork shoulder, reserving the skin to cure for scratchings (see page 62). Depending on the type of pork you are using, there may be a good inch or so of fat under the skin. The more fat that is removed, the better the bark. Bark only occurs from the rub caramelizing on the meat. The fat, however, will produce some lovely dripping and protects the meat during cooking.

Prepare a barbecue for smoking (see The Setup on pages 114–15) and set the temperature to 220°F. A shoulder of pork is pretty forgiving, but keeping a constant temperature will produce the best results. Once a decent bark starts to form, the smoke no longer effectively penetrates the meat, so there is no point continuing to add more wood chunks after the first few hours of cooking.

Evenly massage the meat with 1¼ cups of the house rub, then smoke it on the barbecue, making sure it is fat- (skin-) side up. It can take up to 16 hours but can be ready any time after 14 hours, so keep an eye on it and have your meat probe on hand. Cooking times can vary massively—some pork just takes longer than others. The internal temperature should reach 190 to 194°F. Once it hits this temperature, the butt will have a thick bark and be very dark. It will not be burnt, and will not taste burnt, so don't panic. The blade bone should pull out with little resistance and the shoulder should fall in on itself if pressed gently from above. At this stage remove the pork and set aside to rest, wrapped in foil, for 30 minutes.

PULLED PORK WAS HOW PITT CUE STARTED. OUR SMOKER WAS SMALL AND OUR MENU REFLECTED IT. OFFERING JUST PULLED PORK A LOT OF THE TIME MEANT IT HAD TO BE GOOD. USING WOODLAND-REARED, FREE-RANGE PIGS WAS A GOOD START, BUT KEEPING IT SIMPLE WAS THE KEY. THE PULLED PORK MUST BE SOFT AND MELTING, WITH NUGGETS OF SWEET BARK DOTTED THROUGHOUT, BUT IT MUST ALSO TASTE OF PORK. A PORK SHOULDER COOKED WELL WILL NOT NEED MUCH ATTENTION BEFORE SERVING.

Unwrap the pork and turn it upside down so that the spinal bones are facing upward. Carefully remove the spinal and rib bones from the underside of the shoulder. The small bones are very sharp, so be scrupulous. The meat around these bones is particularly special, so dig deep and work between the bones to find all you can. Remove the blade bone and the piece of tough cartilage that sits at the tip.

Start to work the meat and pull it apart. A correctly cooked shoulder should not take much work. An over-pulled shoulder will be mushy, so keep it in big chunks and strands. Add the remaining rub to taste, sprinkling it evenly like seasoning. Add the Mother Sauce and work this all through the meat. Check for seasoning, adding pepper and sea salt to taste. Serve immediately, in warm Potato Rolls (see page 240), with pickles (see pages 190–7), scratchings, and slaws (see pages 198–203).

BARBECUE MAYO

THIS IS USED AS A CONDIMENT AS WELL AS AN INGREDIENT IN OUR BUNS, TO STOP THE BREAD FROM SOAKING UP TOO MUCH MOISTURE FROM THE FILLING.

MAKES 14 OUNCES

Pitt Cue Barbecue Sauce *(see page 122)*	scant 1 cup
mayonnaise	scant 1 cup

Simply put both the ingredients into a bowl and mix together. Chill in the fridge until needed.

PULLED PORK BUN

YOU WILL NEED TO ASSUME THE TONY SOPRANO SANDWICH STANCE WHEN YOU FINALLY ATTACK THIS. YOUR FEET SHOULD BE SET WIDE APART SO THAT YOU CAN GET A GOOD STABLE LEAN ON A COUNTER TOP, WITH ELBOWS AS YOUR RESTING POINTS. THIS TECHNIQUE WILL SAVE YOU SHIRTS AND EMBARRASSMENT. WHEN SIMON FIRST CAME DOWN TO THE TRAILER, HE MADE THE MISTAKE OF EATING HIS PULLED PORK BUN WITH A STRAIGHT BACK AS WELL AS WEARING A WHITE SHIRT. BAD MOVE.

SERVES 4

Potato Rolls or London Bath Buns *(see page 240)*	4
Barbecue Mayo *(see above)*	¼ cup
Hot Sauce *(see page 124)*	1 tablespoon
Pulled Pork Shoulder *(see page 135)*	1 pound 5 ounces
Mother Sauce *(see page 120)*	2 tablespoons
Bread & Butter Pickles *(see page 191)*	4¼ ounces
Vinegar Slaw *(see page 203)*	4¼ ounces

Slice each roll in half and lightly grill the cut sides.

Spread the barbecue mayo on the base of each roll and spread the hot sauce evenly across the lid. Top each bun base with hot pulled pork and brush lightly with the hot Mother Sauce. Top with pickles and the vinegar slaw. Put the lids on the rolls and serve immediately.

THE TRAILER TRASH

WHEN AN UNUSED BATCH OF MACARONI WAS DEEP-FRIED IN THE RESTAURANT FOR STAFF LUNCH ONE DAY, WE THOUGHT THE KITCHEN MIGHT JUST HAVE HAD PARTICULARLY AGGRESSIVE HANGOVERS THAT REQUIRED DEEP-FRIED MEDICINE. THIS IS A VERY TRASHY BUN THAT WAS A FIXTURE ON THE TRAILER MENU, HENCE THE AFFECTIONATE NAME.

SERVES 4

leftover Hog Mac 'n' Cheese (see page 235), chilled	14 ounces
all-purpose flour	⅓ cup
House Rub (see page 119)	¼ cup
free-range eggs	4
Japanese panko bread crumbs	1½ cups
oil, for deep-frying	
Potato Rolls or London Bath Buns (see page 240)	4
Barbecue Mayo (see page 136)	2 tablespoons
Hot Sauce (see page 124)	2 tablespoons
Pulled Pork Shoulder (see page 135)	7 ounces
Bread & Butter Pickles (see page 191)	2¾ ounces

Take your leftover chilled mac 'n' cheese and cut out four bun-sized disks.

Get ready three shallow bowls. In the first, mix the flour with the house rub, in the second beat the eggs with the milk, and in the third put the panko bread crumbs. Lightly coat the mac 'n' cheese disks with flour, then dip them into the egg and milk mixture, and finally roll them gently in the panko bread crumbs. Do this twice, then put them back into the fridge until needed.

Heat the oil to 355°F in a deep-fryer or large saucepan and deep-fry the mac 'n' cheese burgers for 1 minute, or until golden. Remove from the fryer and drain on paper towels.

To assemble, slice each roll in half. Spread the barbecue mayo on the base of each roll and the hot sauce across the lid. Place a mac 'n' cheese patty on the base of each bun and top with the pulled pork and pickles. Put the lids on and serve.

HOUSE SAUSAGE

MAKES 1 ÜBER SAUSAGE

pork shoulder	1 pound 10 ounces
pork belly	9 ounces
pork fat	4½ ounces
beef flank steak or skirt steak	4½ ounces
small onion	1
mixed peppers	9 ounces
freshly ground black pepper	1½ tablespoons
smoked paprika	1½ tablespoons
Maldon sea salt	2 tablespoons
ground coriander	1½ tablespoons
dried red pepper flakes	2 tablespoons
Pitt Cue Barbecue Sauce (see page 122)	scant 1 cup

WE DEVELOPED THIS SAUSAGE AFTER A TRIP TO THE KANSAS ROYAL BARBECUE CHAMPIONSHIPS. THERE ARE LOTS OF THINGS YOU EXPECT TO LEARN FROM A HARDCORE TWO-WEEK EATING MISSION IN NEW YORK, KENTUCKY, TENNESSEE, KANSAS, AND A THREE-DAY BARBECUE CHAMPIONSHIP, ESPECIALLY WHEN HANGING OUT WITH ONE OF THE TEAMS, BUT WE DIDN'T EXPECT A SAUSAGE TO BE THE THING THAT REALLY STOOD OUT. WE THOUGHT US BRITS, AND EUROPEANS AS A WHOLE, WERE THE KINGS OF SAUSAGE, BUT CLEARLY NOT. WHAT WE ATE AND SAW WAS NOT A SAUSAGE AS WE KNOW IT BUT A MASSIVE LOG OF A THING, A KIND OF MEATLOAF, UNDENIABLY PHALLIC, WHICH WAS SMOKED, LATHERED IN BARBECUE SAUCE AND SLICED INTO THICK DISKS, SIMILAR TO A COTECHINO SAUSAGE. SIMPLY AWESOME.

Before you start, chill your largest meat-grinding attachment.

Dice all the meats and put them into a bowl. Finely dice the onion and mixed peppers, discarding the seeds from the latter, and add them to the meat with all the other ingredients except the barbecue sauce. Refrigerate for 1 hour.

Remove from the fridge and put everything through the chilled grinder attachment on the largest setting. Make sure the ground meat is thoroughly combined, then refrigerate for another hour.

Lay out strips of double-thickness plastic wrap large enough to take the ground meat in a giant sausage, roughly 4 inches thick. Roll up and seal the chilled sausage in the plastic wrap, place in a container of water, and return it to the fridge for at least 1 hour, preferably 2, to chill and set.

Prepare a barbecue for smoking (see The Setup on pages 114–15) and set the temperature to 355°F.

Remove the plastic wrap from the sausage and place it on a baking pan that will fit inside your barbecue. Smoke in the barbecue to let it firm up a little—after 10 minutes, brush the sausage with barbecue sauce, then turn it over and brush again. After a further 10 minutes, remove it from the smoker. You will no longer need the pan.

Lower the barbecue temperature to 230°F, then set the giant sausage directly onto the grill for a further 30 to 45 minutes, brushing with barbecue sauce every 15 minutes until cooked right through. The internal temperature should reach 160°F when ready. Once cooked, slice into ¼-inch rounds and serve, or slice and chill to be grilled at a later date.

SAUSAGE BUN

SERVES 4

Potato Rolls or London Bath Buns *(see page 240)*	4
Barbecue Mayo *(see page 136)*	2 tablespoons
Hot Sauce *(see page 124)*	2 tablespoons
House Sausage slices *(see opposite)*	8
Mother Sauce *(see page 120)* or Pitt Cue Barbecue Sauce *(see page 122)*	⅓ cup
Bread & Butter Pickles *(see page 191)*	
Green Chile Slaw *(see page 203)*	

Slice each roll in half and lightly grill the cut sides. Spread the mayo over the base of each roll and the hot sauce across the lid.

If the sausage slices are cold, grill them for 1 minute each side.

Top each bun base with a hot sausage slice and brush the sausage with hot Mother Sauce. Add pickles, slaw, another sausage slice, and brush with more hot sauce. Finish with more pickles and slaw, put the lids on, and serve.

THE BIG ODE

THE BIG ODE IS AFFECTIONATELY NAMED AFTER ONE OF OUR CORNISH SUPPLIERS.
THIS BUN OFFERS UP A LITTLE BIT OF EVERYTHING. IT IS WORTH NOTING THAT
THERE ARE NOT MANY PEOPLE BLESSED WITH A MOUTH BIG ENOUGH TO ACTUALLY
EAT THIS BUN IN ANY RESPECTABLE MANNER.

SERVES 4

Potato Rolls or London Bath Buns *(see page 240)*	4
Barbecue Mayo *(see page 136)*	1 tablespoon
Pulled Pork Shoulder *(see page 135)*	2¾ ounces
House Sausage slices *(see page 140)*	4
Devil Dip Gravy *(see page 130)*	1 tablespoon
Pitt Cue Burnt Ends *(see page 158)*	2¾ ounces
Vinegar Slaw *(see page 203)*	
Bread & Butter Pickles *(see page 191)*	
Hot Sauce *(see page 124)*	

Slice each roll into three horizontally
and grill the cut sides.

Spread the barbecue mayo on the base of
each roll, and top with the pulled pork
followed by a hot sausage slice. Dip the
middle slice of roll in the devil dip gravy
and place this on top of the sausage slice.

Next up are the burnt ends, followed by
the slaw, pickles, and hot sauce and,
finally, the lids.

PITT CUE BACON

WE GO THROUGH BACON AT AN ALARMING RATE IN THE RESTAURANT, SO A BELLY MAY ONLY LAST US A FEW DAYS, BUT AT HOME IT MIGHT BE WORTH CUTTING IT INTO SMALLER SECTIONS AND FREEZING IT AFTER HANGING.

MAKES 11 POUNDS

black peppercorns	3½ tablespoons
fennel seeds	¼ cup
Muscovado sugar	½ cup
Maldon sea salt	heaping 1½ cups
beautifully fat pork belly, skin removed	1, weighing 11 pounds

Toast the peppercorns and fennel seeds in a dry skillet for a few minutes, shaking the pan, until golden. Remove from the heat and grind to a powder with a mortar and pestle, then combine with the sugar and salt. Rub this dry cure mixture all over the pork belly, then wrap it tightly in plastic wrap. Place the wrapped belly in the fridge and let cure for 5 days.

When ready, rinse off the dry cure mixture (it will be very wet by now) and let dry in the fridge overnight.

At this point the bacon can be wrapped in cheesecloth to hang in a very cool space, or, if your fridge allows it, it can be hung naked in the fridge until it reaches your desired level of maturity. The bacon will mature more quickly outside the fridge and can be brought into the fridge when ready. The longer it hangs, the stiffer, more intense, and more salty the bacon will be. We hang our bacon for 2 to 3 weeks in the fridge.

DEVILED PIGS' FEET

WHEN ONE OF THE MOST IMPORTANT PARTS OF THE PIG MEETS A SUPER SEXY GRAVY THERE IS NOT MUCH YOU CANNOT ACHIEVE. PIGS' FEET ARE GIVEN A LOT OF ATTENTION AT PITT CUE. THEY ARE SMOKED FOR THEIR DRIPPING AND STOCKPILED FOR ALL THE SAUCES. THIS IS SOMETHING OF A "MASTER RECIPE," TO BE MADE IN BULK AND CHIPPED AWAY AT WHENEVER A SAUCE OR DISH IS LACKING AND NEEDS A KICK IN THE PANTS.

MAKES APPROXIMATELY 2 PINTS

pigs' feet, as long as possible	4
Master Chicken Brine (see page 90)	2 cups
onion, peeled	1
carrot, peeled	1
stick of celery	1
leek	1
bulb of garlic	½
mixed herbs (thyme, rosemary, bay, parsley)	bunch
Devil Dip Gravy (see page 130), without mustard or butter	2 cups

Shave the pigs' feet using a disposable razor, and singe any remaining hair over an open flame. Wash the feet thoroughly, then put them into a plastic container and cover with the master chicken brine. Refrigerate overnight.

Prepare a barbecue for smoking (see The Setup on pages 114–15) and set the temperature to 250°F. Alternatively, heat your oven to 250°F.

Drain the pigs' feet and place them in a casserole dish that will fit inside your barbecue, if using. Cover with cold water and bring to a boil, then drain, discarding the water. Put the pigs' feet back into the casserole dish with the vegetables and herbs and cover with the devil dip gravy. Half cover with a lid and either smoke in the barbecue or cook in the oven for 6 hours or overnight.

When cooked, strain the sauce through a fine sieve into a large pan and reserve. Let the pigs' feet cool, then pick all the fat, meat, and skin off of them, add to the sauce, and bring to a boil.

Pack into sterilized jars (see page 78) and seal. When cool, refrigerate until needed.

BELLY CHOPS

A WHOLE PORK BELLY IS A SUCH EXCITING OPTION AND AN INCREDIBLY VERSATILE
CUT. COOKED THIS WAY, THE BELLY GIVES YOU ALL THE ENJOYMENT OF THE RIB,
ALBEIT IN LARGER CHOP FORM, WITH THE THE ADDED BONUS OF THE QUIVERING
FATTY GOODNESS THAT IS TRIMMED FROM THE BELLY WHEN CUTTING SPARE RIBS.
IF YOU FIND A BELLY THAT HAS BEEN HUNG FOR A WEEK OR SO WITH HARD DRY SKIN,
ALL THE BETTER—THIS WILL AID ANY EXTRA-CURRICULAR CRACKLING PURSUITS. WE
SERVE OUR BELLY CHOPS, MOST OFTEN FROM TAMWORTHS, WITH APPLE KETCHUP
TO CUT THE RICHNESS AND SOME PUFFED PIG'S SKIN.

SERVES 4

thick end belly, skin removed	3 pounds 5 ounces
long bushy sprig of rosemary	1

SPICES

cumin seeds	1 teaspoon
celery seeds	1 teaspoon
chilli flakes	1 teaspoon
star anise	1 teaspoon
smoked paprika	1 teaspoon
coriander seeds	1 teaspoon
mustard seeds	1 teaspoon
fennel seeds	scant ¼ cup
black peppercorns	3 tablespoons

MARINADE

ground spices (see above)	2½ ounces
vegetable oil	scant ½ cup
Tabasco	scant ½ cup
English mustard	scant ½ cup
Maldon sea salt	scant ½ cup
cider	scant ½ cup
maple syrup	⅓ cup
blackstrap molasses	½ cup
apricot preserve	⅓ cup

Heat the oven to 350°F. Put all the spices into a roasting pan and roast for 10 minutes, or until golden. Put into a blender and blitz to a powder.

Put all the marinade ingredients into a bowl and mix together. Remove the skin from the ribs and add to the marinade. Massage the ribs well with the marinade and refrigerate overnight.

Prepare a barbecue for smoking (see The Setup on pages 114–15) and set the temperature to 220°F.

Remove the ribs from the fridge and shake off, but do not discard, the excess marinade. Put the ribs, bone-side down, on your barbecue and smoke for 6 to 7 hours, until they reach an internal temperature of 185–188°F. Test them by holding them with tongs to see if they bounce—if they have a bit of resistance, similar to the touch of a medium-rare steak, they are ready.

Cut the ribs into portions. Put the reserved marinade into a pan and simmer until it has reduced slightly. Baste the ribs liberally with the reduced marinade, then let cool and set aside.

To finish, adjust your barbecue for direct grilling (see page 112) and grill the ribs for 2 minutes on each side, using the rosemary sprig as a brush to baste the meat with the reduced marinade as it cooks.

PORK RIBS

SERVES 2

rack of pork spare ribs	1
House Rub *(see page 119)*	scant ½ cup
Mother Sauce *(see page 120)*	scant ½ cup

Remove the membrane on the back of the ribs. Paper towels are the best thing to use for this. Get a blunt knife and carefully prise back the membrane from the tips of the first rib bone. Hold the membrane with some paper towels and it should pull back completely with a little force. (Think skinning a flat fish.) The spare rib rack can be cooked as is, but if the rack is squared up to a St. Louis-style cut, you will be left with the rib tips to play with.

Remove the last four small ribs from the thin end of the rack and trim the rack into a neat, compact rectangle. This will require a section called the "rib tips" to be removed from the base of the rack. The rack will cook more evenly like this. If this seems like too much work, then cooking the rack as spare ribs is absolutely fine. Keep the tips and trim aside.

Prepare a barbecue for smoking (see The Setup on pages 114–15) and set the temperature to 220°F.

Coat the rack all over with the rub. Lay the rack, bone-side down, on the barbecue and smoke for up to 6 hours, checking after 4 hours to see how the ribs are doing. When the internal temperature reaches 186°F, you can start to apply the Mother Sauce.

EVERYONE LOVES A GOOD RIB. JUST AS A CHICKEN SHOULD HAVE BEEN CREATED WITH MORE WINGS, SO SHOULD A PIG HAVE BEEN CREATED WITH MORE BELLY.

WE LIKE OUR RIBS SIMPLE, WITH JUST A TOUCH OF OUR MOTHER SAUCE TO FINISH THEM OFF. THIS RECIPE IS AS SIMPLE AS WE CAN MAKE IT AND WILL PROVIDE GREAT RIBS TO BE EATEN AT HOME. START SIMPLE, THEN EVOLVE AND TRY NEW THINGS ONCE YOU ARE SATISFIED THAT THE BASICS ARE NAILED.

The ribs can be removed at 186 to 194°F. They should have a bit of resistance, similar to the feeling of a medium-rare steak, and the surface of the bark should begin to crack when bounced with tongs. Remove from the grill and let rest in foil.

Adjust the barbecue for direct grilling over high heat (see page 112). At this stage you can either portion the ribs individually or grill the rack whole. Grill the rack or ribs for 1 to 2 minutes on each side. Paint liberally with Mother Sauce, then serve immediately. We like to add a small dusting of rub when serving—Smoked Bacon Rub (see page 119) would be a very good idea.

PORK SHOULDER

THIS IS A BRILLIANT JOINT FROM THE SHOULDER AND MAY JUST BE OUR FAVORITE AMONG THOSE FOUND ON A PIG. IT IS ALSO A GREAT CUT TO SEARCH OUT IF YOU FANCY SOME LAMB OR MUTTON. THE CHOPS FROM THE SHOULDER HAVE JUST ABOUT THE PERFECT RATIO OF MUSCLE TO FAT, WITH MUCH THE SAME SOFTNESS IN THE MUSCLE AS THE BLADE END OF THE LOIN TO WHICH THEY JOIN, BUT ARE AN ALL-ROUND MORE FLAVORSOME PROPOSITION. THE SHOULDER USUALLY PROVIDES SIX OR SEVEN 10½ OUNCE CHOPS, DEPENDING ON THE BREED AND SIZE OF PIG, AND AT THE RESTAURANT WE BREAK IT DOWN IN TWO WAYS: INTO CHOPS, OR INTO TWO LARGER JOINTS THAT EQUATE TO THREE CHOPS EACH. THESE TWO LARGER JOINTS FROM THE SHOULDER MAKE A PERFECT SHARING PLATE AND ARE LARGE ENOUGH TO BE SMOKED SLOWLY TO MEDIUM-RARE BEFORE BEING FINISHED ON THE GRILL.

SERVES 4

pork shoulder, on the bone	1, weighing 2¼ pounds
Maldon sea salt	
freshly ground black pepper	

Prepare a barbecue for smoking (see The Setup on pages 114–15) and set the temperature to 230°F.

Season the shoulder all over with pepper and place in your barbecue. Smoke for 45 minutes to 1 hour, or until the internal temperature reaches 125 to 131°F. Remove from the smoker, seal in plastic wrap, and set aside to rest.

Meanwhile, adjust the barbecue for direct grilling (see page 112). When the grill is hot, season the shoulder with lots of salt and grill for 1 to 2 minutes on each side so that the meat browns evenly. Remove from the grill and let rest for 10 minutes before carving.

To carve, take the meat off of the bone and carve against the grain. Season between the slices and serve, not forgetting the resting juices from the cutting board, or that would be a grave sin. Serve with Fruit Ketchups (see pages 126–7).

—— PITT CUE PORK CHOP ——

SERVES 1

blade end pork chop or shoulder chop	1, weighing 12 ounces
smoked Maldon sea salt	
freshly ground black pepper	

We'd like to assume that you are using a beautiful piece of pork that has ¾ to 1¼ inches of fat between the skin and the first sign of meat. Remove the skin from the chop and set aside. Try to leave a good ¾ inches of fat running along the top of the loin.

Set your barbecue for medium-hot direct grilling (see page 112) and let it cool slightly, with white embers. This is our favorite time to cook a pork chop.

Season the chop with the sea salt and pepper on both sides and place it on the barbecue. Listen to it crackle and pop for a minute. This is perhaps the most comforting sound ever. Cook the chop for 10 minutes, moving it every 20 to 30 seconds to another part of the grill and turning regularly—this will help cook the chop evenly. The surface should be a deep caramel when cooked, with intermittent charring.

Turn the chop onto its edge on the coolest part of the grill and allow the fat to cook for 2 minutes. Be vigilant against flareups. Using a probe, aim for an internal temperature of 127°F. When you reach this will be dependent on the heat of the grill. Remove the chop from the grill and let rest for 10 minutes on a board, turning occasionally. This will produce a chop that is blushing pink all the way through.

> THIS IS ABOUT AS SIMPLE A RECIPE AS ONE CAN FIND BUT IT IS VERY EASY TO GET IT WRONG, STARTING FROM THE WRONG PORK RIGHT THROUGH TO THE MISMANAGEMENT OF THE GRILL WHEN COOKING THE CHOP. ONCE YOU SOURCE, COOK, AND EAT A VERY AWESOME PORK CHOP, THERE ARE FEW THINGS THAT WILL BRING AS MUCH SATISFACTION.

Working along the bone, remove the loin and cut into ½-inch slices across the chop. Season with salt and pepper between the slices and arrange the slices back on the bone of the loin.

Pick up any resting juices from the cutting board by scraping the flat blade of your knife across the board and pour them over the chop. Eat immediately, with a big blob of Apple Ketchup (see page 126), and feel exceptionally good about life.

— HOT GUTS —

THE "HOT GUT" ORIGINATED
FROM SOUTHSIDE MARKET IN
ELGIN, TEXAS, IN 1886.
SADLY, THE HOT GUTS OF TODAY
ARE TAMER AND LEANER THAN
THOSE OF YORE. THEY'RE STILL
QUITE GOOD, THOUGH.

MAKES APPROXIMATELY 40 SAUSAGES

natural sheep's casings	
aged beef flank, chilled	2¼ pounds
aged beef shoulder, chilled	2¼ pounds
beef fat, chilled	9 ounces
bone marrow, chilled	9 ounces
bread crumbs	9 ounces
beer, chilled	1 generous cup
freshly ground black pepper	3 tablespoons
smoked chipotle Tabasco	2 tablespoons
hot mustard	2 tablespoons
light Muscovado sugar	2 tablespoons
garlic cloves, chopped	3
smoked Maldon sea salt	scant ¼ cup
thyme leaves	1 teaspoon

Thoroughly soak and rinse the casing before
using—make sure to rinse through the middle
as well as the outside.

Dice the meat, fat, and bone marrow into
¾-inch cubes. Place in a chilled bowl
and mix together with the remaining
ingredients. Feed the mixture through a
coarse ³/₈-inch grinding attachment into
another chilled bowl.

Beat the mixture for 5 minutes, or until
well bound, then load your sausage stuffer
(or use a sausage-stuffing attachment on
your grinder) and stuff the mixture into
the casings. Tie off the sausages as best
you can. The sausages are now ready to be
cooked, but we suggest to hang them in your
fridge for a few days first, because this
will aid the cooking process.

PORGER SAUSAGE

THIS IS THE GRANDDADDY OF SAUSAGES,
SUPER COMPLEX AND MEATY, OFFERING
ALL THE JUICINESS OF A HERITAGE-
BREED PORK SAUSAGE, WITH SMOKY
PORKINESS FROM THE BACON AND AN
UNDERLYING NUTTINESS FROM WELL-
AGED BEEF. MAKE SURE YOU USE DRY-
AGED BEEF, 30 TO 45 DAYS HUNG, AND
TOP-QUALITY PORK IN THIS RECIPE: IT
REALLY MAKES ALL THE DIFFERENCE.

MAKES APPROXIMATELY 25 SAUSAGES

natural sheep's casings	
fat belly pork, chilled	1 pound 2 ounces
shoulder of pork, chilled	1 pound 2 ounces
dry-aged beef tip roast, chilled	1 pound 2 ounces
dry-aged beef chuck-eye, chilled	1 pound 2 ounces
smoked bacon, rindless, chilled	1 pound 2 ounces
salt	heaping 2 tablespoons
ground white pepper	1 heaping tablespoon
water	scant 1 cup
garlic cloves, peeled and crushed	3 to 4
fennel seeds, toasted and ground	1 teaspoon

Thoroughly soak and rinse the casing before
using—make sure to rinse through the middle
as well as the outside.

Dice all the meat into ¾-inch cubes, place
in a chilled bowl, and mix together with
the remaining ingredients. Feed the mixture
through a coarse ³/₈-inch grinder attachment
into another chilled bowl.

Beat the mixture for 5 minutes, or until
well bound, then feed the mixture through
a ¼-inch grinder attachment. Load your
sausage stuffer (or use a sausage-stuffing
attachment on your grinder) and stuff the
mixture into the casings. Tie off the
sausages as best you can. The sausages
are now ready to be cooked, but we suggest
to hang them in your fridge for a few
days first, because this will aid the
cooking process.

PITT CUE
SMOKED BRISKET

EASY TO GET WRONG BUT UNBELIEVABLE WHEN COOKED PERFECTLY, BRISKET IS LARGELY A LEAN MUSCLE THAT CAN DRY OUT WHEN COOKED, LACKING THE FAT THAT AIDS OTHER CUTS OF BEEF. THE QUALITY OF THE BEEF IS VITAL HERE, AND IT TOOK AN AGE TO FINALLY FIND THE RIGHT BEEF SO THAT WE COULD GET BRISKET ON THE MENU. IT'S A STAPLE IN TEXAS AND REVERED THROUGHOUT THE SOUTH.

GOOD BRISKET SHOULD HAVE 4 TO 5 WEEKS HANGING ON THE BONE, THEN ANOTHER WEEK OFF THE BONE. WE TAKE THE LARGER, OLDER ANIMALS THAT HAVE A LARGER POINT END AND HAVE HAD TIME TO DEVELOP FLAVOR AND INTRAMUSCULAR FAT. TRUST YOUR BUTCHER AND SEE WHAT THEY CAN DO. THE POINT END IS BASICALLY HALF A BRISKET, CUT STRAIGHT ACROSS THE MIDDLE WHERE THE FATTY POINT MUSCLE THAT SITS ON THE LEAN "FLAT" MUSCLE STOPS. THE CUT COMPRISES OF ROUGHLY 70 PERCENT POINT, 30 PERCENT LEAN FLAT MUSCLE.

SERVES 8

brisket, point end cut (see above)	6½ to 8¾ pounds
Beef Rub (see page 119)	scant ½ cup

Prepare a barbecue for smoking (see The Setup on pages 114–15) and set the temperature to 240°F.

Coat the brisket all over with the house rub, then place it, point-side up, in your barbecue. There is a fine line between perfectly cooked brisket and overcooked brisket, so putting a digital thermometer in the meat is very helpful. Smoke the brisket until the internal temperature reaches 186 to 190°F. This can take from 12 to 13 hours, depending on the beef used.

When the beef reaches 186 to 190°F, give it a prod. It should have a somewhat sexy wobble. The sexy wobble is key. Remove the beef from the barbecue and wrap it in plastic wrap and then foil to rest.

To serve the brisket there are a couple of options. The cut contains two separate muscles, the flat and the point. These muscles run in different directions—roughly 45 degrees from each other. If you don't mind having a slice where the two muscles are running differently, slice them together.

We prefer to separate the muscles. They can simply be pulled away gently from each other by working your knife, or fingers, between them. The fat will be so soft that it requires little effort. Be careful—it will be very hot. Once separated, trim any excess fat, but do not remove it entirely, because it is this fat that brings so much joy to the eating. Now slice against the grain of both the flat and the point. You can also slice the point into ¾-inch slabs, then finish both sides by direct grilling on a barbecue (see page 112), painting them repeatedly with Mother Sauce (see page 120) or Devil Dip Gravy (see page 130). The fatty brisket point also browns incredibly well in a hot pan and brings another level of flavor to the brisket.

PITT CUE BURNT ENDS

OUR LOVE AFFAIR WITH BRISKET RUNS DEEP, AND BURNT ENDS ARE OUR REAL GUILTY PLEASURE. WHEN THIS IS ON THE MENU WE'LL CONSTANTLY FIND OURSELVES WITH A PIECE OF GRILLED BREAD IN THE KITCHEN, HUNTING DOWN THE PAN WHERE WE ARE COOKING OUR SMOKED BRISKET. IF YOU IGNORE THE UNWRITTEN RULEBOOK, HOWEVER, THIS RECIPE CAN BE A GREAT WAY OF SAVING THE OCCASIONAL BRISKET THAT DOESN'T COME OUT QUITE RIGHT (AND WHEN COOKING BRISKET FOR THE FIRST TIME, THERE WILL BE A FEW OF THESE). DON'T BE AFRAID TO USE A WHOLE BRISKET, FLAT AND POINT. ENTHUSIASTS MAY SAY IT'S NOT "BURNT ENDS," BUT YOU CAN'T PLEASE EVERYBODY. GREAT BEEF SHOULD HAVE STUNNINGLY TASTY FAT AND THE MORE AVAILABLE THE BETTER, IN OUR OPINION. THE PURISTS MAY DISAGREE … BUT WE ARE NOT PURISTS. WE LOVE THIS RECIPE SO MUCH, WE ADD IT TO EVERYTHING. IT DOMINATES OUR BRISKET BUNS AND MAKES MASHED POTATOES EPIC. IT MAKES A FINE CROQUETTE, A WORTHY NUGGET, EVEN BAO ACCORDING TO ONE CUSTOMER, AND CAN PLAY ITS PART IN A COTTAGE PIE.

SERVES 4 TO 6

Pitt Cue Smoked Brisket (see page 156)	2¼ pounds
Mother Sauce (see page 120)	1¼ cups
Pitt Cue Barbecue Sauce (see page 122)	1¼ cups

Prepare a barbecue for smoking (see The Setup on pages 114–15) and set the temperature to 250°F.

Cut the brisket, flat and as much point end as you wish to use for your burnt ends, into rough ¾- to 1¼-inch square dice. Heat a flameproof pan that will fit inside your barbecue, add the diced brisket, and cook for 10 minutes, stirring occasionally, until evenly browned. There should be a lovely smell of well-browned beef. Add the Mother Sauce and barbecue sauce and cook for a further 15 minutes. Transfer the pan to the barbecue and smoke for 30 minutes, then serve.

Store the burnt ends in the fridge—they keep well and can be reheated when needed.

BRISKET BUNS

THE ONLY THING THAT MIGHT
MAKE THESE BUNS BETTER IS
CHEESE. HEAT SOME OGLESHIELD,
OR OTHER AWESOME CHEDDAR,
THROUGH THE BURNT ENDS FOR
ADDED ENJOYMENT.

SERVES 4

Potato Rolls *(see page 240)*	4
Barbecue Mayo *(see page 136)*	1 tablespoon
Hot Sauce *(see page 124)*	2 tablespoons
Pitt Cue Burnt Ends *(see opposite)*	7 ounces
Pitt Cue Smoked Brisket, sliced *(see page 156)*	14 ounces
Mother Sauce *(see page 120)* or Devil Dip Gravy *(see page 130)*	¼ cup
Bread & Butter Pickles *(see page 191)*	2¾ ounces
Vinegar Slaw *(see page 203)*	2¾ ounces

Slice each roll in half and lightly grill
each the sides. Spread the barbecue mayo
on the base of each roll and the hot sauce
across the lids.

Top each bun base with the sliced brisket
and add the burnt ends on top. Spread the
brisket with warm Mother Sauce or Devil Dip
Gravy. Top with the pickles and slaw.
Put the lids on and serve immediately.

SLOW-GRILLED
DENVER CUT

SERVES 4

Beef Denver cut	1, weighing 3¼ to 4¼ pounds
Beef Rub *(see page 118)*	heaping ¼ cup
smoked Maldon sea salt	
freshly ground black pepper	

Prepare a barbecue for smoking (see The Setup on pages 114–15) and set the temperature to 230°F.

Rub the chuck all over with the beef rub and place in the barbecue to smoke for about 45 minutes, or until the internal temperature of the meat reaches 118°F on your meat probe.

As soon as the beef reaches temperature, remove it from the barbecue, seal in plastic wrap, and let rest for 10 minutes while you adjust the barbecue for direct grilling (see page 112). At this point the whole cut can be grilled and carved, or cut into smaller steaks, as we do in the restaurant, and grilled individually.

When the barbecue is hot, season the beef with salt and pepper and place on the grill. Grill the beef for 2 minutes, turning every 20 seconds or so. Remove from the grill and let rest for 7 to 10 minutes. To serve, carve against the grain into thin slices with a sharp knife, as you would a steak, and serve immediately with an Iceberg Salad (see page 210) and perhaps some Pumpkin Home Fries (see page 232).

BEEF CHUCK IS USUALLY GROUND UP FOR BURGERS OR CUT INTO CHUCK STEAKS, SO CALL YOUR BUTCHER AND ASK HIM TO RESERVE THIS CUT FOR YOU.

JUST AS PORK SHOULDER IS A WONDERFUL CUT TO SLOWLY COOK TO MEDIUM OR MEDIUM-RARE, SO IS ITS BEEF COUNTERPART. THE DENVER CUT IS ONE OF THE MANY MUSCLES THAT MAKE UP THE CHUCK AND SITS ON TOP OF THE EYE OF LOIN AS IT ENTERS THE SHOULDER. AS WITH ALL CUTS THAT ARE SMOKED TO MEDIUM-RARE OR RARE BEFORE GRILLING, THE LEVEL OF SMOKE IN THE BARBECUE NEEDS TO BE MONITORED: TOO MUCH SMOKE CAN QUICKLY RUIN YOUR MEAT AND YOUR DAY.

FEATHERBLADE

IN THE UK, THE CUT KNOWN AS THE FEATHERBLADE COMES FROM THE BEEF SHOULDER AND IS THE FLAT MUSCLE THAT SITS ON THE BLADE BONE ITSELF. IT HAS A THICK BIT OF TENDON THAT RUNS THROUGH THE CENTER THAT SEPARATES WHAT ARE OFTEN CALLED THE FLAT IRON STEAKS. THE STRONG GRAIN ALONG EACH SIDE OF THE CENTRAL TENDON CREATES A FEATHERED EFFECT ALONG THE SIDE OF THE CUT. IT IS A FANTASTIC CUT WITH THE ADDED BONUS THAT IT CAN BE LEFT ON THE BLADE BONE TO DRY-AGE. ANY GOOD BUTCHER SHOULD HAVE NO PROBLEM RESERVING THIS CUT FOR YOU. FEATHERBLADE MAY WELL COME WITH A THICK LAYER OF HARD FAT ON TOP. TRIM THIS TO ¼ TO ½ INCH THICK. THE BETTER THE BEEF WE CAN SOURCE, THE MORE INCLINED WE ARE TO LEAVE MORE FAT ON.

THIS DISH CAN BE COOKED ON OR OFF THE BONE. ON THE BONE WILL REQUIRE A FURTHER 30 TO 45 MINUTES COOKING AT LEAST, AND MAKES FOR A PREHISTORIC SERVING OPTION.

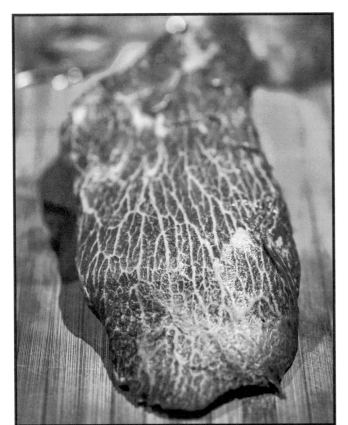

SERVES 4 TO 6

dry-aged beef featherblade	1, weighing about 3¼ pounds
Beef Rub *(see page 118)*	½ cup + 1 tablespoon
Pickled Shiitake *(see page 89)*, to serve	

Prepare a barbecue for smoking (see The Setup on pages 114–15) and set the temperature to 230°F.

Cover the featherblade evenly with the beef rub. Place the featherblade, fat-side up, in your barbecue and smoke for 10 to 12 hours. The internal temperature should reach 188°F when cooked and the meat should be slightly soft to the touch, similar to a well-cooked brisket. If you are unsure, slice off a small chunk and try it.

When ready, remove the meat from the barbecue and let it rest, wrapped in foil, for 20 minutes.

Using a very sharp knife, cut the meat into generous ¼-inch slices and arrange on a plate. You will notice the "feather" when slicing like this. Serve the featherblade slices with pickled shiitake. This recipe is also awesome served in fresh Potato Rolls (see page 240) with some slaw (see pages 198–203).

SMOKED STANDING RIB ROAST
—— WITH DRIPPING TRENCHER ——

THE SMOKED PRIME RIB FROM SMITTY'S MARKET IN LOCKHART, TEXAS,
WAS AWESOME. THEY WENT TO THE EFFORT OF SOURCING REALLY GOOD GRASS-FED BEEF,
AND COMBINED WITH A SIMPLE RUB IT WAS, ALONGSIDE WITNESSING SOME VERY LOOSE
SHOOTING-RANGE ETIQUETTE, ONE OF THE MOST MEMORABLE THINGS ABOUT TEXAS.
WE TESTED THIS RECIPE OUT ON THE TRAILER ONE SUNDAY WITH SOME OF
OUR BEAUTIFUL BEEF FROM CORNWALL.

WE SERVE THIS JUST AS WE DO WITH MOST OF OUR STEAKS IN THE RESTAURANT,
SITTING ON TOP OF A BONE MARROW TRENCHER WITH POPOVERS AND DEVIL DIP GRAVY.
THIS IS OUR ANSWER TO A SUNDAY ROAST.

SERVES 10

Beef Rub (see page 118)	heaping ¼ cup
prime rib of beef	1, weighing about 8¾ pounds
Whipped Bone Marrow, to serve (see page 228)	
Maldon sea salt	
freshly ground black pepper	

Prepare a barbecue for smoking (see The Setup on pages 114–15) and set the temperature to 170°F.

Rub the beef rub all over the joint. Smoke it in the barbecue for 5 hours, or until the internal temperature reaches 131° to 134°F—it will continue to rise even after it has been removed from the barbecue, to around 138°F.

Once the rib reaches temperature, remove it from the barbecue and adjust the barbecue for direct grilling at a medium heat (see page 112).

Season the meat joint with salt and pepper, then cook on the barbecue, turning it over every minute or so, for 5 to 6 minutes, or until the joint has the full Maillard effect (see page 108). It should be evenly browned, but not charred, and have a sweet nutty smell. Rest for 10 minutes and serve on a Dripping Trencher smothered in Whipped Bone Marrow (see page 166) with Devil Dip Gravy (see page 130) and Popovers (see page 243).

DRIPPING TRENCHER

IT IS NICE TO THINK THAT MEDIEVAL DINING STILL HAS A PLACE ON OUR TABLES.
IN MEDIEVAL TIMES, FOOD WOULD OFTEN BE PLACED ON STALE OR DENSE PIECES OF
BREAD. THE BREAD, HAVING SOAKED UP THE MEAT JUICES AND SAUCE, WOULD THEN
EITHER BE EATEN OR HANDED OUT TO THOSE IN NEED OF SUSTENANCE.

OUR DRIPPING TRENCHER IS THE PERFECT FOUNDATION FOR ROAST MEAT. THINK OF IT
AS THE BEST MOP IN THE WORLD. WHENEVER WE PUT A PRIME RIB FOR SHARING ON THE
MENU, WE SET IT ON A TRENCHER SMEARED WITH A LIVELY BONE-MARROW MIXTURE AND
LET IT REST FOR AS LONG AS THE TRENCHER NEEDS TO FULFILL ITS POTENTIAL.

MAKES ENOUGH FOR 1 PRIME RIB ROAST

semiskim milk	scant 1 cup
water	scant ½ cup
fresh yeast	¼ ounce
strong white flour	2 cups
whole-wheat flour	2 cups
beef dripping or bone marrow	½ cup
salt	scant 1 teaspoon
superfine sugar	1 teaspoon

Heat the milk and water to 95°F, then add
the yeast, followed by the sifted flours
and the remaining ingredients. Bring the
ingredients together, then cover with a
damp dish towel and let prove in a warm
place for 20 minutes, or until it has
doubled in size.

Remove the mixture from the bowl and knock
back into a dough, then roll out to the
size of a large plate, big enough to take
your smoked standing prime rib roast. Place
on a baking pan, cover, and let prove for
another 20 minutes.

Heat the oven to 350°F. Bake the trencher
for 20 minutes, or until golden brown.

Slice off the top of the trencher and use
this as a serving platter for the smoked
standing prime rib roast, where you can let
it rest for 10 minutes after cooking.

——— BEEF RIBS ———

THE QUALITY OF THE BEEF HERE IS EVERYTHING. IT TOOK US A YEAR BEFORE A BEEF RIB WAS EVEN SERVED AT PITT CUE. IT WAS ONLY WHEN WE SPENT TIME WITH OUR BUTCHERS IN CORNWALL THAT WE THOUGHT BEEF RIBS SHOULD HAVE A PLACE ON OUR MENU. OUR RIBS COME FROM GRASS-FED, RARE-BREED RIB-EYES THAT ARE KEPT ON THE BONE FOR AT LEAST 4 WEEKS, AND ARE HUNG FOR A FURTHER WEEK OR SO AFTER BEING REMOVED FROM THE RIB-EYE, WHICH DRIES THEM OUT A LITTLE. THE RACK, 4 TO 6 BONES IN LENGTH, SHOULD BE STIFF, FIRM, AND HAVE A DISTINCTIVE SWEET, NUTTY AROMA. TRY TO AVOID RIBS FROM THE WING RIB—THE RIBS FLATTEN OUT TOWARD THE SIRLOIN, ARE GENERALLY CUT LONGER, AND CONTAIN LESS INTERCOSTAL MEAT.

SERVES 2

4- to 6-bone beef rib rack	1, weighing
1 pound 2 ounces to 1 pound 5 ounces	
House Rub (see page 119)	⅓ cup
Mother Sauce (see page 120)	
or Pitt Cue Barbecue Sauce (see page 122), (optional)	

Crucial to the eating of the beef rib is the removal of the membrane on the underside, especially with a well-aged rib. Unlike the pork rib membrane, which is fresh and thin, the membrane on the underside of the beef rib is thick and a bit of a pain. To remove it, score down each side of the individual bones, being careful not to cut into the flesh. Get a proper butcher's knife with some flexibility and work up the rib, removing the membrane with as little flesh as possible. Try to keep the knife as flat as you can to the flesh, just skinning the membrane from it. The removed membrane should be about ¾ inch wide and run the entire length of each rib. All that will remain is a small section of membrane on the rib bone itself, which is a fair compromise.

Cover the rack all over with the rub.

Prepare a barbecue for smoking (see The Setup on pages 114–15) and set the temperature to 230°F, though anything up to 265°F will produce tasty beef ribs.

There is a huge amount of fat running through the intercostal muscles of the beef rib, which can take a bit of a battering through temperature rises without drying out: 230°F is ideal, but don't panic if the barbecue peaks and dips in temperature.

Smoke the rack for 5 to 6 hours, or until the meat has pulled back from the bone. By then the rack will have the French trim effect, with the bone a little bit exposed. The internal temperature should be about 192° to 197°F, the meat squishy and soft with a thick dark crust. We like the ribs naked, but if you prefer them with sauce, give them a good basting with Mother Sauce or barbecue sauce 30 minutes before removing them. Alternatively adjust the barbecue for direct grilling (see page 112) and paint them constantly with the sauce while turning them over the heat.

The smell of a newly smoked beef rib is unbelievable. Serve immediately, with some Pickled Shiitake (see page 89) to boost that amazing umami beefiness while balancing the richness.

LAMB RIBS
—— WITH MOLASSES MOP & ONION SALAD ——

LIVING NEXT TO THE BEST TURKISH OCAKBASI IN LONDON WAS BOUND TO HAVE
AN EFFECT. NOT ONLY DO YOU START TO APPRECIATE ANGRY WAITERS WHO CANNOT WAIT
TO GET YOU OUT THE DOOR, YOU COME TO LOVE THE WAY CITRUS, HERBS, JUST-COOKED
ONIONS, AND ACIDIC FRUITS CAN BENEFIT GRILLED MEAT.

THIS RECIPE IS THE CULMINATION OF TOM'S MANY SUNDAY NIGHT POST-SERVICE PIT STOPS
TO THE TURKISH SUPERMARKET, WHERE HE WOULD GRAB A FEW BOTTLES OF POMEGRANATE
MOLASSES, SOME SUMAC, AND AS MANY LITTLE QUAIL AS HE COULD SAFELY CARRY ON HIS
BIKE. WHILE QUAIL, SUMAC, AND BURNT ONIONS STILL HAVE A PLACE ON THE MENU AT
PITT CUE, THERE ARE FEW THINGS THAT CAN BEAT LAMB RIBS WITH THIS SALAD.

SERVES 2

whole lamb breast on the bone	1, weighing 1 pound 5 ounces
French's mustard	1 tablespoon
Lamb Rub *(see page 118)*	heaping ¼ cup

MOLASSES MOP

Mother Sauce *(see page 120)*	scant 1 cup
blackstrap molasses	1 tablespoon
juice of 1 lemon	

RED ONION & BABY GEM SALAD

firm, small red onions	4
extra virgin olive oil	
baby gem lettuces	2
juice of 2 lemons	
large mint leaves	10
flat-leaf parsley leaves	small handful
pickled pomegranates	2 tablespoons
pomegranate molasses	2 tablespoons
sumac	1 tablespoon
Maldon sea salt	
freshly ground black pepper	

Prepare a barbecue for smoking (see The Setup on pages 114–15) and set the temperature to 230°F.

There is no need to remove the membrane on the lamb breast. It is very thin and doesn't really affect the eating, though the skin on the top side of the breast will need to be removed, because it will become tough and unpleasant to eat. Square off the breast and trim the redundant flap from the smaller end of the breast (rear-end). The yield of a lamb rib is never going to be great, and there is very little meat from the trim, so don't worry if it looks as though you've reduced the rack to a small rectangle. The breast should also be squared off at the shoulder end. The rack of ribs should be nice and neat.

Put all the molasses mop ingredients in a pan and bring to a simmer. Set aside and keep warm.

Rub the rack all over with the mustard and coat evenly with the lamb rub. Smoke the lamb in the barbecue for about 5 hours, or until the meat is just starting to soften and the internal temperature reaches 188°F.

Remove the ribs from the barbecue and set aside. Adjust the barbecue for direct grilling (see page 112). Grill the ribs and baste generously with the molasses mop. Remove the ribs from the grill and keep warm.

To make the salad, peel and quarter the onions and dress lightly in olive oil. Grill the onions on the barbecue for 10 minutes, or until charred and softened, then remove and place in a bowl, cover with plastic wrap, and let steam. Quarter the Baby Gems, season with salt and pepper, and brush with olive oil. Grill for 1 minute on each side, or until the Baby Gems are sporadically dark and charred but not completely burnt. Remove from the grill and set aside.

Lightly peel off most of the burnt outer layer from the onions to leave the lightly charred and soft inner layers, then combine with the Baby Gems. Dress with a tablespoon of olive oil, the lemon juice, torn mint leaves, parsley leaves, pickled pomegranates, and pomegranate molasses. Toss the whole salad gently until well combined and evenly dressed. Season to taste with salt, some sumac, and some freshly ground black pepper.

Serve the ribs sprinkled with the remaining sumac and alongside a nice heap of the grilled onion salad.

LAMB RUMP

LAMB RUMP IS A WICKED LITTLE JOINT FOR THE BARBECUE, COMPACT, EASILY PORTIONABLE AND YET ANOTHER CUT THAT SUITS A COMBINATION OF INDIRECT AND DIRECT COOKING. YOU WANT A RUMP WITH A PROPER COVERING OF FAT (USE MUTTON, IF YOU CAN FIND IT) THAT WILL CHAR AND DEVELOP ALL THOSE COMPLEX SWEET AND SMOKY FLAVORS THAT MAKE GOOD ANIMAL FATS SO RIDICULOUSLY ADDICTIVE WHEN FINISHED ON THE GRILL. YOUR BUTCHER WILL PROBABLY OFFER TO TRIM THE JOINT, WHICH MEANS REMOVING THE THICK END OF THE FILLET THAT ENTERS THE BEGINNING OF THE RUMP. BUT TAKE IT WHOLE AND UNTRIMMED— IT'S MORE INTERESTING TO EAT, KEEPING ALL THE FAT ON IS IMPORTANT, AND THAT BIT OF FILLET IS A BONUS.

SERVES 1 TO 2

lamb rump	1, weighing 14 ounces to 1¼ pounds
Lamb Rub *(see page 118)*	2 tablespoons
Maldon sea salt	
freshly ground black pepper	

Prepare a barbecue for smoking (see The Setup on pages 114–15) and set the temperature to 230°F. Be careful about using too much smoke because this can overpower the lamb.

To prepare the lamb, remove the skin from the top of the rump being careful not to rip off the fat with it. Rub the lamb all over with the lamb rub and put it, fat-side up, inside your barbecue. Smoke for 30 to 45 minutes, or until the internal temperature reaches 122 to 125°F. Remove from the barbecue and let rest while you adjust your barbecue for direct grilling (see page 112).

Season the rump with salt and pepper and grill for 1 minute on each side, or until evenly charred. Let rest for 5 to 10 minutes before carving.

Serve with Crispy Capers (see below).

CRISPY CAPERS

capers, drained	handful
oil, for deep-frying	

Heat the oil to 355°F in a deep-fryer or large saucepan.

Toss the capers into the fryer, and deep-fry for 1 minute, or until puffed and crispy. Drain on paper towels and serve.

LAMB BREAST

PERHAPS OUR FAVORITE PART OF THE LAMB, THIS WAY OF COOKING LAMB BREAST HAS BEEN ALMOST A CONSTANT ON THE MENU SINCE WE FIRST STARTED COOKING IT. LAMB BREAST, ESSENTIALLY THE BELLY OF THE LAMB, IS FANTASTICALLY FATTY, AND ROLLING THE BREAST MEANS THAT ALL THE FAT IS EVENLY SPACED THROUGH THE FINAL ROLLED JOINT. A COOKED CROSS-SECTION OF THE BELLY IS A BEAUTIFUL SIGHT, WITH LAYERS OF MEAT SANDWICHED IN BETWEEN FAT. THE MERGUEZ SAUSAGE, OFTEN LEANER THAN A PORK SAUSAGE, WORKS WELL HERE, BECAUSE THE RENDERING FAT FROM THE BELLY BASTES THE SAUSAGE MEAT DURING COOKING. WE CHILL THE LAMB BREAST AFTER COOKING AND LET IT SET BEFORE SLICING IT INTO THICK SLICES, THEN WE GRILL AND SERVE IT WITH CHEESE CURDS OR SOUR CREAM AND LOTS OF CRISPY CAPERS.

SERVES 4

lamb breast	1, weighing about 2¾ to 3¼ pounds
Lamb rub (see page 118)	2 tablespoons
merguez sausage	¾ pound
Dijon mustard	1 heaping tablespoon
garlic cloves, minced	4

Prepare a barbecue for smoking (see The Setup on pages 114–15) and set the temperature to 230°F.

First, take your lamb breast off the bone. To do this, take the top layer of skin off the breast—it is thin but should be removed; take a sharp thin-bladed knife and find the seam between the skin and the fat that sits just beneath it. Pull the skin away from the fat being careful not to tear any of the fat or flesh on the breast.

To bone the breast, use the same knife and work your way along the breast, keeping as close to the rib bones as possible.

There should be no meat left on the ribs once the breast has been removed. Once the breast bone has been removed, flatten the meat out, skin-side down. Rub the exposed side of the breast evenly with the mustard and cover with half the lamb rub. Remove the sausage meat from the merguez sausage casing and spread it evenly over the mustard and rub, followed by the minced garlic.

Neatly roll up the lamb breast so only the skin side of the breast is exposed. Tie the lambs breast, using cooking twine and make 4 to 5 evenly spaced knots.

Cover the rolled breast with the remaining rub. Smoke in the barbecue for 6 to 7 hours, or until the internal temperature reaches 186 to 190°F and the lamb is soft to the touch.

At this point the breast can be carved with a very sharp knife, or chilled and then cut into slices and browned in a hot pan. Serve with sour cream and pickles and Crispy Capers (see page 172).

MUTTON SHOULDER
& ANCHOVY HOLLANDAISE

MUTTON SHOULDER IS A LITTLE
TOUGHER THAN LAMB BUT HAS
TWICE THE FLAVOR AND, IF
SLOW-COOKED OVER MANY HOURS, IT
WILL DELIGHT.

SERVES 8

good Cantabrian anchovy fillets	¼ ounce
capers	scant 1 tablespoon
zest of 2 lemons	
zest of 1 orange	
apricot conserve	½ tablespoon
Dijon mustard	2 teapoons
shoulder of mutton or lamb	1, weighing 4½ pounds
Lamb Rub (see page 118)	scant ½ cup
salt and pepper	
Pitt Cue Barbecue Sauce (see page 122),	(optional)
Anchovy Hollandaise (see below)	½ cup

Blitz the anchovies, capers, citrus zests, apricot conserve, and mustard in a blender to a thick paste. Rub the paste all over the mutton shoulder and refrigerate overnight.

Prepare a barbecue for smoking (see The Setup on pages 114–15) and set the temperature to 230°F.

Take the mutton out of the fridge and cover it with the lamb rub. Put it in your barbecue and smoke for 10 to 11 hours, or until the internal temperature reaches roughly 188°F and the meat is very soft. Remove the meat from the barbecue and let rest, wrapped in foil, for 30 minutes. Pull the shoulder apart, season to taste (add barbecue sauce if necessary), and serve in Potato Rolls or London Bath Buns (see page 240), with lots of Anchovy Hollandaise and Burnt Leeks (see page 223).

ANCHOVY HOLLANDAISE

SERVES 8

good tinned anchovy fillets	5½ ounces
garlic cloves	3
thyme leaves	1 teaspoon
basil leaves	2
good mustard	1 tablespoon
unsalted butter	2 sticks
free-range egg yolks	4
white wine vinegar	scant ½ cup
shallots, peeled and sliced	3

Blitz the anchovies, garlic, thyme, basil, and mustard in a blender to a smooth paste or on a board using a knife. Set aside.

Gently heat the butter in a small pan, then let stand. Skim off the solids on the top and pass the clarified butter through a fine sieve.

Place a heatproof bowl over a pan of gently simmering water. Add the egg yolks and vinegar and whisk together to form a hot foam, then remove from the heat. Slowly pour in the warm clarified butter in a steady stream, whisking constantly until all the butter is incorporated. Whisk the anchovy paste into the mixture and serve immediately.

HOT MUTTON RIBS

MUTTON BREAST IS ONE OF OUR FAVORITE CUTS FROM THE SHEEP.
MUTTON IS LARGER THAN SPRING LAMB AND HAS A GREATER DEPTH OF FLAVOR.

Prepare a barbecue for smoking (see The Setup on pages 114–15) and set the temperature to 230°F.

Carefully remove the top layer of skin from the breast, then rub the mutton with the lamb rub. Put it in your barbecue and smoke for 5 to 6 hours, or until the breast has a thick bark but is gelatinous and soft, and the internal temperature of the meat reaches 186°F. Remove from the barbecue and let cool slightly. When cool enough to handle, portion the belly into ribs.

Adjust the barbecue to direct grilling (see page 112), then grill the ribs for 1 minute on each side until well browned. Meanwhile, heat the hot sauce and barbecue sauce together in a pan and keep warm. When the ribs are cooked, toss them in the sauce and serve at once.

A side of curd and Poor Man's Capers (see page 193) would be welcome accompaniments.

SERVES 2

mutton or lamb breast	1 pound 2 ounces
Lamb Rub (see page 118)	heaping ¼ cup
Hot Sauce (see page 124)	3 tablespoons
Pitt Cue Barbecue Sauce (see page 122)	3 tablespoons

WHOLE SPICY SMOKED ROAST CHICKEN

WE BELIEVE IT'S ALMOST IMPOSSIBLE TO IMPROVE ON A SIMPLE ROAST CHICKEN, BUT THIS IS JUST AS GOOD AND A BIT DIFFERENT. THE MOST IMPORTANT THING TO REMEMBER IS TO BUY A GOOD BIRD—FREE-RANGE, AND AS OLD AS YOU CAN FIND. INTENSIVE FARMING PUTS BIRDS ON THE SHELF AT SIX WEEKS OLD (NOT GOOD), SO IF YOU CAN FIND A BIRD THAT HAS LIVED FOR A FEW MONTHS, YOU'LL BE REWARDED.

SERVES 3 TO 4

chipotle chile paste	3 tablespoons
unsalted butter	½ stick
maple syrup	3 tablespoons
roasted garlic paste	1¾ ounces
House Rub (see page 119)	heaping ¼ cup
free-range chicken	1, weighing 3¼ pounds

Blitz the chipotle chile paste, butter, maple syrup, roasted garlic paste, and house rub in a blender to a paste. Make slashes about ½ inch deep in the thighs of the chicken with a sharp knife, then rub the chicken thoroughly inside and out with the paste. Put it into a dish, cover, and leave overnight in the fridge.

Prepare a barbecue for smoking (see The Setup on pages 114–15) and set the temperature to 300°F.

Put the chicken, breast-side up, into a roasting pan that will fit inside your barbecue and smoke/roast for 1½ hours, or until the internal temperature of the meat reaches 158°F and the juices run clear when the chicken is pricked with a knife at the thickest point of the thigh area.

Remove the chicken from the barbecue and let rest for 10 minutes before carving. Serve with Iceberg Salad (see page 210) and Anchovy Salad Cream (see page 205).

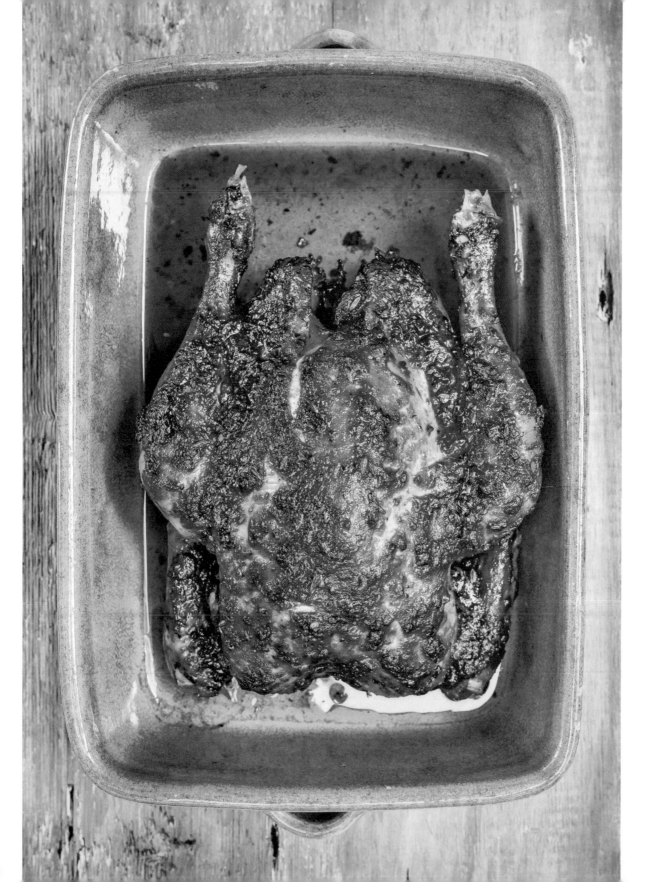

DEVILED CHICKEN BUN

AS BUNS GO THIS IS A REAL BEAUTY. IT STANDS VERY PROUD AND PRETTY ON A PLATE, SERVED AS WE DO IN THE RESTAURANT WITHOUT THE LID IN PLACE SO THE BRIGHT AND BEAUTIFUL PICKLED SALAD SITS ON FULL SHOW. THE EATING OF IT HOWEVER, IS NOT SO PRETTY. THIS WAY OF FRYING CHICKEN WORKS REALLY WELL, WITH THE PRESMOKING ALLOWING FOR A LIGHT CRUNCHY COATING THAT KEEPS THIS BUN NICE AND CLEAN (ISH).

SERVES 2

free-range boneless chicken thighs	4
Master Chicken Brine *(see page 90)*	2 cups
breakfast radishes, cleaned and leaves removed	¾ ounce
Smashed Cucumber and Pickled Watermelon Salad *(see page 213)*	2¾ ounces
House Rub *(see page 119)*	2 tablespoons
all-purpose flour	heaping ¾ cup
whole milk	scant ½ cup
oil, for deep-frying	
Chipotle and Maple Wings Marinade *(see page 93)*	3 tablespoons
London Bath Buns, sliced	2
Chipotle Mayonnaise *(see page 198)*	

Prepare a barbecue for smoking (see The Setup on pages 114–15) and set the temperature to 230°F.

Load the chicken thighs into the brine and refrigerate for 1 hour. Meanwhile, finely shave the radishes into a bowl of iced water. Once cold, drain the radishes and toss through the cucumber and watermelon salad.

Remove the thighs from the brine, dry on paper towels, then rub all over with the house rub. Smoke the thighs in the barbecue for 1 hour, or until the internal temperature reaches 158°F. Remove from the smoker and let rest for 10 minutes.

Get ready two shallow bowls. In the first put the flour and in the second put the milk.

Coat the thighs in flour, shaking off any excess. Then dip the thighs into the milk, and then back into the flour. Heat the oil to 355°F in a deep-fryer or large saucepan, and deep-fry the thighs for 1 to 2 minutes, or until golden and crispy. Remove the thighs from the fryer, drain on paper towels, and brush all over with the chipotle and maple marinade.

To construct the bun, toast the cut sides of the buns under a broiler. Spread the chipotle mayonnaise on the base of the buns and top with the chicken thighs. Press the thighs down a little so the buns retain some structural integrity—these have a tendency to topple so a little force does it some good. Finish with the pickled salad on top and serve with the bun lids on the side.

WHOLE SMOKED
── DUCK ──

WE STARTED OFFERING WHOLE
DUCK FOR TWO OR THREE PEOPLE
TO SHARE, REMOVING THE CROWN
FOR SMOKING, DEEP-FRYING THE
WINGS, AND MAKING SMOKED
CONFIT NUGGETS FROM THE LEGS.
AFTER THAT YOU ARE LEFT WITH
ALL THE LOVELY VARIETY MEATS
TO GRILL, SPREAD ON TOAST,
AND PICK AT AS YOU WISH. IT
IS A GREAT WAY TO ENJOY A
DUCK, WITH LOTS OF DIFFERENT
FLAVORS AND TEXTURES, BUT
UNFORTUNATELY IT IS TIME-
CONSUMING AND A LOT EASIER TO
DO IN A RESTAURANT KITCHEN
THAN AT HOME.

THIS METHOD OF SMOKING DUCK
IS INSPIRED BY THE TEA-
SMOKED DUCK OR ZHANGCHA
THAT IS A STAPLE OF BANQUETS
AND FEASTING IN THE CHINESE
PROVINCE OF SICHUAN. IT IS A
BRILLIANT WAY TO TREAT A DUCK
BUT REQUIRES A LITTLE BIT
OF ATTENTION. IN SICHUANESE
COOKING, THE DUCK IS
MARINATED, BLANCHED, AND AIR-
DRIED BEFORE BEING SMOKED,
STEAMED, AND DEEP-FRIED. EVEN
THE GREATEST DUCK FANATIC
IS GOING TO BE PUSHED TO DO
THIS ON A REGULAR BASIS, SO
THIS RECIPE IS SLIGHTLY MORE
SUBDUED, MAKING A MIGHTY FINE
FEAST ALL THE SAME.

SERVES 4

fresh duck	1, weighing about 5½ pounds
Duck Rub (see page 118)	½ cup + 1 tablespoon

TEA BRINE

water	3 pints
tea leaves (Oolong, Darjeeling or Lapsang Souchong)	½ cup (about 1¾ ounces)
fresh ginger, peeled	1-inch piece
bulb of garlic	1
star anise	2
soy sauce	scant ½ cup
honey	¼ cup
smoked Maldon sea salt	3½ tablespoons

In a large pan, whisk together all the brine ingredients over low heat until well combined and the salt has dissolved. Chill in the refrigerator.

Place the duck in a large bowl and add the the brine. Set aside and let stand overnight. Next day, remove the duck from the brine and let dry in the fridge for an hour.

Prepare a barbecue for smoking (see The Setup on pages 114–15) and set the temperature to 340°F.

Rub the duck thoroughly inside and out with the duck rub. Place it in the barbecue and smoke for 45 minutes to 1 hour.

Remove the duck from the barbecue and let rest for 10 minutes. Carve or pull the duck apart, and serve hot with Potato Rolls (see page 240), sour cream, and pickles.

PULLED DUCK & CAVIAR BUNS

RICHARD CAME ACROSS THIS COMBO WHILE STAYING IN A POSH HOTEL IN ST. PETERSBURG, IN RUSSIA. THERE, IT WAS ROAST DUCK AND CAVIAR, SERVED IN PANCAKES WITH A SHOT OF ICE-COLD VODKA. OUR VERSION SHOULD, OF COURSE, BE EATEN WITH A PICKLEBACK OR BOILERMAKER.

WE USE ETHICALLY FARMED CAVIAR, WHICH IS PRODUCED BY MILKING THE FISH OF THEIR EGGS RATHER THAN GUTTING THEM … LIKE A FISH.

SERVES 4

cucumber	1
leftover Smoked Duck *(see page 178)*	4¼ ounces
Mother Sauce *(see page 120)*	2 tablespoons
Potato Rolls or London Bath Buns *(see page 240)*	4
sour cream	2 tablespoons
sturgeon caviar (Ossetra)	1 ounce

Shave the cucumber lengthwise into very thin strips. Place in iced water and set aside.

Pick the duck off the bone and heat through in a small pan with the Mother Sauce.

Drain the cucumber. Slice the buns in half and arrange a few strips of cucumber on the bottom half. Top this with the hot pulled duck, and finish with sour cream and caviar. Put the lid on and eat at once.

— DUCK GIBLET SAUSAGES —

IT'S NOT POSSIBLE TO GET MUCH MORE DUCK INTO A SAUSAGE THAN THIS, AND FOR THAT WE SHOULD ALL BE VERY HAPPY.

IF PICKLED CHERRIES ARE NOT IN YOUR KITCHEN CUPBOARD, GET PICKLING. AND IF YOU ARE NOT YET PICKLING, SUBSTITUTE THE CHERRIES WITH SOME PRUNES. IDEALLY, CONFIT DUCK MEAT SHOULD REMAIN IN THE FRIDGE FOR SEVERAL WEEKS TO ALLOW THE FLAVORS TO DEVELOP, BUT WHO KNOWS WHERE WE WILL BE IN SEVERAL WEEKS? SO GET GOING!

SERVES 6

duck necks, with skin	6
duck gizzards	12
duck wings	6
Duck Rub (see page 118)	2 teaspoons
duck fat	1 cup
duck hearts	12
duck livers	12
Pickled Cherries (see page 197), pitted	12
sprigs of thyme, leaves picked	2
Maldon sea salt	

Prepare a barbecue for smoking (see The Setup on pages 114–15) and set the temperature to 230°F.

Carefully remove the skin from the duck necks and try to keep the skin in one piece so that you can stuff them later. Season the gizzards, wings, and skinned duck necks with some of the duck rub and place in a small cocotte dish. Cover with the duck fat, then place in the barbecue and smoke gently for 3 hours.

Season the duck hearts with more duck rub, add to the dish, and cook for another 2 hours, then season the duck livers and add to the dish for a further 20 minutes. Remove everything from the barbecue and let cool slightly.

Take the duck necks and wings out of the dish, and leave any duck fat in the bottom of the dish. Pick all the meat from the bones and place in a bowl, then chop the other giblets and roughly chop the pickled cherries and thyme. Add to the bowl, season with salt, and mix together, then refrigerate until needed.

Tie one end of each duck neck skin with string and stuff with the giblet mixture, then tie the other end. Place the sausages in the cocotte dish with the reserved duck fat and smoke for a further 30 minutes at 212°F. If you are not cooking these immediately, then drain on paper towels, and chill until you are ready to cook them.

Prepare a barbecue for direct grilling (see page 112). Remove the sausages from the dish, dry on paper towels, and grill them until crisp and golden. Serve hot with salads and Pickled Pomegranate (see page 197) or chutney.

SMOKED QUAIL

WE STARTED SERVING QUAIL WHEN WE FIRST OPENED THE TRAILER, BUT A SINGLE SERVING OF ONE OR TWO BIRDS WAS NEVER REALLY ENOUGH. IT IS MUCH MORE SATISFYING TO HAVE A BIG PILE OF QUAIL IN FRONT OF YOU, KNOWING WHAT NEEDS TO BE DONE. QUAIL HAS SINCE BEEN DRESSED UP IN MANY WAYS ON OUR MENU, BUT THIS RECIPE IS SUPER SIMPLE AND TAKES ITS LEAD FROM THE LEGENDARY MENU AT ST JOHN, IN LONDON, WHERE WE HAVE ENJOYED MANY A QUAIL. ONCE YOU HAVE MASTERED SMOKING QUAIL DOWN TO A FINE ART, THEN IT IS DEFINITELY WORTH SUBSTITUTING ANY OF THE SMOKED WING SAUCES (SEE PAGES 92–3) FOR OUR MOTHER SAUCE.

SERVES 4

large oven-ready quail	8
Our Pickle Brine *(see page 78)*	4 ¼ pints
House Rub *(see page 119)*	½ cup + 1 tablespoon
Mother Sauce *(see page 120)*	scant 1 cup

Load the quail into the brine and refrigerate for 2 hours. Remove from the brine and let dry.

Prepare a barbecue for smoking (see The Setup on pages 114–15) and set the temperature to 230°F.

Rub the quail inside and out with the house rub. Place them on the barbecue and smoke for 30 to 40 minutes, or until the internal temperature reaches 147°F.

Remove the quail from the heat and adjust the barbecue for direct grilling (see page 112). Grill the quail for 30 seconds on each side, basting occasionally with the Mother Sauce, until well browned.

Remove from the grill and pile the quail into a serving bowl. Eat immediately.

CHAPTER

04

SLAWS
{&}
SIDES

SLAWS {&} SIDES

· · · · · · · · · · · · ·

Side dishes can really be anything you want them to be, and for this reason they are one of the most exciting things to cook and be faced with in a restaurant. Unfortunately, though, when it comes to barbecue, they are often neglected. Barbecue, as culture and technique, is based on meat and the cooking of it over fire, so the neglect of side dishes is not entirely surprising. However, this neglect is a grave shame; for us, barbecue most definitely requires some satisfying respite and clean juxtapositions to the main meaty event. Side dishes are there to provide this balance.

The side dishes we have eaten on our trips to Texas, the neighboring Southern states, and the barbecue in NYC have largely been disappointing, consisting mostly of sweet baked beans and overcooked greens. The vast majority of people eating barbecue, and traveling the great distances that they do to eat at the most respected places, are not doing so for great side dishes, or even for any side dishes at all. We are guilty of the same thing when visiting Texas, largely in search of great smoked beef, but it was only through doing this that we began to realize the need for side dishes that offset and match the great meats on offer.

Perhaps our desire to focus a lot of time on side dishes and pickles comes from the fact that we have been brought up in restaurants where vegetables and fruits are given as much attention as the meat they sit alongside.

As a devout green hater, Simon would probably disagree, but whenever eating barbecue in the US, however awesome the meal may have been, we often exited the building on the brink of giving birth to a food baby—and this was down to the lack of balance in the meal. Delicious as it is, a tray of meat with no vegetables and just a small cup of meaty beans is not balanced and leads to some textbook post-meal lethargy shortly afterward. That is not to say that our customers do not get into this state after eating with us, but we at least try to give them the option of a more civilized or balanced meal if they so wish.

The Soho kitchen has a small induction cooktop and no service oven, so the side dishes on our menu are dictated by what cooking equipment we can use during service and what can be used during the day. The one piece of equipment that is often available is the grill, so grilling vegetables was an obvious avenue for us to go down. Lettuces, onions, greens, and brassicas have become some of our favorite vegetables to grill, developing sweet, complex, smoky flavors, and open up a huge number of options when it comes to delicious and simple side dishes. Next time you are making a salad or side dish, think seriously about using the grill. For us, the parameters of what can be a side dish are fairly loose. As long as you are using something seasonal and it helps to complete the meal, not becoming a meal unto itself, you are on the right track.

· · · · · · · · · · · · ·

PICKLES

PICKLING, FOR US, IS AN ESSENTIAL PART OF WHAT WE DO. SMOKED MEATS NEED SOME ASSISTANCE—A BIG MOUND OF MEAT IS A VERY ATTRACTIVE PROPOSITION, BUT WITHOUT GOOD SIDES AND PICKLES, KEY FOILS AND JUXTAPOSITIONS, THE MOUND BECOMES A MOUNTAIN.

PICKLING HAS ALWAYS BEEN AN OCCUPATION DICTATED BY THE SEASONS. THESE RECIPES CAN BE MADE BY ANYONE THROUGHOUT THE YEAR WITH WHATEVER FRESH VEGETABLES OR FRUIT IS AVAILABLE, BUT THEY WILL ALSO WORK TO FULFILL ANY IMMEDIATE DESIRE. IF YOU FIND YOURSELF IN NEED OF A PICKLE, YOU CAN EASILY THROW TOGETHER A PICKLE BEFORE LUNCH, AT ANY TIME OF YEAR. ON THE OTHER HAND, IF THERE IS A HUGE AMOUNT OF FRESH PLUMS OR SLOE BERRIES IN THE MARKET IN FALL, YOU CAN GET PICKLING FOR THE WINTER.

THE PICKLE BRINE WE USE (SEE PAGE 78) IS A SIMPLE PICKLING BRINE AND IS IDEAL FOR A QUICK PICKLE THAT WILL LAST A WEEK, SOMETIMES A MONTH; HOWEVER, IT IS NOT A FULLY FLEDGED FERMENTATION, SO BEST NOT TO LEAVE IT IN YOUR CUPBOARD FOR NEXT YEAR.

BREAD & BUTTER PICKLES

THESE ARE INTEGRAL TO THE
RESTAURANT AND HAVE BEEN SERVED
SINCE DAY ONE. THEY'RE SUPER
EASY TO MAKE AND THEY STORE
VERY WELL. THERE ARE NO EXCUSES
NOT TO HAVE THEM IN YOUR
FRIDGE JUST IN CASE. THEY'RE
PURE JOY TO MAKE AND TO EAT.

RESERVE ALL THE PICKLING
JUICE FOR MAKING PICKLEBACKS
(SEE PAGE 23).

MAKES 2 PINTS

large cucumbers	5
onion	1
salt	heaping ¼ cup

BRINE

cider vinegar	1¼ cups
soft brown sugar	1 cup
ground turmeric	2 teaspoons
cloves	5
black mustard seeds	½ tablespoon
fennel seeds	2 teaspoons
coriander seeds	1 tablespoon

Wash the cucumbers and onion, then cut into slices ⅛ inch thick.

Layer the cucumber and onion slices in a container, distributing the salt between the layers. Cover with plastic wrap and put a heavy weight on top to help extract the water from the vegetables. Leave for at least 4 hours, until limp but crunchy.

When ready, pour away the liquid and rinse the cucumber and onion under running water, tossing constantly for 5 to 10 minutes, until no longer salty. Let dry.

Put the vinegar, sugar, and spices into a stainless steel pan and stir over medium heat until the sugar has dissolved. Bring to a boil, then add the cucumber and onion and cook for 3 minutes, or until the cucumbers have browned through but are not cooked. This is important, because overcooked cucumbers will soften. Remove from the heat and let cool.

Transfer the pickles to a sterilized jar (see page 78) and store in the fridge until needed, preferably leaving them for 2 to 3 weeks for a fuller flavor.

POOR MAN'S CAPERS

MAKES 2 PINTS

water	scant 2 cups
Maldon sea salt	3½ tablespoons
green nasturtium seeds	1 pound 2 ounces
Our Pickle Brine *(see page 78)*	2 cups

Pour the water into a bowl, add the salt, and stir to dissolve. Pick the nasturtium seeds while still green, put them into the water, then let stand for 24 hours.

Drain and rinse the seeds, then pack them into sterilized glass jars (see page 78). Pour the pickle brine into a pan and bring to a boil. Pour the hot brine into the jars to cover the seeds, then seal. Let stand for 2 weeks to mature before using.

PICKLED PLUMS & SLOE BERRIES

MAKES 2 PINTS

plums or sloe berries	1 pound 2 ounces
soft light brown sugar	1½ cups
red wine	¾ cup
red wine vinegar	½ cup
small stick of cinnamon	1
cloves	4
coriander seeds	½ teaspoon
black peppercorns	5
small bay leaf	1

First, discard all the leaves and stalks from the fruit. Wash the fruit gently under running water, but don't let it sit in the water for any length of time. Let dry, then prick each fruit individually with a needle—a couple of pricks each is ideal.

Put the remaining ingredients into a pan and bring to a boil, then continue to boil for 10 minutes. The mixture will thicken just slightly. Take the pan off of the heat and add the fruit. The aim here is not to burst or split the fruits and create chutney, but to keep them whole. Return the pan to low heat and very gently bring back to a boil. If the fruit begins to split, lower the heat. Remove the pan from the heat once the mixture has come to a boil.

Transfer the fruit and liquid to sterilized glass jars (see page 78). Cover the exposed surface at the top of each jar with a disk of waxed paper, then seal and let cool. Store in the fridge for at least 2 months before using.

PICKLED BEETS

MAKES 2 PINTS

beets (chioggia, golden, or red)	1 pound 2 ounces
water	scant 1 cup
white wine vinegar (or red, for red beets)	1¼ cups
sugar	scant 1 cup
Maldon sea salt	2 teaspoons
shavings of fresh horseradish	¼ ounce
star anise	1
black peppercorns	3
small bay leaf	1

Steam the beets over a pan of simmering water until a skewer slides easily through the center—this will take about 45 minutes to 1 hour, depending on size. When they're ready, remove them from the steamer, place in a bowl, and cover with plastic wrap. Let stand for 15 to 20 minutes, or until the beets are cool enough to be handled and you can remove the skin easily with your fingers. Cut the beets whichever way you wish—wedges, slices, or cubes all work well. Bring all the remaining ingredients to a boil in a large pan, then set aside to cool.

Put the beets into a sterilized 2-pint jar (see page 78) or plastic containers and add the pickling liquid. The chioggia and golden beets will discolor if they are used alongside red beets, so use separate containers for different colors.

Remove the horseradish shavings and bay leaf after a day, and let the beets stand for a further 2 to 3 days before using. Keep refrigerated for up to 2 weeks.

· Alternatively, for a fresh instant pickle, pour cold Pickle Brine (see page 78) over shaved chioggia beets, add a pinch of ascorbic acid to hold the color, and serve. This makes for super good salads.

PICKLED CELERY

MAKES 2 PINTS

whole head of celery	1
Our Pickle Brine (see page 78)	2 cups
black peppercorns	5
coriander seeds	1 teaspoon

Separate the celery into sticks. Cut about ¼ inch off the top and the entire white section off the bottom, about ¾ inch. Peel each stick to remove the outer fibers. This is important because the pickled celery will be unpleasant if it contains a lot of stringy parts. Slice the celery lengthwise into ½-inch thick batons.

Put the pickle brine into a large pan and add the peppercorns and coriander seeds. Bring to a boil, then remove from the heat and add the celery. Let cool, then transfer to a sterilized 2-pint jar (see page 78) and refrigerate for 2 to 3 days before serving.

PICKLED CARROTS

MAKES 1½ PINTS

large carrots	5
Maldon sea salt	2 tablespoons
superfine sugar	scant 1 cup
water	scant 1 cup
rice wine vinegar	scant 1 cup
star anise	1
fennel seeds, toasted	1½ tablespoons
coriander seeds, toasted	1 tablespoon
black peppercorns	1 tablespoon

Chop the carrots into batons or slices. Put them into a container and sprinkle with the salt and 2 tablespoons of the sugar.

Move the carrots around so that they are evenly coated, then let stand for 10 minutes, or until the carrots are bendy. Wash them thoroughly and let dry.

Bring the rest of the ingredients to a boil in a stainless steel pan and drop in the carrots. Remove from the heat, let cool, then transfer to a sterilized 1½-pint jar (see page 78) or plastic containers and refrigerate for 3 to 4 days before eating.

· As an alternative, try adding the zest of ½ an orange, 2 cardamom pods, 1 cinnamon stick, and 2 bay leaves to the brine.

PICKLED WATERMELON RIND

THIS IS A BRILLIANT PICKLE
TO MAKE FOR YOUR KITCHEN
CUPBOARD WHEN WATERMELONS COME
INTO SEASON. IT IS POPULAR
THROUGHOUT THE SOUTHERN
STATES, BUT WE FIRST TRIED IT
AT FATTY CRAB IN NEW YORK'S
MEATPACKING DISTRICT. THEY
SERVED IT WITH PORK BELLY,
CHILI, AND CILANTRO. PORK
BELLY AND PICKLED WATERMELON,
AS IT TURNS OUT, IS AWESOME.

MAKES 2½ GENEROUS CUPS

rind of ½ a medium watermelon, including ½ inch of red flesh	
good cider vinegar	1 cup
water	½ cup
superfine sugar	½ cup
Maldon sea salt	2 teaspoons
star anise	1
fresh ginger, peeled	1 small piece
stick of lemongrass, crushed	½

Cut the watermelon rind into slices 1 inch
thick. Carefully slice the skin off and cut
the slices into 1-inch chunks.

Put the remaining ingredients into a large
pan and bring to a boil. Add the watermelon
rind and continue to boil for 1 minute.
Carefully transfer everything to a container,
then cool and refrigerate.

The pickles are ready in a few hours and
will keep for at least 2 weeks.

PICKLED POMEGRANATE

PICKLED CHERRIES

THIS IS A MIGHTY FINE PICKLE.
WE SERVE IT WITH SMOKED
QUAIL, GRILLED DUCK HEARTS,
AND SMOKED LIVER AT THE
RESTAURANT. THE PICKLED SEEDS
LOOK LIKE JEWELS AND CAN
TRANSFORM A LIVER PÂTÉ OR ANY
SALAD INTO A THING OF BEAUTY.
TRY SHOOTING THE RESERVED
PICKLE JUICE AFTER A BOURBON
FOR AN INTERESTING PICKLEBACK.

THE CHERRY FARMS OF KENT, IN
ENGLAND, ARE AMAZING PLACES
TO VISIT WHEN FRUITING IS IN
FULL SWING. YOU WILL ARRIVE
INNOCENT AND LEAVE LOOKING LIKE
A SLIGHTLY SICK VAMPIRE. THE
CHERRY IS ONE OF OUR FAVORITE
FRUITS, AND IT'S ANOTHER ONE
THAT PICKLES VERY WELL.

MAKES 4 x 1-PINT JARS

large ripe pomegranates	4
good red wine	1¾ cups
red wine vinegar	1¾ cups
turbinado sugar	2 cups
cloves	5
pink peppercorns	5
cardamom pods	3
star anise	1
stick of cinnamon	1
coriander seeds, toasted	1 tablespoon
pared zest of ½ a large orange	

Cut the pomegranates in half and remove all the seeds by tapping the back of the pomegranate halves with a spoon. Put the seeds into a bowl and discard any pith.

Put the remaining ingredients into a large pan and bring to a boil, then set aside to cool and infuse overnight. Pass the liquid through a sieve, then add the pomegranate seeds. Transfer to sterilized jars (see page 78) and refrigerate for 2 to 3 days before using.

MAKES 2 x 14-OUNCE JARS

cherries	1 pound 5 ounces
white wine vinegar	2 cups
water	1 cup
light Muscovado sugar	1¼ cups
stick of cinnamon	1
bay leaf	1

Rinse, dry, and prick the cherries, then put them into a plastic container.

Put the remaining ingredients into a large pan and bring to a boil. Simmer for 5 minutes, then pour over the fruit and let stand for 3 minutes.

Pour into sterilized jars (see page 78), cool, then put in the fridge to chill. Allow to pickle for at least 2 weeks before opening.

SLAWS

SLAW IS ONE OF THE MOST VERSATILE SALADS YOU CAN FIND. STARTING WITH A SIMPLE BASE OF CABBAGE AND ONION YOU CAN DO PRETTY MUCH ANYTHING YOU WANT AND BE INSPIRED BY FOOD FROM ALL OVER THE WORLD, ADAPTING AND ADDING TO THE BASIC INGREDIENTS TO MAKE YOUR PERFECT SLAW.

CHIPOTLE & CONFIT GARLIC SLAW

SERVES 4 TO 6

white cabbage, finely shredded	½
red cabbage, finely shredded	¼
corn kernels	1¼ cups
finely grated zest of 1 lime	
juice of 2 limes	
cilantro, leaves picked	1 bunch
Chipotle Mayonnaise (see right)	¾ cup
confit garlic cloves, puréed	6
Maldon sea salt	
freshly ground black pepper	
sour cream, to serve	
Pork Rub (see page 118), to serve	

Put the shredded cabbages into a large bowl and add the corn kernels, lime zest, lime juice, and cilantro, and gently mix together.

Whisk together the chipotle mayonnaise and garlic purée, add to the slaw, and mix well. Season with salt and pepper to taste. To finish, top the slaw with a dollop of sour cream and a generous shake of pork rub before serving.

CHIPOTLE MAYONNAISE

MAKES 5½ OUNCES

mayonnaise	¾ cup
chipotles in adobo, puréed	1½ tablespoons

Put the mayonnaise and puréed chipotles into a bowl and whisk together. Store in the fridge until needed.

RED SLAW

SERVES 6 TO 8

large red cabbage, shredded	1
large red onion, finely sliced	1
large red bell pepper, seeded and thinly sliced	1
large beet, peeled and cut into julienne strips	1
Pitt Cue Barbecue Sauce *(see page 122)*	1 cup
Hot Sauce *(see page 124)*	scant ½ cup
salt and freshly ground black pepper	
sour cream, to serve	

Put the cabbage, onion, red bell pepper, and beet into a large bowl.

Mix together the barbecue sauce and hot sauce and pour over the vegetables. Combine thoroughly, season to taste, and refrigerate until chilled. Serve topped with sour cream.

KIMCHI SLAW

SERVES 4 TO 6

smoked garlic clove	1
mayonnaise	scant ½ cup
lemon juice, to taste	
Napa cabbage, finely shredded	1
red onion, finely shredded	1
carrot, julienned	1
radishes, shaved and quartered	small bunch
Kimchi Hot Sauce *(see page 124)*	scant ½ cup

Make a smoked garlic mayonnaise by processing the garlic with the mayo in a blender and adding lemon juice to taste. Combine the Napa cabbage, red onion, carrot, and radishes in a bowl. Add the kimchi hot sauce and the smoked garlic mayo, mix gently together, then serve.

MUSTARD SLAW

SERVES 6 TO 8

large white cabbage, shredded	¾
large white onion, finely sliced	1
large carrots, peeled and cut into julienne strips	2
sticks of celery, chopped	2
dill, chopped	bunch
hot mustard (English or Dijon)	3½ tablespoons
cider vinegar	3 tablespoons
superfine sugar	¼ cup
mayonnaise	¼ cup
sour cream	¼ cup
salt	
freshly ground pepper	

Put the cabbage, onion, carrots, celery, and dill into a large bowl.

In a separate bowl, mix together the mustard, vinegar, sugar, mayonnaise, and sour cream, and season to taste. Pour the dressing over the vegetables, adjust the seasoning, and refrigerate until chilled.

GREEN SLAW

SERVES 6 TO 8

large Savoy cabbage, shredded	1
onions, finely sliced	2
large green bell pepper, seeded and finely sliced	1
large Granny Smith apple, skin on, cored and julienned	1
large jalapeño chile, seeded and finely sliced	1
cilantro, chopped	½ small bunch
mint, chopped	½ small bunch
plain yogurt	scant ½ cup
finely grated zest and juice of 2 limes	
salt and sugar, to taste	

Add the cabbage, onions, green bell pepper, apple, jalapeño, and herbs to a large bowl.

Mix together the yogurt, lime juice and lime zest, and add salt and sugar to taste. Pour over the vegetables, adjust the seasoning, and refrigerate until chilled.

GREEN CHILE SLAW

SERVES 6 TO 8

white cabbage, finely sliced	½
red cabbage, finely sliced	¼
small bulb of fennel, finely sliced	1
mayonnaise	½ cup
cilantro leaves	small handful
Maldon sea salt	

GREEN CHILE DRESSING

green chiles	2
fresh ginger, peeled and roughly chopped	1 ounce
garlic cloves	3 tablespoons (about 10 cloves)
soft light brown sugar	2½ tablespoons
zest and juice of 1 lime	
cilantro stalks, chopped	small handful
soy sauce	1½ tablespoons

To make the dressing, grill the chiles over direct heat on the barbecue or in a ridged grill pan until charred and blistered. Discard the stalks. Blitz all the remaining dressing ingredients except the soy sauce in a blender, adding the soy gradually until emulsified and smooth.

Lightly salt the cabbage and let it sit for 1 hour in a colander to allow the excess moisture to drain off. Transfer to a serving bowl and stir in the fennel. Add the mayo, cilantro leaves, and 3 tablespoons of the green chile dressing and toss, then season with salt to taste. Add more dressing if you like, then serve.

VINEGAR SLAW

SERVES 6 TO 8

fennel seeds	1½ tablespoons
small white cabbage	¾
small red cabbage	½
bulb of fennel	7 ounce
red onions	2
mint tips	10
mixture of parsley, cilantro, and chervil	handful
Maldon sea salt	
freshly ground black pepper	

DRESSING

cider vinegar	½ cup
white wine vinegar	½ cup
extra virgin olive oil	⅓ cup
superfine sugar	heaping ⅓ cup
juice of 2 lemons	

Put the dressing ingredients into a bowl and whisk together until the sugar has dissolved. Set aside.

Toast the fennel seeds in a small pan until golden. Set aside.

Slice the cabbages, fennel, and onions on the thinnest setting of a mandoline slicer (the thinner the better) and add to a large bowl. Finely chop the mint with a very sharp knife, pick the herb leaves, and add to the bowl with the fennel seeds, making sure the herbs are distributed evenly.

Half an hour before serving, whisk the dressing again and pour over the slaw. Toss thoroughly and check for seasoning.

DRESSINGS

SALAD DRESSING

WE HAVE SIMPLE, FRESH SEASONAL
SALADS ON THE RESTAURANT MENU
ALL YEAR ROUND, AND WE ALMOST
ALWAYS DRESS THEM SIMPLY—GREAT
OIL, LOTS OF LEMON JUICE, AND
A FEW DROPS OF GOOD VINEGAR.
THIS DRESSING CAN BE MADE IN
ADVANCE, LEFT ALONE, AND JUST
GIVEN A FINAL WHISK BEFORE
YOU DRESS YOUR SALAD. BETTER-
QUALITY INGREDIENTS WILL
IMPROVE IT GREATLY. POOR OIL
AND VINEGAR WILL NOT MAKE FOR
A GOOD DRESSING.

MAKES ABOUT 2/3 CUP

extra virgin olive oil	scant ½ cup
juice of 1 lemon	
sherry vinegar	1 tablespoon
light brown sugar	1 tablespoon
garlic clove, crushed	1
Maldon sea salt	
freshly ground black pepper	

Put all the ingredients into a bowl and
whisk together until fully emulsified.
Add salt and pepper to taste. Just before
you dress your salad, give the dressing
another whisk.

MEAD SALAD DRESSING

WE WENT THROUGH A BIT OF A
MEAD OBSESSION WHEN TOM FOUND
AN OLD BOTTLE AT HOME, AND A
WINERY NEARBY WAS PRODUCING
SOME FANTASTIC MEAD. THIS
SIMPLE SALAD DRESSING
WAS ONE OF THE MANY MEADY
THINGS BORN OUT OF THIS
SLIGHTLY UNUSUAL CRAZE AND
HELPS ADD COMPLEXITY TO
SIMPLE, FRESH SALADS.

MAKES ABOUT 2/3 CUP

extra virgin olive oil	scant ½ cup
cider vinegar	1 tablespoon
juice of 1 lemon	
medium-sweet mead	1 tablespoon
Maldon sea salt	
freshly ground black pepper	

Put all the ingredients into a bowl and
whisk together until fully emulsified,
seasoning to taste.

APPLE DRESSING

THIS IS A SIMPLE DRESSING,
BUT DELIGHTFUL. A VERY GOOD
APPLE JUICE IS ESSENTIAL,
AND NOT TOO SWEET. APPLE
JUICES AND VINEGARS VARY,
SO THIS RECIPE IS MORE OF A
GUIDELINE. TASTE AND ADJUST
IT UNTIL IT SUITS.

MAKES 1 CUP

extra virgin olive oil	scant ½ cup
unfiltered apple juice	½ cup
cider vinegar	1 tablespoon
juice of 1 lemon	
Maldon sea salt	
freshly ground black pepper	

Put all the ingredients into a bowl and
whisk together until fully emulsified.
Add salt and pepper to taste.

This dressing can be stored in a sterilized
bottle (see page 78) in the fridge but will
need a good whisk before use.

ANCHOVY SALAD CREAM

HEINZ ALWAYS HELD THE SALAD
CREAM CROWN FOR US. NO ONE
COULD BEAT THAT INDUSTRIALLY
MADE, NUTRITIONALLY DUBIOUS
BOTTLE OF FILTHY GOODNESS.
THIS RECIPE GIVES IT A GOOD
TRY, THOUGH, AND CONTINUES ON
THE ANCHOVY THEME.

MAKES 3 CUPS

cider vinegar	scant ½ cup
Dijon mustard	3½ tablespoons
superfine sugar	1 tablespoon
Maldon sea salt	2 teaspoons
ground white pepper	¼ teaspoon
Cantabrian anchovy fillets	5½ ounces
garlic cloves	3
thyme leaves	1 teaspoon
heavy cream	1¾ cups

Put all the ingredients except the cream
into a blender and blitz for 30 seconds.
Slowly add the cream, blitzing until
just incorporated.

Pass through a fine sieve and refrigerate
until needed.

APPLE, FENNEL, WATERCRESS —— & RADISH SALAD ——

APPLE AND FENNEL MAKE A SIMPLE BUT GREAT BASE FOR A SIDE SALAD TO ACCOMPANY SMOKED PORK. BY ADDING PEPPERY RADISHES AND A MEAD SALAD DRESSING, THIS HAS BECOME ONE OF OUR MOST POPULAR SIDE SALADS IN THE RESTAURANT.

SERVES 3 TO 4

bulbs of fennel, tops removed, fronds reserved	2
watercress	1½ cups
apples, cored	2
radishes, quartered	1½ ounces
mint leaves, torn	6
parsley leaves	10
chervil leaves	1 tablespoon
Mead Salad Dressing (see page 204)	
salt, to taste	

Fill a small bowl with ice and water.

Wash the fennel, watercress, apples, and radishes. Shave the fennel into the iced water, using a mandoline slicer. Slice the apples into very thin slices, then cut into batons. Drop the apples into the iced water, along with the radishes for 10 seconds.

Drain the apple, fennel, and radishes and put them into a serving bowl with the fennel fronds. Add the herbs and watercress and toss together. Season with salt and dress lightly with the salad dressing. Serve immediately.

NASTURTIUM & TOMATO SALAD

SERVES 3 TO 4

bulbs of fennel	2
apples, cored	2
nasturtium leaves	2¼ ounces
sweet cherry tomatoes, halved	10
Poor Man's Capers *(see page 193)*	1 ounce
Mead Salad Dressing *(see page 204)*	
Maldon sea salt	
freshly ground black pepper	

Shave the fennel into a bowl of iced water, using a mandoline slicer. Cut the apple into very thin slices, then cut into batons and add to the iced water. Drain the fennel and the apple. If the nasturtium leaves have thick stalks, slice these finely.

To assemble the salad, put the fennel, apple, nasturtium stalks and leaves, tomato halves, and poor man's capers into a serving bowl and toss with the salad dressing. Season with salt and pepper and serve.

THIS SALAD OWES ITS PLACE TO SEAN, THE AMAZING VEGETABLE GROWER AND ALL-ROUND LEGEND, WHOSE FARM IS IN CORNWALL, IN THE FAR WEST OF ENGLAND. ONE DAY, OUT OF THE BLUE, A PACKAGE ARRIVED AT PITT CUE ADDRESSED TO "MAJOR TOM" CONTAINING LOTS OF SWEET LITTLE TOMATOES AND PEPPERY NASTURTIUMS. THESE ARE PARTICULARLY GOOD SERVED WITH SMOKED MEAT.

BOSTON BIBB LETTUCE & HERB SALAD

WE LOVE BIG FLAVORS BUT HAVE
REALIZED THE IMPORTANCE OF
HAVING SOME GREAT "FOILS" UP
OUR SLEEVE, SIDE DISHES THAT
BALANCE THE BIG FLAVORS IN THE
MEATS. AN HERB SALAD MAKES A
GREAT JUXTAPOSITION FOR ALL
THE FLAVORS ASSOCIATED WITH
BARBECUED FOOD. SIMPLE AND
FRESH CERTAINLY HAS ITS PLACE,
AND GOOD-QUALITY HERBS
ARE ESSENTIAL.

SERVES 3 TO 4

Boston Bibb lettuce	1
Salad Dressing *(see page 204)*	1 tablespoon
chopped scallions	1 tablespoon
chopped cilantro	1 tablespoon
chopped parsley	1 tablespoon
chopped mint	1 tablespoon
Maldon sea salt	
freshly ground black pepper	

Pick and wash the lettuce leaves, then
gently dry.

Just before serving, toss the leaves in
the dressing with the chopped scallions and
herbs. Season to taste and serve.

ICEBERG SALAD

SERVES 4

iceberg lettuce	1
scallions, trimmed and sliced	1 bunch
onions, trimmed and sliced	1¾ cups
pulled bread (bread torn into rough chunks)	2¾ ounces
olive oil, for frying	
Pulled Pork Shoulder (see page 135)	3½ ounces
blue cheese	3½ ounces
buttermilk	scant ½ cup

Cut the iceberg lettuce into quarters and trim them into four small brick shapes. Cut the scallions into very fine rings and set aside. Slice the onions.

Toast the pulled bread to make croutons.

Heat a little oil in a pan over low heat, add the onions, and cook, stirring until they are a lovely brown caramel color. Remove them from the heat and mix with the pulled pork.

Put the blue cheese and buttermilk into a small bowl and mix with a fork, leaving the cheese slightly chunky.

Place each iceberg brick on a plate. Dress liberally with the buttermilk blue cheese dressing. Top with the onion and pulled pork mixture, scatter with the scallions, and crumble the pulled bread croutons on top. Serve with a knife and fork.

PICKLED CARROT SALAD

LIGHTLY PICKLED VEGETABLES WORK REALLY WELL IN SALADS, BRINGING FRESHNESS AND AROMATIC NOTES FROM THE PICKLING BRINE. THIS CAME ABOUT BY ACCIDENT WHEN MAKING ANOTHER SALAD THAT WAS CLEARLY FAR LESS MEMORABLE!

SERVES 4

medium carrots, peeled and shaved	5
Our Pickle Brine (see page 78)	2 cups
star anise	1
coriander seeds, toasted	2 tablespoons
fennel seeds, toasted	1½ tablespoons
mint leaves, torn	10
cilantro, finely chopped	small bunch
Maldon sea salt	

DRESSING

large garlic cloves, peeled and puréed	2
fresh ginger, peeled and puréed	thumb-sized piece
cider vinegar	3 tablespoons
superfine sugar	1 tablespoon
sesame oil	1 teaspoon
Maldon sea salt	

Put the carrot shavings into a container. Put the pickle brine into a pan with the star anise, coriander seeds, and fennel seeds, and bring to a boil. Pour the boiling pickle brine over the carrot and let cool, then refrigerate for 3 hours.

To make the dressing, combine the garlic, ginger, vinegar, sugar, and sesame oil in a bowl, and season with salt.

To assemble, put the carrot into a bowl, shaking off the excess pickle juice. Toss with the herbs, then season to taste and dress lightly. Toss again and serve.

SMASHED CUCUMBER & PICKLED WATERMELON SALAD

SERVES 6

cucumbers, peeled	4
watermelon flesh	7 ounces
Pickled Watermelon Rind *(see page 196)*	7 ounces
Pickled Carrots *(see page 195)*	3½ ounces
scallions, sliced	5
green chiles, finely sliced	3
chopped cilantro	3 teaspoons
chopped mint	5 teaspoons
salt	
freshly ground black pepper	

DRESSING

large garlic cloves, peeled and puréed	2
ginger, peeled and puréed	thumb-sized piece
cider vinegar	3 tablespoons
superfine sugar	1 tablespoon
sesame oil	1 tablespoon
Maldon sea salt	

To make the dressing, combine the garlic, ginger, vinegar, sugar, and sesame oil in a bowl, and season with sea salt.

Peel the cucumbers, cut them into 2½-inch chunks, then crush them with the flat blade of a large knife. Chop the watermelon flesh into 1¼-inch chunks and put them into a serving bowl with the cucumbers, pickled watermelon rind, pickled carrots, and scallions.

Just before serving, add the chiles, cilantro, and mint, season, and toss with enough of the dressing to coat the salad.

THIS IS A GREAT LITTLE REFRESHMENT AMID THE MEAT FRENZY AT PITT CUE. IT WORKS REALLY WELL IN A PULLED PORK SANDWICH, BRINGING TO IT A HINT OF A VIETNAMESE BANH MI, WHICH THEMSELVES ARE AMONG THE BEST PORKY DELIGHTS TO BE HAD. IN FACT, A HUGE NUMBER OF ASIAN SALADS GO REALLY WELL WITH PULLED PORK AND BARBECUE FLAVORS.

KIMCHI

KIMCHI HAD NOT FEATURED AT PITT CUE UNTIL RICHARD BREWED UP A BATCH FOR US ON THE TRAILER AND WE BEGAN TO REALIZE HOW MAGICAL THE COMBINATION OF BARBECUED MEAT AND KIMCHI CAN BE. IT CUTS THROUGH THE RICHNESS, AND ADDS LAYERS AND LAYERS OF FLAVOR, TEXTURE, AND HEAT AT THE SAME TIME. IT HAS MAGICAL BALANCING POWERS FOR EVEN THE FATTIEST OF PORK, SO IT'S NO SURPRISE THAT OUR PIG'S HEAD BUN HAS A HEALTHY AMOUNT OF KIMCHI IN IT.

IT'S IMPORTANT TO FIND THE RIGHT JARRED SALTED SHRIMP AND KOREAN CHILI POWDER. WE MADE THE MISTAKE OF SUBBING IN SHRIMP PASTE FOR ONE BATCH. GRAY FISHY KIMCHI IS NOT WHAT YOU WANT. ON WHICH NOTE, USE THE BEST ANCHOVIES YOU CAN FIND.

SERVES 8 TO 10

small to medium Napa cabbage	1
Maldon sea salt	2 teaspoons
superfine sugar	heaping ⅓ cup
garlic cloves, minced	10
fresh ginger, peeled and minced	10 slices
Korean chili powder	scant ½ cup
canned anchovy fillets	1¾ ounces
light soy sauce	3 tablespoons
jarred salted shrimp	1¾ ounces
scallions, cut into ¾-inch batons	3½ ounces
carrots, cut into julienne strips	3½ ounces

Discard the outer leaves of the Napa cabbage. Cut it lengthwise in half, then cut the halves crosswise into pieces 1½ inches wide. Add to a bowl and toss with the salt and 2 tablespoons of the sugar. Put into the refrigerator and let stand overnight.

Put the garlic, ginger, chili powder, anchovies, soy sauce, shrimp, and remaining sugar into a large bowl and mix together. If the mixture is very thick, add water a little at a time until the mixture is just thicker than a creamy salad dressing but no longer a sludge. Stir in the scallions and carrots.

Wash, drain, and dry the Napa cabbage and add to the bowl. Cover and refrigerate. Though the kimchi will be tasty after 24 hours, it will be better in a week and at its prime in 2 weeks. It will still be good for another couple of weeks after that, though it will grow stronger and funkier.

MEAD BRAISED LETTUCE
— CARROTS & ONIONS —

MEAD IS HONEY WINE, AND IS ONE OF THE EARLIEST FORMS OF ALCOHOL TO BE RECORDED IN HISTORY. IT IS MADE BY FERMENTING A SOLUTION OF HONEY AND WATER, WITH SPICES, HOPS, AND FRUITS OCCASIONALLY BEING USED AS FLAVORINGS. IT IS PROBABLY BEST KNOWN FOR BEING THE TIPPLE OF CHOICE FOR FRIAR TUCK, ROBIN HOOD, AND THE MERRY MEN OF SHERWOOD FOREST, BUT IS HAVING A WELCOME RESURGENCE NOW.

THIS RECIPE CAME ABOUT OVER A SUCKLING PIG AND COCKEREL DINNER IN PITT, WHEN WE FOUND A DUSTY OLD BOTTLE OF MEAD AND TRIED IT. FOR GOOD REASON, EVERYONE KEPT GOING BACK FOR THE BRAISED VEGETABLES.

SERVES 6 TO 8

large shallots	4
small carrots	7 ounces
olive or canola oil	1 tablespoon
garlic cloves	3
sprigs of thyme	3
smoked bacon lardons	3½ ounces
chicken wings	5½ ounces
chicken necks	3
Little Gem lettuces	8
cider vinegar	1 tablespoon
medium-sweet mead	scant ⅔ cup
chicken stock	scant 1 cup
Maldon sea salt	
freshly ground black pepper	

Peel the shallots and carrots and cut into quarters. Toss them with the oil, garlic, and thyme, season with black pepper and a good teaspoon of sea salt, and place them in a large casserole dish. Cook over low heat on the stove, stirring occasionally, for 45 minutes, or until the shallots are darkly caramelized and sweet and the carrots are almost cooked through. Set aside.

In another pan, fry the bacon lardons, chicken wings, and chicken necks until golden and crispy. Add the halved Little Gems and lightly fry in the bacon fat until golden. Transfer everything to the casserole dish, then add the vinegar and the mead.

Heat the oven to 350°F.

Allow the vinegar and mead to reduce by one-third, then pour in the chicken stock and cook in the oven for 30 minutes. Season to taste and serve.

GRILLED ZUCCHINI & TUNWORTH

WHEN ZUCCHINI ARE AT THEIR PRIME IN SUMMER, THEY ARRIVE IN THE KITCHEN BY THE BOX LOAD. SIMPLY DRESSING LIGHTLY WITH OIL AND SALT BEFORE GRILLING IS ONE OF THE BEST WAYS TO ENJOY THEM. HOWEVER, THIS HAS NOW BEEN TRUMPED BY THE INCLUSION OF TUNWORTH, A BRILLIANT ENGLISH CAMEMBERT-STYLE CHEESE THAT BECOMES SOFT AND GOOEY WHEN RIPE. OBVIOUSLY IT IS NOT TOO FOND OF A GRATER, SO ROLLING THE CHEESE INTO A SAUSAGE SHAPE AND FREEZING GETS AROUND THIS PROBLEM NICELY.

SERVES 6

ripe Tunworth or camembert cheese	1
zucchini	2¼ pounds
parsley leaves, finely chopped	10
thyme leaves	½ teaspoon
olive oil	1 tablespoon
juice of ½ a lemon	
Maldon sea salt	
freshly ground black pepper	

First, remove your Tunworth or camembert cheese from its packaging and wrapper. Spread out several large layers of plastic wrap, then put the cheese on top and squeeze it into a rough sausage. If the cheese is very ripe you may have some leakage. Roll up the cheese in the plastic wrap into a tight sausage and freeze.

When you are ready to cook, prepare a barbecue for medium-hot direct grilling. Alternatively, heat a ridged grill pan on the stove.

Cut the zucchini into ½-inch slices—sharp diagonal slices always look best—and lightly oil them. Put them on the grill or grill pan and cook for 5 minutes, or until they are well charred but not cooked entirely through. Toss them in a bowl with the parsley, thyme, olive oil, and lemon juice, and season to taste.

To serve, remove the cheese from the freezer and, while the zucchini are piping hot, grate as much of the cheese onto them as you wish. More the merrier.

SPROUT TOPS

SERVES 6

smoked bacon	1¾ ounces
Brussels sprout tops	1¾ pounds
smoked ham stock	1¼ cups
cloves of garlic, peeled	3
Maldon sea salt	
freshly ground black pepper	

ANCHOVY BUTTER

Cantabrian anchovy fillets	4½ ounces
unsalted butter, softened and diced	9 ounces
cayenne pepper	pinch
ground nutmeg	pinch
freshly ground black pepper	pinch
ground cinnamon	pinch
lemon juice	1 tablespoon
Worcestershire sauce	1 tablespoon
water	1 tablespoon

First make the anchovy butter. Put all the ingredients into a blender and blitz to a very smooth paste. Place the mixture on a few sheets of plastic wrap and roll into a sausage about 1¼ inches thick. Chill in the fridge (this will keep for up to 1 week).

Cut the bacon into small lardons and fry in a skillet until crisp and golden. Drain on paper towels and reserve any fat from the bacon. It is not really needed for this recipe, but having bacon fat in the fridge is a bonus.

Remove the leaves of the sprout tops, discarding any very tough or damaged outer leaves, and cut the larger leaves into ¾-inch ribbons. The core of the sprout tops can be cut in half. Wash thoroughly to remove any dirt and grit. Blanch the cut leaves in boiling salted water for 10 seconds, then remove and plunge them into a container of iced water to cool. Once cold, drain thoroughly.

Put the ham stock into a pan and bring to a boil. Grate in the garlic and cook for 5 minutes. Reduce to a very gentle simmer and add the blanched sprout tops. Cook over low heat for 15 to 20 minutes, or until the leaves are softening but have not lost their freshness and color. At the very last minute, season to taste with salt and pepper—although be warned that the bacon and anchovy will do much of the seasoning for you—and serve with ¼ cup of cubed anchovy butter and the lardons on top.

BROCCOLI RABE
WITH ANCHOVY & CHILE

SERVES 4

butter	½ stick
red chiles, very finely sliced lengthwise	2
Tabasco sauce	
broccoli rabe	14 ounces
parsley, finely chopped	small bunch
anchovy fillets	8
juice of 1 lemon	
Maldon sea salt	
freshly ground black pepper	

ANCHOVY IS A TRULY MAGICAL INGREDIENT THAT GOES WITH ALMOST ANYTHING. IT IS FANTASTIC WITH GRILLED MEATS, AND AS SUCH, WE CAN'T RESIST USING A LOT OF IT IN OUR SIDE DISHES. HOWEVER, IT'S VERY IMPORTANT TO BUY THE BEST YOU CAN AFFORD. A BAD ANCHOVY SHOULD NOT BE LET OUT OF ITS CAN.

Prepare a barbecue for medium-hot direct grilling (see page 112). Alternatively, heat a ridged grill pan on the stove.

In a small pan, melt the butter and add the chiles and 5 drops of Tabasco. Keep warm.

Wash the broccoli, and trim the stalks if necessary. Bring a pan of well-salted water to a boil and fill a container with cold water and ice. Add the broccoli to the boiling water and cook for 2 minutes, or until just starting to soften but still firm. Drain, then drop it into the iced water. Remove as soon as it is cold and drain on paper towels.

Grill the broccoli for 2 minutes, until just charred. The florets will char quickly, so keep moving the broccoli so that it grills evenly. Remove from the heat and put the broccoli into a serving bowl with the parsley, melted butter and chiles, anchovy fillets, and lemon juice. Toss together and season to taste with salt and pepper (you may not need any salt, because the anchovies are already salty). Serve immediately.

BURNT POINTED CABBAGE
WITH RAMPS

IN THE UK, GREEN POINTED
CABBAGE SEASON COINCIDES NICELY
WITH RAMP SEASON, WHICH STARTS
IN THE WEST COUNTRY FROM LATE
FEBRUARY ONWARD.

SERVES 2

green pointed cabbage, quartered with outer leaves removed,	1
ramps	2¾ ounces
extra virgin olive oil	
juice of ½ a lemon	
Maldon sea salt	
freshly ground black pepper	

Prepare a barbecue for medium-hot direct grilling. Alternatively, heat a ridged grill pan on the stove.

Bring a pan of salted water to a boil and fill a container with cold water and ice. Add the cabbage to the boiling water and cook for 1 minute, or until the core has softened only slightly—you want it just undercooked. Drain, then drop the cabbage into the iced water, removing it as soon as it is cold.

Grill the cabbage for 1½ minutes on each side, or until evenly charred. While it's still hot, put it into a serving bowl and add the ramps, a good glug of olive oil, and salt and pepper. Toss the cabbage with the ramps immediately so that the ramps wilt with the residual heat. Drizzle with the lemon juice and serve.

BURNT LEEKS
—— WITH ANCHOVY HOLLANDAISE ——

> WE SERVE THIS AS A SIDE DISH AT
> THE RESTAURANT, BUT IT WILL
> ALSO MAKE A VERY FINE APPETIZER
> OR SNACK, CONTINUING OUR AFFAIR
> WITH OUR FISHY FRIEND.

Prepare a barbecue for medium-hot direct grilling. Alternatively, heat a ridged grill pan on the stove.

Wash the leeks and peel off the outer layer. Trim ½ inch off at the root end and leave just a couple of inches of green at the top.

Bring a pan of well-salted water to a boil, and fill a container with cold water and ice. Add the leeks to the boiling water. Cook for 5 minutes, or until softened. Drain, then add them to the iced water. Remove when cold and drain on paper towels. Brush the leeks with olive oil. Grill for 2 to 3 minutes, turning occasionally, until charred. Put them into a bowl with the basil and lemon juice and toss together, then season to taste. Spoon the anchovy hollandaise on top, sprinkle with basil, and serve.

SERVES 2

leeks, the younger the better	4
olive oil, for brushing	
basil, finely chopped, plus extra to serve	small handful
juice of 1 lemon	
Anchovy Hollandaise (see page 174)	scant ½ cup
Maldon sea salt	
freshly ground black pepper	

— BURNT CORN ON THE COB —

THIS WAS, IN FACT, ONE OF THE FIRST SIDES EVER SERVED AT THE PITT CUE TRAILER. A FRIEND OF OURS SHOWED US A NEAT TRICK OF COOKING THE COBS WITH THE HUSKS ON, THEN PEELING THEM BACK AND TWISTING THEM AROUND THE VERY BASE OF THE COB TO MAKE A TEMPORARY HANDLE. THE HUSKY HANDLE WORKS MUCH BETTER THAN THOSE USELESS MINI FORK THINGS THAT ARE ALWAYS SOLD IN JULY WHEN CORN IS PROLIFIC.

SERVES 1

corn on the cob, husk still intact	1
unsalted butter	1½ tablespoons
House Rub *(see page 119)*	2 teaspoons

Prepare a barbecue for medium-hot direct grilling. Grill the corn, husk on, for 20 minutes, until almost all the layers of husk and fiber have burnt through and the kernels are nearly exposed.

Remove from the grill and peel back the remaining pieces of husk. Brush the corn with the butter and sprinkle with the house rub before serving.

— GRILLED BABY GEMS —

THE BABY GEM DEVELOPS A REAL MEATINESS ONCE COOKED, WHICH IS OBVIOUSLY SOMETHING THAT APPEALS TO US.

SERVES 6

Baby Gem lettuces	6
olive or canola oil	1 tablespoon
Maldon sea salt	
freshly ground black pepper	

Prepare a barbecue for medium-hot direct grilling.

Cut the Baby Gems in half. Rub the cut sides with some of the oil and season with salt and pepper. Place the Baby Gems, cut-side down, on the hot grill and close the lid. Cook for 5 minutes, untouched.

Open the barbecue and check the Baby Gems. Their faces will be slightly blackened. Turn them over and cook for a further 2 minutes, then remove from the grill, dress with the remaining oil, season to taste, and serve.

— MASH —

MASHED POTATOES HAVE NEVER REALLY LEFT THE MENU AT PITT CUE, ALBEIT APPEARING IN DIFFERENT GUISES. IT IS MADE FRESH FOR EVERY SERVICE, ALWAYS BY HAND, AND THE POTATOES ARE ALWAYS BAKED. THE BENEFITS OF BAKING THE POTATOES ARE TWOFOLD: FIRSTLY, THE POTATOES DRY OUT BETTER, MAKING FOR A SMOOTHER RESULT WITH A SMOKY BAKED NOTE; SECONDLY, YOU WILL HAVE LOTS OF EMPTY POTATO SKINS TO FILL WITH WHATEVER DELIGHTS YOU DESIRE. LONG LIVE BAKED MASHED POTATOES.

SERVES 6 TO 8

baking potatoes	5½ pounds
heavy cream	scant 1¼ cups
chilled unsalted butter, diced	1½ sticks
Maldon sea salt	

Heat the oven to 400°F.

Wash the potatoes and let them dry, then bake them in the oven for roughly 45 minutes to 1 hour, or until cooked through. When they are ready, gently heat the cream in a large pan. Remove the potatoes from the oven, cut them in half, then let stand for 1 minute to allow some of the moisture to evaporate.

Scoop the potato flesh from the skins (reserve the skins for loading, see opposite) and pass it through a fine sieve into the cream, pushing it through with the back of a spatula or a pastry scraper. Work quickly, because the potato needs to be sieved while still hot. Start to beat the mix together with the spatula while adding the diced butter, until it is smooth and silky. Season to taste with salt. Keep warm. Baked mashed potatoes need to be eaten fresh and do not keep well.

· One of the many joys of a baked potato is the skin it leaves behind; the perfect potato "spoon" to be filled with whatever you want. We deep-fry our leftover skins, give them a liberal shake of dry rub when they leave the fryer, then load then with all sorts of tings. Brisket, picked beef ribs, ox cheek, pig's head, confit duck, duck variety meats, and pulled pork have all been topped with bone marrow, kimchi, pickles, fruit ketchup, cheese sauce, piles of chopped herbs, and anything else we can find. More a meal than a mouthful, but that is yet to cause complaint. Another excuse to make more mashed potatoes then.

LARDO & ROSEMARY MASH

SERVES 6 TO 8

Mash *(see page 226)*	2¼ pounds
Mother Sauce *(see page 120)*	scant 1 cup
lardo di Colonnata, chilled	5½ ounces
small garlic clove, minced	1
sherry vinegar	1 teaspoon
sprig of rosemary, leaves finely chopped	1
freshly ground black pepper	

Heat the mashed potatoes and Mother Sauce in two separate pans.

Put the lardo through the smallest setting on a meat grinder and add it to a bowl. Add the garlic and vinegar and begin massaging air into the lardo with a spatula, as if you were making mashed potatoes. As you work with the meat, folding in air, it will get softer. Beat continuously for 5 minutes, until the lardo is light and fluffy. Add the rosemary and pepper to taste.

Top each portion of hot mashed potatoes with a teaspoon of whipped lardo, pour over the hot Mother Sauce, and serve.

BURNT ENDS MASH

SERVES 6 TO 8

Mash *(see page 226)*	2¼ pounds
Pitt Cue Burnt Ends *(see page 158)*	7 ounces
Mother Sauce *(see page 120)*	scant 1 cup

Heat the mashed potatoes, Burnt Ends, and Mother Sauce in separate pans. Accompany each portion of mashed potatoes with a good spoonful of the Burnt Ends and pour over the sauce. Serve immediately.

BONE MARROW MASH

SERVES 6 TO 8

Mash *(see page 226)*	2¼ pounds
Mother Sauce *(see page 120)*	scant 1 cup
Whipped Bone Marrow *(see below)*	5½ ounces

Heat the mashed potatoes and Mother Sauce in two separate pans. Get the marrow up to room temperature.

To serve, dot teaspoons of marrow all over the mashed potatoes and pour over the hot Mother Sauce. Watch the marrow melting slowly into the sauce before diving in!

WHIPPED BONE MARROW

split shafts of center-cut shank bone, marrow scooped out	4
juice of ½ a lemon	
garlic clove, minced	1
flat-leaf parsley, finely chopped	small handful
Maldon sea salt	
freshly ground black pepper	

Put the raw marrow, lemon juice, and garlic into a blender and blitz for 10 minutes, until very smooth, glossy, and nicely whipped. Everything should be fully combined. Pass through a sieve, then fold the parsley into the mixture and season to taste.

DUCK & HOMINY HASH

A HASH RUNS VERY CLOSE TO CROSSING THE LINE BETWEEN A SIDE DISH AND A FULL MEAL UNTO ITSELF. IN FACT, IT PROBABLY DOES CROSS THE LINE, AND THUS RENDERS ALL OUR TALK OF WHAT MAKES THE PERFECT SIDE DISH REDUNDANT. IT IS THE EGGS' FAULT. REMOVE THE EGG AND IT IS A SIDE DISH, BUT THE EGG IS WHAT REALLY MAKES THIS HASH HAPPEN, LEAKING INTO THE SWEET SHALLOTS, DUCK, AND CRISPY POTATOES. THIS HASH IS ALSO THE COMPLETE BREAKFAST, AND THEREFORE THE PERFECT ALL-ROUNDER!

SERVES 6

potatoes	9 ounces
sweet potatoes	9 ounces
reserved duck fat	heaping ¼ cup
banana shallots, diced	4
garlic cloves, minced	2
cooked or canned hominy	9 ounces
leftover Smoked Duck (*see page 178*)	9 ounces
thyme leaves	½ teaspoon
free-range duck eggs	6
Maldon seas salt	
freshly ground black pepper	
chopped parsley, to finish	1 tablespoon

Peel and chop the potatoes and sweet potatoes into ¾-inch dice, and steam until just cooked.

Put 1 tablespoon of the duck fat into a pan with the shallots and garlic and cook until they are soft and beginning to caramelize. Set aside.

Heat another 2 tablespoons of duck fat in a large nonstick skillet and add the cooked potatoes, hominy, smoked duck, thyme leaves, shallots, and garlic. Cook for 25 minutes, tossing occasionally to evenly crisp and caramelize the hash.

Heat the remaining duck fat in a hot nonstick skillet and fry the duck eggs. The yolks should still be runny.

Season the hash with salt and pepper to taste and serve each helping with a fried egg and a good amount of parsley on top.

PUMPKIN HOME FRIES
—— WITH NDUJA MAYONNAISE ——

NDUJA IS A DEEP RED, SPICY
CALABRIAN SALAMI MADE FROM
PORK FAT AND THE JOWLS OF
THE PIG, AND SOMETIMES THE
TRIPE. UNLIKE A FRENCH SEC
OR MOST ITALIAN SALAMIS IT
REMAINS SPREADABLE, THUS
LENDING ITSELF TO RUNNING
THROUGH SAUCES AND AS A
CANDIDATE FOR AN
AWESOME MAYONNAISE.

SERVES 6

lardo di Colonnata, cut into ¼-inch dice	1¾ ounces
pumpkin flesh, cut into ½-inch dice	1 pound 2 ounces
baking potatoes, cut into ½-inch dice	1 pound 2 ounces
rosemary leaves, finely chopped	1 teaspoon
salt and pepper	

NDUJA MAYONNAISE

nduja	1¾ ounces
Dijon mustard	1 tablespoon
lemon juice	1 tablespoon
garlic clove, minced	1
free-range egg yolks	2
peanut oil	scant 1 cup
olive oil	3 tablespoons
salt	

Bring all the mayonnaise ingredients to room
temperature. Put the nduja into a blender
with the mustard, lemon juice, and garlic and
blitz to a purée. Set aside.

Whisk the egg yolks in a bowl, then add a
pinch of salt and continue to whisk until
thick, roughly 45 seconds. Slowly add the
peanut oil, whisking continuously until
the mixture begins to thicken. When it
has thickened and the groundnut oil is
incorporated, add the olive oil and whisk
until thick and glossy. Whisk in the nduja
mixture and season to taste. Refrigerate
until needed.

Heat 1¾ ounces of lardo in a large nonstick
skillet. When it's hot and melted, add the
pumpkin and potatoes and cook over high heat
for 15 minutes, or until the vegetables are
crisp and cooked through. Remove from the
heat, toss in the chopped rosemary leaves,
and season to taste. Serve immediately,
with a large dollop of nduja mayonnaise.

HOG MAC 'N' CHEESE

A DOUBLE DOSE OF PORK—CRISP
BACON RUB BREAD CRUMBS ON TOP
AND QUIVERING CHUNKS OF BELLY
WITHIN—ADDS RICHNESS AND
TEXTURE TO ELBOW MACARONI.
THE SAUCE IS A COMBINATION
OF STILTON, CHEDDAR, AND
OGLESHIELD CHEESES.

SERVES 6

dried elbow macaroni	1 pound 2 ounces
cooked bacon or pork belly (or any leftover smoked meat), cut into chunks	7 ounces
bread crumbs	2 cups
Smoked Bacon Rub (see page 119)	3½ tablespoons
cheddar, grated	3½ ounces

CHEESE SAUCE

whole milk	generous 2½ cups
butter	½ stick
shallots, minced	2
garlic cloves, minced	2
sprigs of thyme, leaves picked	2
all-purpose flour	½ cup
Colston Bassett Stilton or Stichelton cheese, grated	4½ ounces
Montgomery cheddar cheese, grated	4½ ounces
Ogleshield (or Gruyère) cheese, grated	4½ ounces
salt	1 teaspoon
ground white pepper	½ teaspoon

Bring a large pan of salted water to a boil and cook the pasta until al dente. Drain, then refresh in cold water and drain again. Put into a large bowl and add the cooked bacon or pork belly.

To make the cheese sauce, put the milk into a medium pan, bring to a foamy boil, then reduce the heat to low and keep warm.

In another pan, melt the butter over medium heat. Add the shallots, garlic, and thyme leaves, and cook for 10 minutes, or until the onions and garlic are just caramelizing and soft.

Whisk in the flour and continue to cook until a pale "roux" has formed. Then, whisking steadily, ladle the hot milk into the roux a cupful at a time, completely incorporating each amount before adding the next. After all the milk has been added, continue to whisk until the sauce thickens and bubbles gently (about 2 minutes).

Add the stilton, cheddar, Ogleshield (or Gruyère), salt, and pepper, and stir until completely melted.

Heat the oven to 350°F.

Stir three-quarters of the cheese sauce into the cooked pasta and bacon. Layer the pasta in a large ovenproof gratin dish and spread the rest of the cheese sauce evenly over the top. Lightly toast the bread crumbs and mix with the bacon rub and grated cheddar, then scatter evenly over the top layer of cheese sauce.

Bake in the oven for 20 minutes, or until golden and bubbling. Serve with a side of Deviled Pigs' Feet for pouring over (see page 145). Any leftovers can be used in Trailer Trash (see page 138).

HOG 'N' HOMINY

THIS IS A DUBIOUSLY TERMED "SIDE DISH." WE ORIGINALLY MADE THIS FOR SHARING, WITH A WHOLE SMOKED HOG JOWL SUNK INTO THE TOP OF THE HOMINY AND CHEESE MIXTURE AND DEVIL DIP GRAVY POURED OVER. ABSOLUTELY FILTHY: A PORK OVERLOAD. SO NUTRITIONALLY QUESTIONABLE WAS THIS AS AN ACCOMPANIMENT TO MEAT, IT WAS ARCHIVED IN FAVOR OF SOMETHING A TOUCH MORE RESERVED, AN ACTUAL SIDE DISH UP TO THE TASK AND ONE THAT DOESN'T LEAVE YOU FULL FOR A DAY OR TWO. THIS MAKES A GREAT ALTERNATIVE TO MAC 'N' CHEESE.

SERVES 6

butter	½ stick
shallots, sliced	2
spring of thyme	5
garlic cloves, crushed	2
smoked bacon, diced	7 ounces
Cheese Sauce (see page 235)	1 pound 5 ounces
sour cream	⅔ cup
hominy, drained	2 x 16-ounce cans
Maldon sea salt	
freshly ground black pepper	

Melt the butter in a large saucepan, add the shallots, thyme, and garlic, and cook over gentle heat for 10 minutes, or until soft and beginning to caramelize.

In a separate nonstick skillet, cook the bacon over high heat for 5 to 10 minutes, or until golden and crispy.

Add the cooked bacon, cheese sauce, sour cream, and hominy to the shallot mixture, season with salt and pepper, and continue cooking gently over low heat for 10 minutes.

Meanwhile, heat the oven to 350°F.

Put the hominy mixture into a baking dish, then cook in the oven for 30 minutes, or until golden.

BAKED BEANS

EVERYONE LOVES A BAKED BEAN. FEW OTHER THINGS CAN BE BREAKFAST, SECOND BREAKFAST, BRUNCH, LUNCH, AFTERNOON SNACK, AND DINNER. CANNED PRECOOKED BEANS WORK WELL, BUT THEY WILL NEVER BE AS GOOD AS DRIED BEANS. THE LITTLE EXTRA EFFORT IS WELL WORTH IT. SIMILARLY, BUYING READY-MADE TOMATO SAUCE WILL WORK, BUT IT WILL NOT COMPARE.

THIS RECIPE CALLS FOR THE TOMATO SAUCE TO BE SMOKED. THAT'S WHAT WE DO IN THE RESTAURANT. HOWEVER, AN OVEN-BAKE ALSO WORKS VERY WELL.

SERVES 4 TO 6

BEANS

dried mixed beans, soaked overnight	9 ounces
Whipped Bone Marrow (see page 228)	1¾ ounces
bacon, finely diced	1¾ ounces
ham stock	scant ½ cup
leftover Smoked Brisket (see page 156)	2¾ ounces
Pitt Cue Barbecue Sauce (see page 122)	⅓ cup
Maldon sea salt	
freshly ground black pepper	

TOMATO SAUCE

olive oil	2 teaspoons
large onion, diced	½
garlic cloves, minced	3
smoked paprika	1 teaspoon
cloves, crushed	5
tinned tomatoes	9 ounces
cider vinegar	2 teaspoons
light brown sugar	1 tablespoon

Drain the soaked beans, then cover them with fresh water and boil until just tender. Drain and set aside.

If using a barbecue, prepare it for smoking (see The Setup on pages 114–15) and set the temperature to 300°F.

To make the tomato sauce, heat the olive oil in a flameproof pan that will fit inside your barbecue and sweat the onion in the oil for 5 minutes, or until soft. Add the garlic, paprika, and cloves, and cook for a further 5 minutes. Add the tomatoes, vinegar, and sugar, stir, then smoke in the barbecue for 1 hour, or until the tomato sauce is smoky and thickened.

Adjust the temperature of the barbecue to 340°F, or preheat your oven to 300°F.

Fry the bacon in a skillet for 10 minutes, or until golden and crispy. Put the bacon into an ovenproof pan that will fit inside your barbecue, along with any bacon fat rendered during frying, and add all the other ingredients as well the tomato sauce. Mix the bean mixture thoroughly, then smoke or oven-bake for 30 minutes, or until a crust begins to form and most of the liquid has been absorbed.

Remove the beans from the oven and stir. The sauce should be thick. If the beans are too dry, loosen the sauce with some more ham stock or water. Season to taste. The beans can be served immediately, but will improve after 2 days in the fridge. We reheat them with Mother Sauce (see page 120) and whisk through more whipped bone-marrow paste before serving.

POTATO ROLLS

MAKES 12

dried active yeast	1 tablespoon
sugar	2½ teaspoons
warm water	scant ½ cup
free-range egg	1
warm milk	scant ⅔ cup
warm Mash (see page 226)	3½ ounces
all-purpose white flour	4 cups
Maldon sea salt	2 teaspoons
warm rendered bacon fat	scant ½ cup
butter	½ stick

GLAZE

milk	3 tablespoons
free-range egg yolks	2
Maldon sea salt	2 teaspoons

Combine the yeast, sugar, and water in a small bowl and set aside for 15 minutes.

Knead together the egg, milk, mash, and yeast mixture on slow speed. Add the flour and salt and knead for a further 5 minutes.

Add ⅓ cup of the bacon fat, 1 tablespoon at a time, until the dough is smooth and homogenous. Transfer to an oiled bowl and let stand in a warm place for about 40 to 60 minutes, until doubled in size.

On a lightly floured surface, punch the dough down, then knead it for a minute. Divide it into 12 equal pieces. Roll each piece into a ball in the palm of your hand and gently press it down. The dough will be very soft, so it may not form perfect rolls.

Melt the butter and pour it onto a baking tray along with the remaining bacon fat. Place the dough balls, seam-side down, on the baking tray 2½ inches away from one another, and let stand in a warm place for 45 minutes, or until doubled in size again.

Heat the oven to 375°F. Gently whisk together the milk and egg yolks for the glaze. Bake the rolls in the oven for 15 minutes, then brush the tops of the rolls with the glaze and sprinkle with the salt. Return to the oven and bake for a further 10 to 15 minutes, until lightly brown. Let cool on a wire rack for 15 minutes and serve.

LONDON BATH BUNS

MAKES 12

milk	1¼ cups
fresh yeast	½ ounce
all-purpose flour	3¾ cups
granulated sugar	1 teaspoon
Maldon sea salt	1 teaspoon
butter, diced	1¾ sticks

Put the milk into a pan and warm to blood temperature. Crumble in the yeast.

In a separate bowl, mix the flour, sugar, and salt. Add the butter and rub it in, using your fingertips. Add the milk mixture and mix to form a dough, then cover the bowl and let stand in a warm place for an hour to prove.

Grease a baking pan with butter and dust it with flour. Divide the dough into 12 equal pieces and place them on the baking pan. Let stand in a warm place to prove for a further 30 minutes.

Meanwhile, heat the oven to 375°F. Bake the buns for 20 minutes, then remove from the oven, and set aside to cool.

JALAPEÑO & SOUR CREAM CORNBREAD

THIS IS A GREAT CORNBREAD RECIPE AND COMES FROM A FAMILY FRIEND IN CALIFORNIA (A FELLOW MIDDLE WHITE AND MANGALITZA BREEDER, FUNNILY ENOUGH). IT WORKS REALLY WELL WITH HOT WINGS, NOT LEAST BECAUSE CORNBREAD, HOT MEATY THINGS, AND CURD ARE LOVELY TOGETHER.

SERVES 4 TO 6

baking powder	2 teaspoons
Maldon sea salt	1 teaspoon
yellow cornmeal	1¼ cups
hot chiles, i.e. jalapeño (pickled jalapeños work well), finely chopped	2
vegetable oil	¾ cup
free-range eggs, gently beaten	2
sour cream	1 cup
canned cream-style sweet corn	2 x 8½-ounce cans
onion, grated	1
good cheddar cheese, grated	3½ ounces

Heat the oven to 325°F and butter an 8- or 9-inch ovenproof baking dish or cake pan.

Put the baking powder, salt, cornmeal, and chiles into a medium bowl and mix together. In another bowl, mix together the oil, egg, sour cream, and cream-style sweet corn. Mix the grated onion into the wet ingredients, then quickly mix this into the dry ingredients.

The batter will be a little lumpy and clumpy—this is a good thing. Pour half of the batter into the pan and scatter with 2½ ounces of the grated cheddar. Pour in the remaining batter and scatter with the rest of the grated cheddar.

Bake in the oven for 45 minutes, or until the surface feels firm and a skewer inserted comes out clean. Let stand for 10 minutes to cool a little, then cut into wedges. This is best served hot, and don't refrigerate it or it will ruin the texture.

POPOVERS

THE POPOVER IS AN AMERICAN VERSION OF YORKSHIRE PUDDING, WHICH HAS BEEN MADE IN ENGLAND SINCE THE SEVENTEENTH CENTURY, THOUGH IT HAS EVOLVED AND IS NOW TYPICALLY BAKED IN MUFFIN PANS. THE NAME "POPOVER" COMES FROM THE FACT THAT THE BATTER SWELLS OR "POPS" OVER THE TOP OF THE PAN WHILE BAKING.

MAKES 12

all-purpose flour	scant 1¾ cups
free-range eggs, beaten	scant 1 cup
fennel seeds, ground	pinch
freshly ground black pepper	pinch
skim milk	scant 1 cup
beef dripping, for greasing	

Put the flour, eggs, ground fennel seeds, black pepper, and milk into a bowl and mix together. Put into the fridge and let stand, covered, overnight.

Next day, heat the oven to 425°F. Put a little dripping into 12 individual mini muffin pans set on a cookie sheet, or into each hole in a muffin pan, then place in the oven until the dripping is smoking hot. Pour in the batter to come halfway up each hole, and bake until the tops pop over like muffin tops. After another 15 minutes, remove the pan from the oven and turn out and invert the popovers. Put them back into the oven directly on the oven shelf for a couple of minutes to crisp them up underneath.

Serve with the Smoked Standing Rib Roast (see page 164).

SWEET STUFF

SWEET STUFF

·············

We have a love affair with desserts: the creamy, the cakey, the sticky, the clean, the buttery, the set, the soft, the cold, the hot, the elegant, and the slutty. Especially the slutty.

The kitchen in Soho has no identifiable pastry section. A small corner on top of a boxed-in boiler, a covered vegetable sink that doubles up as our bun-making area next to the dishwasher that hands out free steam facials every five minutes—this area constitutes the pastry section and it has been the bane of everyone who has worked there. This, combined with a domestically inept oven constantly full of baked potatoes that tries to sabotage any decent pastry work, meant the odds were against us when it came to offering a little post-meat sweetness.

In Soho we started by offering two desserts every day each service, and that is something we stick to, keeping them simple, with one often offering some clean, fruity respite, and the other a bit of dessert sluttiness. Whether or not eating in a dark Soho basement affects the sensibilities, it would seem that the slutty desserts tend to outsell the more restrained ones. That said, a slightly camp posset seems to go down well.

·············

BANOFFEE MESS

SERVES 4

Meringues *(see below)*	2
Bourbon Caramel Sauce *(see page 276)*	scant 1 cup
bananas, sliced	2
Whipped Custard *(see page 254)*	scant 1 cup
Shortcakes *(see below)*	4
frozen chocolate candy bar (we use Snickers)	1

MERINGUES

free-range egg whites	about ½ cup (4 to 5 eggs)
superfine sugar	1¼ cups
chopped nuts of your choice, toasted and cooled	½ cup (about 1¾ ounces)

SHORTCAKES

butter	3 sticks
superfine sugar	heaping ¾ cup
all-purpose flour	1¾ cups
toasted bread crumbs	1 cup
ground almonds	1¾ cups
finely grated zest of 2 oranges	

First, make the meringues. Heat the oven 275°F. Using an electric stand mixer, whisk the egg whites until almost stiff, then slowly add half the sugar and continue mixing until the whites become stiff and glossy. Using a metal spoon, fold in the remaining sugar and whichever toasted nuts you are using.

Line a cookie sheet with waxed paper, using a little of the meringue mixture underneath to stop the paper from moving around. Spoon neat individual meringue portions onto the waxed paper. Place in the oven and immediately reduce the temperature to 230°F. Bake for 45 minutes, then remove from the oven and let cool. These meringues store well in a sealed container for up to 2 days.

Next, make the shortcake. Using an electric stand mixer, cream the butter and sugar for 10 minutes, or until fluffy and pale. Fold in the remaining ingredients and combine well. Take three sheets of waxed paper and divide the mixture equally between them. Roll up the dough in the waxed paper into sausages about 2¾ inches thick, then tie the ends. Chill in the fridge for 2 to 3 hours, or until firm.

Meanwhile heat the oven to 300°F and line two cookie sheets with waxed paper. Unwrap the dough, slice it into ¼-inch disks and set the disks on the cookie sheets. Bake for 15 minutes, or until golden, then let cool. You will need 2 or 3 shortcakes, crumbled, for the mess.

In a large bowl, gently fold together 2 crushed meringues, one-quarter of the bourbon caramel sauce, 8 slices of banana, and the whipped custard.

To assemble the mess, make a ½-inch layer of crumbled shortcake in the bottom of four small glass dessert dishes. Layer some of the banana slices on top, followed by a thin layer of bourbon caramel sauce. Top this with 2 tablespoons of the custard meringue mixture and then another layer of crumbled shortcake. Finish with a layer of whipped custard, more slices of banana, and a drizzle of the remaining sauce. Take the chocolate candy bar straight from the freezer, grate generously over the top of each portion, and serve.

THIS IS BEST EATEN AT A TIME WHEN
YOU WILL NOT FEEL GUILTY ABOUT
IT. HANGOVERS, BREAKUPS, AND
ILLNESS CAN ALL BE REMEDIED WITH
A GOOD MESS.

DO NOT FORGET TO GRATE THE FROZEN
CHOCOLATE CANDY BAR ONTO THE TOP
OF THE MESS.

THIS IS NOT A PRODUCT PLUG—"PEANUT, BOURBON, MALT,
CHOCOLATE, AND CARAMEL MESS" IS JUST TOO SCARY A
PROSPECT TO EAT. WE ARE NOT AFTER A LIFETIME SUPPLY
OF SNICKERS—THE ENJOYMENT WOULD BE FAR OUTWEIGHED
BY DENTAL BILLS. THERE IS NO DENYING A DEEP LOVE
FOR THIS BAR, THOUGH. EATING ONE STRAIGHT FROM THE
FRIDGE, WHEN THE CHOCOLATE AND CARAMEL NEED EXTRA
WORK TO GET THROUGH, IS THE ONLY WAY TO DO IT.
THIS IS A SLUTTY SALUTE TO THE GREAT BAR AND THAT
FRIDGE-COLD ENJOYMENT.

"SNICKERS" MESS

SERVES 4

vanilla bean	1
heavy cream	scant ½ cup
malt powder (such as Ovaltine)	1 tablespoon
Meringues *(see page 248)*	2
Brownies *(see below)*	1¾ ounces
Bourbon Caramel Sauce *(see page 276)*	⅓ cup
Peanut Butter Ice Cream	
(see page 268)	2 tablespoons
frozen milk chocolate candy bar, or a Snickers	1

Split the vanilla bean, scrape out the seeds and discard the bean pod. Make a malt cream by beating the heavy cream with the malt powder and vanilla seeds until it forms soft folds. Set aside.

To assemble the mess, break the meringues into bite-sized chunks and break the brownies into small pieces. Put them into a mixing bowl, add the malt cream and half the bourbon caramel sauce, and gently fold together.

To serve, spoon the meringue mixture into four serving bowls. Top with the ice cream, drizzle with the remaining sauce, and finish with some shavings of the frozen candy bar.

BROWNIES

MAKES 12 TO 16

unsweetened chocolate	
(70% cocoa solids)	10½ ounces
butter	3 sticks
vanilla bean	1
large free-range eggs	5
superfine sugar	1½ cups
all-purpose flour	1¼ cups
cocoa powder	½ cup
Maldon sea salt	1 teaspoon

Preheat your oven to 350°F and line an 8 x 12-inch baking pan with parchment paper.

Melt the chocolate and butter in a heatproof bowl set over a pan of gently simmering water, making sure the base of the bowl doesn't touch the water. Remove and set aside.

Split the vanilla bean, scrape out the seeds, and discard the bean pod. Beat the eggs in a bowl with the sugar and vanilla seeds until thick enough to coat the back of a spoon. In a separate bowl, mix the flour, cocoa, and salt together. Stir the melted chocolate mixture into the egg mixture, then fold in the flour mixture.

Pour the batter into the baking pan and bake for about 20 to 25 minutes, or until just set on top.

Remove from the oven. Let cool, then put into the fridge overnight to firm up.

FRUIT & WHIPPED CUSTARD MESS

THIS RECIPE AND THE PROCESSES INVOLVED REMAIN PRETTY MUCH THE SAME FOR MOST FRUITS WHEN THEY ARE IN SEASON. WHILE WE ADD HOMEMADE MARSHMALLOWS IN THE RESTAURANT, THEY CAN BE TIME-CONSUMING TO MAKE AND ARE DEFINITELY OPTIONAL FOR THOSE WHO ARE PUSHED FOR TIME.

SERVES 3 TO 4

fresh fruit, plus extra to decorate	
(see below)	1 pound 2 ounces
superfine sugar	½ cup
juice of 2 lemons	
turbinado sugar	¼ cup
Peanut Meringues *(see page 248)*	2
Marshmallows *(see page 254)*, (optional)	
Whipped Custard *(see page 254)*	scant ½ cup

First, purée the fruit. Put 10½ ounces of fruit into a pan with the superfine sugar and the juice of 1 lemon and cook gently over low heat for 10 minutes, stirring occasionally. Pass the mixture through a fine sieve and set aside. (For plums and sloe berries, combine in a roasting pan with three times the amount of sugar and a scant ½ cup of water, and bake in the oven at 300°F for 15 minutes.)

Put the rest of the fruit into a container. Add the juice of the remaining lemon and the turbinado sugar, and set aside for a few hours to macerate.

To assemble the mess, put 2 crushed meringues into a bowl and gently combine with 2 tablespoons of fruit purée, 1 tablespoon of macerated fruit, a few marshmallows (if using), and 3 tablespoons of whipped custard. Spoon into a serving bowl and top with the fruit, the remaining macerating liquid, and a good helping of marshmallows. If you like, light a chef's torch and toast the marshmallows until dark and molten.

· This mess undoubtedly works best with berry fruits. Strawberries, raspberries, blueberries, red currants, black currants, blackberries, and gooseberries all create a lovely mess. Stone fruits like sloe berries and plums also work well, and rhubarb is a fixture on the menu throughout its forced season.

· Walnuts, almonds, and pistachios all work well instead of peanuts in the meringues.

· Substitute vanilla cream for the custard if you are running out of time or are in a hurry.

MARSHMALLOWS

MAKES LOTS

gelatin leaves	¼ ounce (about 1 to 2)
water	2 tablespoons
superfine sugar	1 cup
liquid glucose	1 tablespoon
fresh free-range egg whites	4 (about 2¾ ounces)
finely grated zest of 1 lemon	
fruit purée, optional	⅓ cup (about 2¾ ounces)
cornstarch, for dusting	½ cup
powdered sugar, for dusting	heaping ½ cup
Maldon sea salt	pinch

Line a baking pan with waxed paper. Put the gelatin leaves into a bowl, cover with cold water, and let soak until soft. Put the 2 tablespoons water, superfine sugar, and glucose into a large pan, and heat until the temperature reaches 250°F on a candy thermometer.

In an electric stand mixer, slowly beat the egg whites and lemon zest on medium speed until they reach stiff peaks.

When the sugar mixture reaches temperature, take the pan off the heat. Squeeze out the gelatin leaves and add to the pan, mixing gently. Be careful: the mixture may bubble and spatter a bit. Turn the mixer to the lowest setting. With the mixer running, gently pour the hot sugar mixture down the side of the bowl into the egg whites, then increase the speed to medium and continue to mix until the whites are cool, glossy, and stiff, about 8 to 10 minutes. Fold in the fruit purée, if using, until well combined.

Scoop the mixture into a pastry bag with the smallest tip available. Combine the cornstarch and powdered sugar and sift it evenly over the prepared baking pan (this will stop the marshmallows from sticking). Pipe little marshmallow teardrops onto the waxed paper, about the width of a quarter (coin), with a nice quiff on top. Put the pan into the fridge for 1 hour to let the marshmallows set.

WHIPPED CUSTARD

MAKES 1¾ PINTS

large free-range egg yolks	6
superfine sugar	heaping ¼ cup
vanilla bean	1
heavy cream	3 cups

Beat the egg yolks and sugar in a very large bowl until light and fluffy. When you lift the beater, it should leave a trail of thick ribbons behind in the mixture.

Split the vanilla bean, scrape out the seeds, and discard the bean pod. Put a 2½ cups of the cream into a large pan with the vanilla seeds and heat slowly until steaming, just below boiling point. Slowly beat the hot cream into the egg-yolk mixture until well combined.

Half-fill a very large bowl or a sink with water and ice and set a smaller bowl in the water to chill. Keep the bowl upright, because the cream will need to be strained into this chilled bowl.

Return the mixture to the pan over low to medium heat and beat slowly and continuously until thickened, about 5 to 7 minutes. If it begins to boil, remove from the heat and beat to ensure it does not split. The custard should be very thick.

Pass the custard through a sieve into the chilled bowl and stir for a few minutes to cool it down as quickly as possible. Cover the bowl with plastic wrap and refrigerate until well set.

When you are ready to serve the custard, beat in the rest of the cream until it forms thick peaks.

PIMM'S MESS

WHEN THE CLEVER CHAPS AT THE ICE CREAM UNION DROPPED OFF A CARTON OF PIMM'S SORBET DURING OUR FIRST SUMMER IN SOHO WE THOUGHT THEY WERE JOKING. WHAT KIND OF EVIL GENIUS WOULD PRODUCE A PIMM'S SORBET, NOT ONE THAT TASTES OF THE LIQUOR ITSELF, BUT OF THE FINISHED CONCOCTION; THE STEEPED CUCUMBER, STRAWBERRIES, AND TORN MINT THAT MAKE A WELL MADE PIMM'S SO GOOD? IT HAD TO BECOME A DESSERT, AND SO THIS CLEAN LITTLE MESS WAS BORN. IT BEGAN WITH VERY FINE SLICES OF APPLE, BUT WAS MADE AGAIN AT THE END OF THE SUMMER USING OUR CERAMIC BARBECUE AND SOME SLOWLY COOKED PEARS THAT TURN SUPER SWEET AND A LITTLE BIT SMOKY WHEN COOKED THIS WAY.

SERVES 2

Comice or Bartlett pear	1
superfine sugar	2 tablespoons
strawberries	½ cup
balsamic vinegar	2 teaspoons
zest of ½ an orange	
juice of ½ a lemon	
mint leaves	10
Meringue *(see page 248)*, broken up	1
Pimm's Sorbet *(see page 280)*	2 scoops

Prepare your barbecue for medium-heat direct grilling, about 300°F. Chop ¼ inch off of the base of the pear so that it sits flat, with the flesh exposed on the bottom. Dip the exposed base into the superfine sugar, then place the pear on buttered waxed paper on the grill and close the lid. Cook for 30 minutes, or until the pear is soft and the skin has begun to shrivel. Remove from the heat and set aside.

Put half the strawberries into a pan and add the balsamic vinegar, orange zest, lemon juice, and 1 tablespoon of the superfine sugar. Cook over low heat until the strawberries are just softening, then remove from the heat and blitz in a blender until smooth. Pass through a sieve and set aside.

Finely chop 6 of the mint leaves, then use a pestle and mortar to grind them thoroughly with the remaining superfine sugar to make a mint sugar. Cut the rest of the strawberries in half, place in a bowl with the mint sugar and let macerate for 1 hour, tossing occasionally.

To serve, cut the pear into quarters and remove the seeds, peel, and core. Slice the quarters in half. Arrange these slices in a shallow bowl and add the macerated strawberries and shards of meringue alongside. Place a scoop of Pimm's sorbet on top and scatter with the rest of the mint leaves, torn roughly, then drizzle with the strawberry coulis.

ORANGE & CHOCOLATE
—— CHEESECAKES ——

SERVES 8

water	1¼ cups
superfine sugar	1 cups
large oranges	5
Grand Marnier	3 tablespoons
package of chocolate cookies (we use Oreos)	1
milk chocolate, for grating	

CHEESECAKE TOPPING

vanilla bean	1
cream cheese (Philadelphia is best)	2¾ pounds
free-range eggs	6
free-range egg yolks	4
heavy cream	scant 1 cup
superfine sugar	1 cup
finely grated zest of 1 lemon	
finely grated zest of 1 lime	
finely grated zest of 1 orange	

THIS IS NOT A CONVENTIONAL CHEESECAKE IN ANY SENSE, BUT RATHER MORE OF A CUSTARD MADE WITH CREAM CHEESE. THE RECIPE CAME ABOUT IN THE KITCHEN WHEN WE BEGAN MAKING OUR OWN CREAM CHEESE BUT, AS IT TURNS OUT, IT'S PRETTY HARD TO BEAT PHILADELPHIA.

THE FINISHED MIXTURE WILL BE THICKER THAN A CUSTARD BUT BY NO MEANS SET. WE PIPE THE MIX ONTO POACHED FRUITS AND FRUIT-FLAVORED GELATINS, AND ADD SHORTCAKES AND CRUMBS TO BUILD A "CHEESECAKE." ONCE YOU HAVE THIS RECIPE NAILED, THE OPTIONS FOR VARIATIONS ARE ENDLESS.

To make the cheesecake topping, split the vanilla bean lengthwise and scrape out the seeds. Discard the bean pod and add the seeds to a heatproof bowl with the rest of the cheesecake topping ingredients. Set over a pan of gently simmering water for 20 minutes, whisking constantly until smooth and thickened. Pass through a fine sieve and chill in the refrigerator.

Pour the 1¼ cups water into a large pan, add the sugar, and heat gently to dissolve.

Peel and segment the oranges, removing any skin and pith, put the segments into a bowl, and set aside. Squeeze any orange juice remaining in the debris into the pan with the sugar syrup. Add the Grand Marnier to the pan and bring to a boil, then remove from the heat and pour the mixture over the orange segments. Let cool slightly, then cover with plastic wrap and set aside to cool completely.

To make each cheesecake, put 5 or 6 orange segments in the bottom of 8 small clean jars and add a little of the liquid. Crumble a cookie evenly over the top of each one, and use a pastry bag to pipe the cheesecake topping mixture onto the crumbled cookies, to reach just below the surface of the jar.

Grate the top evenly with the milk chocolate and serve.

LEMON & CHERRY POSSETS
— WITH FRUIT MARSHMALLOWS —

A CUTE, CITRUSY, AND VELVETY
POST-PORK REFRESHMENT.
THESE POSSETS CAN BE MADE
WELL IN ADVANCE AND WILL SUIT
ALL SORTS OF FRUIT, WHICH
MAKES IT A PRETTY PERFECT
GET-ME-OUT-OF-TROUBLE DESSERT
CANDIDATE.

SERVES 5 TO 6

cherries	1 pound 2 ounces
turbinado sugar	3½ tablespoons
black currant jam	1 tablespoon
vanilla bean, split lengthwise	1
heavy cream	2½ cups
superfine sugar	heaping ¾ cup
lemon juice	scant ½ cup (about 2 lemons)
Marshmallows *(see page 254)*	

Set aside a cherry for each posset, to decorate. Remove the pits and halve the remaining cherries. Put half of these cherries into a bowl with half of the turbinado sugar and set aside to macerate for 1 hour.

Put the rest of the cherries into a pan with the remaining turbinado sugar, the black currant jam, and the split vanilla bean. Cook on low heat for 10 minutes, or until softened. Remove the vanilla bean, blitz the cherries to a thick pulp in a blender, and pass through a sieve to make a thick purée. There should be about 2½ to 2¾ ounces. Set the purée aside.

Divide the macerated cherries evenly between serving glasses, reserving the juices. The cherries should just cover the bottom of the glass. Put the glasses into the refrigerator to chill.

To make the posset, bring the cream and sugar to a boil in a pan, whisking them to ensure that the sugar is well combined. Take the pan off the heat and pour in the lemon juice, then pass the mixture through a fine sieve. Take the glasses out of the fridge and pour the posset on top of the cherries. Let cool, then return the glasses to the fridge for 4 hours to set.

To serve, arrange the marshmallows on top of each posset. If you like, you can use a chef's torch on the marshmallows until just browned and melting. Finish by placing a reserved cherry on top.

OLD-FASHIONED GELATIN

ONE OF OUR FAVORITE
COCKTAILS MADE INTO A
DESSERT. SERVE WITH A BIG
SCOOP OF ICE CREAM FOR
A NIGHTCAP AND A DESSERT
ALL IN ONE. MAKE SURE YOU
USE THE RIGHT KIND OF
CHERRIES, BECAUSE IT MAKES
A BIG DIFFERENCE TO THE
FINAL RESULT.

SERVES 4 TO 5

gelatin leaves	1
soda water	⅓ cup
bitters syrup *(see below)*	⅓ cup
maraschino cherry juice	2 tablespoons
bourbon	⅓ cup
maraschino cherries, halved and pitted	5

BITTERS SYRUP

water	¾ cup
granulated sugar	½ cup
Angostura bitters	3 tablespoons

First, make the bitters syrup. Put the water, sugar, and bitters into a medium pan. Place over medium heat and let the sugar dissolve completely, then bring to a boil, stirring occasionally, and boil for 5 minutes. Remove from the heat and let cool to room temperature.

To make the dessert, put the gelatin into a bowl, cover with cold water, and let soak until soft. Combine the soda water, bitters syrup, and cherry juice in a small pan. Squeeze out the gelatin, add to the pan, and heat over very low heat for about 5 minutes, stirring constantly, until it has dissolved. Remove from the heat, add the bourbon, and stir until combined.

Pour the liquid into individual ramekins or a mold. Evenly distribute the cherry halves through the mixture and refrigerate until fully set. Serve with Prune & Whiskey Ice Cream (see page 268).

── TOFFEE APPLE GRUNT ──

THIS DESSERT SHARES MANY OF THE SOOTHING QUALITIES THAT A COBBLER OR CRISP HAS, BUT IS, FOR SOME REASON, MORE APPEALING. IT IS EQUALLY GOOD COLD, SO MAKE A LARGE GRUNT AND FINISH IT OFF FOR BREAKFAST. THIS RECIPE WAS WRITTEN ON A RAINY DAY AND FEELS LIKE IT SHOULD BE EATEN ON THAT SORT OF DAY WITH SOME SWEET MULLED HARD CIDER OR JUST SOME DECENT BOURBON FOR COMPANY. IT IS LIKE A HOT TODDY AND PILLOW ALL ROLLED INTO A SMALL DESSERT POT.

SERVES 4

superfine sugar	1 cup
Northern Spy, Gravenstein, or similar apples, peeled, cored, and sliced into $1/8$ slices	1¾ pounds
vanilla beans, split lengthwise	2
cinnamon stick	1
star anise	1
finely grated zest of 1 lemon	
pine nuts, toasted	¾ cup
bourbon-soaked agen prunes, roughly chopped	12
rum	2 tablespoons
blackberries	7 ounces

ALMOND COOKIE TOPPING

free-range egg whites	2
ground almonds	2 cups
superfine sugar	½ cup
almond extract	2 teaspoons

ALTERNATIVE BUTTERMILK BATTER TOPPING

all-purpose flour	heaping ½ cup
ground almonds	⅔ cup
baking powder	1 teaspoon
bicarbonate of soda	¼ teaspoon
Maldon sea salt	1 teaspoon
cinnamon sugar	2½ tablespoons
unsalted butter, melted	½ stick
buttermilk	generous ½ cup

Put the sugar into a pan over medium heat and let it cook without stirring until it turns into a thick, golden caramel. Add the apples, split vanilla beans, cinnamon, star anise, and lemon zest to the pan. Cook for 10 to 15 minutes, stirring occasionally, until the apples just retain some shape and take on some color and the mixture is thick. Add the prunes, pine nuts, and rum, stir gently, and cook for a further 5 minutes. Set aside to cool.

For the almond cookie topping:
Heat the oven to 340°F.

Beat the egg whites until stiff peaks form. Gently fold in the ground almonds and sugar, then add the almond extract and fold gently until well combined. Set aside.

Half-fill four ramekins or mini casserole dishes or cast-iron pot with the apple mixture. Sprinkle the apple mixture with the fresh berries and then place tablespoons of the almond batter topping on top. Bake in the oven for about 15 minutes, or until the batter topping is golden and slightly puffed up. Let cool for 10 minutes, then dust with powdered sugar and eat with ice cream, fresh berries, and cold custard.

For the buttermilk batter topping:
Heat the oven to 350°F.

Sift together the flour, ground almonds, baking powder, baking soda, salt, and sugar. Stir in the melted butter and add enough buttermilk to form a soft and fairly wet dough.

Half-fill four mini casserole dishes or cast-iron pots with the apple mixture. Scatter with the fresh berries and place tablespoons of the batter on top. Bake for about 20 minutes, or until the dough has puffed up slightly and turned golden.

Let cool for 10 minutes, then dust with powdered sugar. Serve with ice cream, fresh berries, and some cold custard.

DOUGHNUTS

BROOKE SMITH, A SPOKESPERSON FOR
KRISPY KREME SAYS, "DOUGHNUTS
ARE A NORMAL PART OF A HEALTHY,
BALANCED DIET."

OUR ADVICE WOULD BE TO EAT UNTIL
JUST BEFORE THE POINT OF REGRET—
ABOUT THREE DOUGHNUTS, WE RECKON.

MAKES 25

warm milk	scant 1 cup
dried active yeast	1 heaping tablespoon
light Muscovado sugar	2 tablespoons
butter	2 sticks
free-range eggs	5
Maldon sea salt	pinch
all-purpose flour	3¾ cups
oil, for deep-frying	
superfine sugar and ground cinnamon, for rolling	

Place the warm milk, yeast, and half the Muscovado sugar in a bowl and mix well to combine. Cover with a damp dish towel and let stand in a warm place for 15 minutes.

In a large bowl, beat the remaining Muscovado sugar with the butter until creamy, then add the eggs one by one until each are incorporated. Add the yeast mixture, the flour, and salt and beat until smooth. Cover the bowl with the damp dish towel and refrigerate overnight.

When you're ready to cook the doughnuts, heat the oil to 340°F in a deep-fryer or large saucepan.

Turn the dough out onto a lightly floured surface and roll out until 1¼ inches thick. Use a 2-inch cookie cutter to cut out circles, then drop them straight into the oil. Deep-fry the doughnuts in batches, 3 to 4 at a time, for 2 minutes each side, or until golden. Place on paper towels to drain, then roll them in superfine sugar and cinnamon while still hot.

Alternatively, use a pastry bag with a fine plain tip to fill the doughnuts with Creamy Vanilla Filling or Chocolate Frosting (see page 266) and let set.

CREAMY VANILLA FILLING

MAKES ENOUGH TO FILL 25 DOUGHNUTS

vanilla bean	1
free-range egg yolks	6
maple syrup	scant ½ cup
heavy cream, chilled	2 pints
bourbon	scant ½ cup

Split the vanilla bean, scrape out the seeds and discard the bean pod. Put the egg yolks and maple syrup into a large bowl and whisk until light and fluffy. When you lift the whisk, it should leave a thick ribbon trail behind.

Pour half the cream into a bowl and put into the fridge to use later. Pour the other half into a large pan and add the vanilla seeds and bourbon. Heat slowly until steaming, just below boiling point. Slowly whisk the hot cream into the egg mixture until well combined.

Half-fill a very large bowl or sink with water and ice and let a smaller bowl chill in the water. Keep it upright—the custard will be strained into this chilled bowl.

Return the cream and egg mixture to the pan and set over low—medium heat. Slowly whisk until thickened, about 5 to 7 minutes. Do not let it boil. If it does, remove from the heat and whisk hard to ensure it does not split. It should become a thick custard. Pass the custard through a sieve into the chilled bowl and stir for a few minutes to cool it as quickly as possible. Add the remaining chilled cream and beat until lightly whipped.

Pierce a hole in the side of the doughnuts and pipe the filling into the center, then serve.

TWO CHOCOLATE FROSTINGS

MAKES ENOUGH TO COAT & FILL 25 DOUGHNUTS

good-quality milk chocolate, broken into pieces	3½ ounces
heavy cream	scant ½ cup
Maldon sea salt	¼ teaspoon
peanut butter	scant ¼ cup
light Muscovado sugar	¼ cup, packed

Melt the chocolate with the heavy cream and salt in a heatproof bowl set over a pan of gently simmering water, making sure the base of the bowl does not touch the water.

Divide the chocolate mixture between two bowls and add the peanut butter to one bowl and the sugar to the other. Stir both mixtures thoroughly with a wooden spoon until smooth. Spoon the peanut butter frosting into a pastry bag with a fine plain tip.

Pierce a hole in the side of the doughnuts and pipe the peanut butter frosting into the center, then dip the top into the salted caramel frosting. Transfer to a wire rack to set, then serve at room temperature.

Once cooled, these frostings will set hard and can be stored in the fridge for a few days.

— ICE CREAMS & SORBETS —

PRUNE & WHISKEY ICE CREAM

MAKES APPROXIMATELY 3½ CUPS

prunes, soaked in whiskey (see method)	⅓ cup
free-range egg yolks	4 (about 2¾ ounces)
superfine sugar	scant ¾ cup
milk	2 cups
heavy cream	scant ½ cup
whiskey	1 tablespoon

PEANUT BUTTER ICE CREAM

MAKES APPROXIMATELY 3½ CUPS

egg yolks	2 (about 1½ ounces)
superfine sugar	heaping ½ cup
milk	2 cups
heavy cream	3 tablespoons
peanut butter	heaping ⅓ cup
salt	a pinch

For this recipe use prunes that have been soaked in whiskey for 1 month.

Beat together the egg yolks and ½ cup of the sugar in a large bowl using an electric hand mixer, until frothy and pale.

Put the milk, cream, and remaining sugar into a pan and heat to 140°F. Slowly pour the hot milk mixture into the egg yolk and sugar mixture, beating continuously. Cover the bowl, put into the fridge, and chill to 39°F. Once chilled, add the whiskey (ideally chilled to 39°F too), then transfer to an ice-cream maker and churn according to the manufacturer's instructions. Fold in the prunes after churning.

Beat the egg yolks with ¼ cup of the sugar in a large bowl.

Put the milk, cream, peanut butter, salt, and remaining sugar into a pan and heat to 140°F. Slowly pour the hot milk mixture onto the egg yolks, stirring with a whisk. Cover the bowl, then put into the fridge and chill to 39°F.

Once chilled, transfer to an ice-cream maker and churn according to the manufacturer's instructions.

SALTED CARAMEL
ICE CREAM

MAKES 2 PINTS

milk	1¼ cups
heavy cream	1¼ cups
milk chocolate	1¾ ounces
free-range egg yolks	6
light Muscovado sugar	¾ cup, packed
Maldon sea salt	1 teaspoon

Put the milk, cream, and chocolate in a saucepan over medium heat and bring to a simmer.

Beat together the egg yolks, sugar, and salt in a large bowl using an electric hand mixer, until they have doubled in volume.

Pour the hot milk mixture onto the egg yolk mixture and stir to combine. Pour through a fine sieve and let cool. Once cooled, transfer to an ice-cream maker and churn according to the manufacturer's instructions.

RASPBERRY SORBET

MAKES APPROXIMATELY 1 PINT

fresh raspberries	2¼ pounds
lemon juice, to taste	
superfine sugar	1 cup + 2 tablespoons
water	generous 1½ cups

First, make a raspberry purée. Put the raspberries in a saucepan over low heat and cook until they begin to break down. Increase the heat and bring to a boil. Add lemon juice to taste. Remove from the heat, pass through a fine sieve, and let cool before refrigerating.

Pour 2¼ cups of the raspberry purée into a pan and add the sugar and water. Bring to a boil, then pass through a fine sieve and let cool.

Once cooled, transfer to an ice-cream maker and churn according to the manufacturer's instructions.

WHITE PEACH SORBET

MAKES APPROXIMATELY 1 PINT

white-flesh peaches	1 pound 2 ounces
superfine sugar	½ cup + 2 tablespoons
water	scant ¾ cup
lemon juice	1 tablespoon

Before you start, put the peaches into the fridge and chill to 39°F.

Put the sugar into a bowl. Heat the water in a pan to 140°F, then add to the sugar. Cover the bowl, put into the fridge, and chill to 39°F.

Pour the lemon juice into a container (use plastic or glass; do not use metal). It must be large enough to hold all of the remaining ingredients.

Leaving the skins on, juice the cold peaches and immediately pour the juice into the container of lemon juice to prevent the juice from oxidizing. This must be done just prior to churning.

Add the cold sugar syrup to the container, stir to combine, then transfer to an ice-cream maker and churn according to the manufacturer's instructions.

PEANUT BUTTER & CHOCOLATE TART

SINCE OPENING WE HAVE HAD A NUMBER OF LOVE AFFAIRS WITH ALL MANNER OF TRASHY CHOCOLATE CANDY BARS, SOME JUST WEEK-LONG FLINGS, OTHERS BECOMING LENGTHY AND FRUITFUL RELATIONSHIPS, AND SOME JUST TOO FILTHY AND WRONG TO REPEAT. JUST LIKE OUR "SNICKERS" MESS, THIS TART IS THE BEAUTIFUL LOVE-CHILD OF ONE OF THE MORE LONG-LIVED RELATIONSHIPS.

TRY GOING OVER THE SURFACE OF THE PORTIONED TART WITH A CHEF'S TORCH TO BRING BACK ITS FULL GLOSS.

SERVES 10 TO 12

butter	1 stick
hazelnuts	heaping ¼ cup
chocolate cookies (we use Oreos)	4¾ ounces
smooth peanut butter	scant 1 cup
superfine sugar	3½ tablespoons
Maldon sea salt	1 teaspoon
unsweetened chocolate (70% cocoa solids)	9 ounces
heavy cream	1 cup
clotted cream	scant ¼ cup
olive oil	1 tablespoon

Heat the oven to 400°F.

Melt 3 tablespoons of the butter in a pan. Add the nuts and cookies to a blender and blitz to a powder. Add the melted butter and combine. Press firmly and evenly into the bottom of a 10-inch loose-bottomed tart pan. Bake in the oven for 3 to 4 minutes, then remove and let set.

Put the peanut butter and sugar into a bowl. Melt the remaining butter in a pan, add to the bowl. Beat until thick and a ribbon is left behind in the mixture when you lift the beater up. Stir in the salt, then pour the mixture into the tart pan on top of the crust, and put it into the fridge to set.

Make a ganache by melting the chocolate in a heatproof bowl set over a pan of gently simmering water, making sure the base of the bowl does not touch the water. Remove from the heat, add the cream and clotted cream, and stir until smooth and glossy. Add the olive oil and stir again until shiny and emulsified. Pour the ganache evenly over the peanut butter layer and let cool, then refrigerate for 2 hours, or until set. Serve with Raspberry Sorbet (see page 271).

— RHUBARB & LEMON TART —

WHEN THE FORCED RHUBARB SEASON STARTS IN JANUARY WE GO A BIT CRAZY
IN THE RESTAURANT, WITH MESSES, PICKLES, JAMS, CHEESECAKES, TARTS,
SORBETS, AND BIG POACHING SESSIONS KEEPING THE PASTRY SECTION HAPPY.
THIS IS A CLASSIC LEMON TART GIVEN A RHUBARB MAKEOVER, AND MAKES FOR A
VERY CLEAN DESSERT AFTER SOME PIG.

SERVES 12

lemons	4
forced pink rhubarb	1 pound 2 ounces
superfine sugar	1½ cups
free-range eggs	9
heavy cream	1¼ cups
seeds from 1 vanilla bean	

TOPPING

unsalted butter	2½ sticks
powdered sugar, sifted	scant 2 cups
eggs, beaten	2
all-purpose flour	4½ cups

First, make the pastry. Beat the butter and powdered sugar in a mixing bowl until just beginning to come together. Mix in the eggs slowly, until thoroughly combined, scraping down the sides of the bowl as you go.

Carefully add half of the flour and mix to a smooth paste, making sure not to overmix, then add the remaining flour and mix gently until a light dough is formed.

Seal the dough in plastic wrap and chill for at least 2 hours before using.

Finely grate the zest of the lemons directly into a large bowl and set aside. Juice the lemons and set aside a scant ¾ cup of juice.

Put the rhubarb through a centrifugal juicer and set aside a scant ¾ cup of juice.

Place the rhubarb pulp, the leftover rhubarb juice, the leftover lemon juice, and ¼ cup of the superfine sugar in a small pan. Cook down gently over low heat for 10 to 15 minutes to make a rhubarb compote as thick and as dry as possible, trying not to let it stick to the bottom of the pan. Set aside.

Roll out the pastry on a lightly floured surface as thinly as possible. Use it to line the bottom and sides of a 10-inch loose-bottomed tart pan. Place the crust in the fridge for 10 minutes to firm up.

Meanwhile, heat the oven to 400°F.

Line the crust with waxed paper and fill with baking beans. Blind bake for 15 minutes, or until the edges just start to color. Remove the paper and beans and bake for a further 5 minutes, or until the bottom of the crust is dry. Remove from the oven and reduce the temperature to 260°F.

Spread a thin layer of rhubarb compote evenly over the crust and flatten.

Add the eggs to the bowl containing the lemon zest, then whisk together with the remaining superfine sugar, cream, vanilla seeds, and reserved lemon and rhubarb juices. Pour this mixture carefully into the crust on top of the rhubarb compote layer. Bake in the oven for 40 minutes, or until just set. Let cool and fully set before serving.

STICKY BOURBON — & COLA PUDDING —

SERVES 12

dates, pitted and chopped	9 ounces
prunes, pitted and chopped	9 ounces
cola	3¼ cups
unsalted butter	1½ sticks
maple or light Muscovado sugar	1¾ cups
large free-range eggs	4
all-purpose flour	5 cups
baking powder	2½ tablespoons
baking soda	2 teaspoons
Maldon sea salt	1 teaspoons

BOURBON CARAMEL SAUCE

milk chocolate	3½ ounces
unsalted butter	2 sticks
maple or light Muscovado sugar	1¾ cups
heavy cream	1 cup
Maldon sea salt	¾ teaspoon
bourbon	⅓ cup

BASED ON STICKY TOFFEE PUDDING, A QUINTESSENTIAL BRITISH DESSERT, THIS RECIPE GRACIOUSLY BASTARDIZES IT WITH A NOT-SO-GRACIOUS DOSE OF BOURBON AND COLA.

NO MATTER WHAT DESSERTS ARE ON THE MENU, THIS HAS THE KNACK OF OUTSELLING THEM. IT'S STICKY TOFFEE PUDDING IN OVERDRIVE, JUST TOO MUCH OF A TEMPTATION FOR ANYONE WHO HAS EVER HAD A MOMENT WITH, OR FALLEN COMPLETELY FOR, A STICKY TOFFEE PUDDING IN THEIR LIFE.

FOR THIS RECIPE YOU WILL NEED A 10- OR 12-INCH SPRINGFORM CAKE PAN, LINED WITH WAXED PAPER SO THAT NONE OF THE PRECIOUS SAUCE CAN LEAK OUT.

Line a 10- or 12-inch springform cake pan with waxed paper.

To make the bourbon caramel sauce, put the chocolate, butter, and sugar into a pan and heat gently until melted. Remove from the heat and whisk in the cream, salt, and bourbon. Pour some of the sauce into the bottom of the pan and chill it in the fridge for 20 minutes. Set aside the rest of the sauce and keep warm.

Put the chopped dates and prunes into a pan with the cola and simmer over low heat for 5 minutes. Meanwhile, using an electric stand mixer, beat together the butter and Muscovado sugar. Mix in the eggs gradually, followed by the flour and baking powder. Add the baking soda and salt to the hot date and prune mix, then add the mixture to the batter.

Heat the oven to 340°F.

Pour the batter into the chilled pan, then bake in the oven for 40 minutes, or until risen and just cooked through.

Remove from the oven and make holes in the crust of the pudding with a skewer. Heat a little more sauce and pour it evenly over the top, then return the pudding to the oven for 5 minutes.

Invert the pudding onto a deep serving dish and serve with more of the sauce and clotted cream or ice cream.

BOURBON BABA

ORIGINALLY A SOBER AND DRY POLISH CAKE, IN THE EARLY NINETEENTH CENTURY THE BABA MADE ITS WAY TO FRANCE WHERE PÂTISSIERS INTRODUCED IT TO SYRUPS AND GLAZES, AND THE "BABA AU RHUM" OR "RUM BABA" WAS BORN. IT IS NOW A FRENCH CLASSIC, AND THE SAVARIN DOUGH WITH WHICH IT IS MADE IS A FUNDAMENTAL OF FRENCH PÂTISSERIE. THIS RECIPE OMITS THE BOOZY SOAKED FRUITS THAT OFTEN APPEAR IN RUM BABAS AND TRADES IN RUM FOR BOURBON. IF FOR SOME REASON BOURBON DOES NOT TURN YOU ON, USE RUM. BABAS CAN BE TRICKY LITTLE THINGS TO GET RIGHT.

MAKES 8

all-purpose flour	1 cup
salt	pinch
dried active yeast	1 teaspoon
eggs	3
maple syrup	2 teaspoons
unsalted butter, melted	⅓ cup

SYRUP

maple syrup	scant 1 cup
water	scant ½ cup
vanilla bean, split	1
bourbon	scant ½ cup
finely grated zest and juice of 1 lemon	
finely grated zest and juice of 1 orange	
finely grated zest and juice of 1 lime	

GLAZE

apricot conserve	⅓ cup
water	1 tablespoon

In a large mixing bowl, mix together the flour, salt, yeast, eggs, and maple syrup, then beat for 5 minutes, or until the mixture becomes a smooth batter. Pour the melted butter slowly into the batter in a fine stream, beating to fully incorporate. Continue to beat for another 5 minutes, until the savarin dough is completely smooth and free of any lumps. Leave the dough in the mixing bowl, covered, for 45 minutes, until doubled in size.

Knock back the dough. (When you first make a batch, the dough will probably seem far too wet—don't be tempted to add flour when knocking back the dough after it proves, because it can result in an overly "cakey" baba that will please nobody.) Transfer to a piping bag and divide the batter between eight dariole molds, putting approximately 1 ounce into each one. The molds need be no more than half full, because the dough will rise. Let prove at room temperature for 30 to 45 minutes, until the dough has doubled in size again. It will be bulging at this stage.

Heat the oven to 350°F and bake the babas for 12 to 15 minutes, or until golden brown. Once baked, remove them from the molds and let cool.

To make the syrup, put all syrup ingredients into a pan and bring to a boil. Reduce to a simmer for 15 minutes, then remove from the heat and let cool slightly for 20 minutes.

Add the babas to the syrup, turning them over to make sure they are evenly coated. Remove them from the syrup and refrigerate on a wire rack until needed.

To make the apricot glaze, put the apricot conserve into a small pan with the water and warm through, stirring. To serve, brush the babas evenly with the glaze, then serve in a few more tablespoons of the syrup with ice cream and poached fruits.

SMOKED PEACHES

WHEN BEAUTIFULLY RIPE PEACHES ARE COOKED LIKE THIS, THEY NEED VERY LITTLE HELP. IF COOKED WELL THE SKINS PEEL OFF WITH BARELY ANY EFFORT AT ALL, WHICH IN ITSELF MAKES THE WHOLE THING WORTHWHILE—SUCH IS THE SATISFACTION OF A PERFECTLY NAKED PEACH! WE SERVED THEM AS IS, BUT WHEN WE DISCOVERED PIMM'S SORBET WE COULD THINK OF NO BETTER PARTNER FOR IT THAN A WARM, SMOKED PEACH. VERY LITTLE SMOKE IS NEEDED FOR THIS RECIPE; JUST A HINT IS ALL YOU WANT.

SERVES 4

ripe peaches	4
Maldon sea salt	pinch

Prepare a barbecue for direct grilling over medium heat—around 300°F is best—and add a small handful of wood chunks (see page 112). Place a sheet of buttered paper on the grill, butter-side up, then arrange the peaches on top and close the lid. Cook for 20 minutes, until the peaches are just soft to the touch.

Remove the peaches from the barbecue and let cool for 5 minutes. The skin should peel off without much effort, though the very bottom of the peach may need to be removed with a knife, because the skin on the surface touching the butter paper is less forgiving.

Serve the peaches with a pinch of sea salt and Pimm's Sorbet (see below).

PIMM'S SORBET

MAKES APPROXIMATELY 1 PINT

good-quality lemonade	1¾ cups
mint leaves	10
superfine sugar	scant 1 cup
juice of ½ a large orange	
juice of ½ a large lemon	
cucumber, juiced	¾-inch piece
fresh strawberries, quartered	2
Pimm's	scant ½ cup

Put the lemonade into a large pan and add the mint leaves. Heat slowly over low heat to 104°F, then add the sugar. Stir until the sugar has completely dissolved, then remove from the heat.

Add the orange juice, lemon juice, cucumber juice, and strawberries to the lemonade mixture. Let the mixture cool to 39°F in the refrigerator. When cold, remove the mint leaves and strawberries, then transfer to an ice-cream maker and churn according to the manufacturer's instructions. After 4 minutes, add the Pimm's and continue to churn until the sorbet is frozen.

INDEX

Bold page numbers indicate the main recipe.

A

Adams, Tom   10
Amaretto   32, 55
anchovies
  butter   220
  hollandaise   **174**, 223
  pickled   80-1
  with broccoli rabe   221
  salad cream   99, 176, **205**
  smoked   74
Anderson, Simon   13, 188
apple
  dressing   205
  fennel, watercress, and radish salad   206-7
  ketchup   **126**, 152
  nasturtium & tomato salad   208
  toffee apple grunt   262-3
Applejack brandy   34, 38
Argentina   10
asador   10

B

baba, bourbon   278-9
bacon
  baked beans   239
  Hog Mac 'n' Cheese   235
  Hog 'n' hominy   236
  lardons   217
  Pitt Cue   144
  in porger sausage   155
  smoked bacon rub   119, 148, 235
  with sprout tops   220
  vodka   50
baked beans   129, **238-9**
banoffee mess   248-9
barbecue jelly   121
barbecue mayo   136, 138, 141, 143, 159
barbecues
  cooking time   116, 117
  direct cooking/grilling   112-13, 117
  equipment   116, 117
  evolution/spread   9, 10
  fuel   114
  indirect cooking   113-17
  setting up   114-15

  temperature control   114, 115, 117
barbecue sauce   72, 101, 122, 129, 136, 140, 158, 168, 174, 175, 199, 239
b****** hot sauce   90, **125**
beef
  brisket, smoked   156-7, 158, 159, 239
  brisket buns   159
  burnt ends (brisket)   143, 158, 159, 228
  cuts   111
  cuts for grilling   113
  cuts for smoking   113-14
  Denver cut, slow-grilled (chuck)   160-1
  dry-aging   107
  featherblade   162-3
  genetics/feed   105, 106
  hot guts sausage   154-5
  in porger sausage   155
  rib roast, smoked standing   164-5
  ribs   168-9
  rub   **118**, 160, 164
beer
  the Boilermaker   23
  Boom Town   48
  mean shandy   45
beets
  pickled   78, 194
  pickled eggs   86-7
  in red slaw   199
Berger, Jamie   10, 21
Big Mac 'n' Rye   26
blackberries   252-3, 262
Bloomfield, April   7
the Boilermaker   23
bone marrow
  lamb marrow with anchovy   74-5
  mash   228
  trencher   164, 166
  whipped   228, 239
Boom Town   48
bourbon
  baba   278-9
  caramel sauce   248, 251, 276
  and cola pudding   276-7
  history   20-1
  old-fashioned jelly   260
  see also drinks
Bourboroni   40
Boxer, Jackson   55

bread
  dripping trencher   164, 166
  jalapeño & sour cream cornbread   242
  London Bath buns   132, 136, 138, 141, 143, 180, **240**
  potato rolls   129, 132, 135, 136, 138, 141, 143, 159, 163, 180, **240**
  toast   72-3, 94-5
bread and butter pickles   136, 138, 141, 143, 159, **191**
broccoli rabe   221
brownies   251
butter, anchovy   220
Buzz cut   34

C

cabbage
  burnt pointed, with garlic   222
  kimchi   129, 132, **214**
  see also slaws
Camp America   40
Campari-based cocktails   40-1
capers   172, 175, **193**, 208
caramel
  bourbon caramel sauce   248, 251, **276**
  salted caramel ice cream   269
carrots
  mead braised lettuce & onions   217
  in mustard slaw   202
  pickled   **195**, 210, 213
caviar & pulled duck buns   180-1
celery, pickled   90, **194**
Chambord   37
charcoal   112, 114, 115, 117
cheeks, ox   72-3
cheese
  Cheddar   235, 242
  cream   257
  curd   66, 90, 198
  goat   87
  Gruyère   235
  Hog Mac 'n'   234-5
  Ogleshield   68-9, 235
  sauce   235, 236
  Stichelton   235
  Stilton   66, 235
  Tunworth   218

cheesecakes, orange & chocolate 256–7
cherries
  Cherry Cola 46
  and lemon possets 259
  maraschino jelly 260
  pickled 77, 182, 197
Cherry Heering 46
chicken
  apricot & green chile wings 92
  chipotle & maple wings 93
  deviled chicken buns 178
  hot wings 90–1
  kimchi hot wings 92
  master chicken brine **90**, 92, 93, 145
  skin, with deviled eggs 98–9
  whole spicy smoked roast 176–7
  wings in gravy 130
  wings with mead-braised lettuce 217
chimney starter 115, 117
chipotle
  chile paste 176
  and confit garlic slaw 198
  ketchup 122, **125**, 130
  and maple chicken wings 93
  mayonnaise 198
chocolate
  brownies 251
  frosting 266
  and orange cheesecakes 256–7
  and peanut butter tart 272–3
  "Snickers" mess 250–1
cider
  in Mapple 38
  sour 33
  vinegar 57, 78, 191, 196, 204, 205
cocktails see drinks
Cointreau 34, 37, 38, 42
cola
  and bourbon pudding 276–7
  syrup 45, 46, 48, **56**
collagen 108, 113, 116
combread, jalapeño & sour cream 242
corn on the cob 224–5
cow see beef
crackers, saltine 96–7
crubeen, pulled pig's head 132–3
corn
  corn on the cob 224–5
  Hog 'n' hominy 236
cucumber
  bread and butter pickles **191**
  and pickled watermelon salad 212–13
  Cue Jumper 27
  curd cheese 66, 90, 198

custard, whipped **254**
  in banoffee mess 248
  mess with fruit 252–3

D

dates, sticky bourbon & cola pudding 276
desserts 244–81
  bourbon baba 278–9
  brownies 251
  doughnuts 264–7
  iced 268–71, 280
  lemon & cherry possets 258–9
  messes 248–55
  old-fashioned gelatin 260
  orange & chocolate cheesecakes 256–7
  puddings 262–3, 276–7
  smoked peaches 281
  tarts 272–5
Devil dip gravy 129, **130**, 143, 145, 159, 164
deviled eggs 87, 98–9
deviled pigs' feet 132, **145**
direct cooking 112–13, 117
doughnuts 264–7
dressings 204–6, 208, 210, 213
drinks
  Big Mac 'n' Rye 26
  the Boilermaker 23
  Boom Town 48
  bourbon 20–1
  bourbon hot toddy 53
  Bourboroni 40
  Buzz cut 34
  Camp America 40
  Campari-based cocktails 40–1
  Cherry Cola 46
  Cider sour 33
  Cue Jumper 27
  French toast 37
  the Ganton 34
  Godfather 55
  Hair of the Hog 50
  hard lemonade 42
  Indian Summer 37
  the J-Dawg 26
  Kentucky libre 45
  LBC 41
  lemonade syrup 42, 45
  Manhattans 24–7
  Mapple 38
  mean shandy 45
  New Port sour 31
  New York sour 31

  the Pickleback 23
  Pink Pig 50
  Pitt Pony 48
  Red Rye 27
  the Side Truck 38
  Soho sour 32
  sours 29–39
  Trash 46
  whiskey sour 29
drippings 108
dripping trencher 164, 166
dry-aging 107
dry cure 62, **119**, 144
duck
  giblet sausages 182–3
  and hominy hash 230–1
  pulled, and caviar buns 180–1
  rub 77, **118**, 179, 182
  smoked livers 70–1
  whole smoked 179

E

ears, habanero pigs' 64–5
eggs
  beet-pickled 86–7
  deviled, with roast chicken skin 98
  deviled beet-pickled 87
equipment 116, 117
ethical concerns 15–16, 77, 106

F

fat, pork 104, 105, 107–8
feet, deviled pigs' 132, **145**
fennel
  apple, watercress, and radish salad 206–7
  nasturtium & tomato salad 208
Fernet Branca 27
foie gras 70, 77
French toast cocktail 37
frosting, chocolate 266
fruit
  and chocolate cheesecakes 257
  ketchup **126–7**, 151
  lemon & cherry possets 258–9
  old-fashioned gelatin 260–1
  pickled 196–7
  Pimm's mess 255
  with whipped custard mess 252–3

G

the Ganton   34
gin   42, 50
ginger syrup   33, 48, 53, **56**
goat cheese, beet-pickled eggs   87
the Godfather   55
goose livers, foie gras   70, 77
Grandfield, Colin   26
Grand Marnier   257
gravy, Devil dip   129, **130**, 143, 145,
                                159, 164
green chile slaw   141, **203**
grill grate, cast iron   117
grilling
    direct cooking   112–13, 117
    maillard & drippings   108
    suitable cuts   113

H

habanero rub, pigs' ears   64–5
Hair of the Hog   50
hash, duck & hominy   230–1
Hog Mac 'n' Cheese   **138**, 235
Hog 'n' hominy   236
hominy   230–1, 236
honey syrup   53, **56**
horseradish   72, 194
hot sauce   66, 90, 92, 101, **124**, 132,
        136, 138, 141, 143, 159, 175, 199
hot toddy, bourbon   53
House Rub   66, 72, 92, 93, 101, **119**,
            129, 135, 138, 148, 157,
            168, 176, 184, 224
House sausage   **140–1**, 143

I / J / K

iced desserts
    peanut butter ice cream   251, **268**
    Pimm's sorbet   255, **280**
    prune and whiskey ice cream 260, **268**
    raspberry sorbet   270, 271
    salted caramel ice cream   269
    white peach sorbet   271
Indian Summer   37
indirect cooking   113

jalapeño & sour cream cornbread   242
Japan   10
jars, sterilizing   78
the J-Dawg   26

jelly
    barbecue   121
Kentucky   20, 45
Kentucky libre   45
ketchup
    chipotle   122, **125**, 130
    fruit   **126–7**, 151, 152
kimchi   129, 132, **214**
    hot sauce   92, 99, **124**, 199
    slaw   199

L

lamb
    hot ribs   175
    marrow with anchovy   74–5
    ribs, with molasses mop   170–1
    rub   **118**, 170, 172, 174, 175
    rump   172–3
    sausage casings   155
    see also mutton; sheep
    shoulder   151
lardo di Colonnata
    pumpkin home fries   232
    and rosemary mashed potatoes   228
LBC cocktail   41
leeks, burnt, with anchovy hollandaise 223
lemon
    and cherry possets   258–9
    and rhubarb tart   274–5
lemonade
    hard   42
    syrup   42, 45
lettuce
    Boston Bibb, and herb salad 129, 209
    grilled baby gems   224–5
    grilled red onion & baby gem salad
                                170, 171
    Iceberg salad   160, 176, **210**
    mead braised, carrots & onions   217
    see *also* salads; slaws
liver
    foie gras   70, 77
    smoked duck   70–1
London Bath buns   132, 136, 138, 141,
                        143, 180, **240**

M

macaroni, deep-fried   138
mackerel, pickled   80–1, 190
maillard   108, 117
Mangalitza pigs   105, 106, 108

Manhattans   24–7
Mapple   38
marmalade   40
marshmallows   252, 254, **254**, 259
mashed potatoes   226, 228
master chicken brine   **90**, 92, 93, 145
mayonnaise
    barbecue   **136**, 138, 141, 143, 159
    chipotle   198
    nduja   232
mead
    braised lettuce, carrots & onions 217
    and pear ketchup   127
    salad dressing   **204**, 206, 208
meat
    collagen   108, 113, 116
    cuts   109–11
    dry-aging   107
    fat   104, 105, 107–8
    genetics/feed   104–5
    grilling   112–13
    maillard & drippings   108
    probes   116, 117
    pulled   132–9, 142–3, 180–1
    slaughtering/eating   9, 106
    smoking   113–17
    sourcing   15, 16, 104
meatloaf   140
meringues   **248**, 251, 252, 255
Middle White pigs   105, 106
molasses mop   170–1
Mother Sauce   69, **120**, 135, 136, 141,
            148, 158, 159, 168, 170,
            180, 184, 228, 239

mushrooms
    penny bun rub   119
    pickled shiitake   **88–9**, 163, 168
mustard slaw   202
mutton   106
    hot ribs   175
    rump   172
    shoulder   151
    shoulder, with anchovy hollandaise 173
    see also lamb; sheep

N / O

nasturtium
    leaves, in salad   208
    seeds, pickled   **193**, 208
nduja mayonnaise   232
New Port sour   31
New York sour   31
nuggets, oxtail & ogleshield   68–9

ocakbasi 10, 112, 170
onions
  grilled, in salad 171
  mead, braised lettuce & carrots 217
  in red slaw 199
orange & chocolate cheesecakes 256-7
ox cheek, on toast 72-3
oxtail & ogleshield nuggets 68-9
oysters, pickled 83

P

pâté, smoked livers 70-1, 197
peach
  ketchup 126
  smoked 280
  white peach sorbet 271
peanut butter
  and chocolate tart 272-3
  ice cream 251, **268**
pears
  and mead ketchup 127
  Pimm's mess 255
penny bun rub **119**
the Pickleback 23
pickle brine 78, 184, 190, 193
  as drink 23, 26, 74
pickles 188, 190-7
  beet 78, **194**
  beet eggs 86-7
  bread and butter 136, 138, 141, 143,
    159, 191
  carrots **195**, 210, 213
  celery 90, **194**
  cherries 77, 182, **197**
  fruit 196-7
  plums/sloe berries 193
  pomegranate 27, 170-1, 182, **197**
  poor man's capers 193
  seafood 80-3, 190
  shiitake **88-9**, 163, 168
  vegetables 78
  watermelon rind **196**, 213
  wieners 84-5
pig/pork
  belly chops 146-7
  the Big Ode 142-3
  buffalo pigs' tails 66-7
  cuts 109
  cuts for grilling 113
  cuts for smoking 113-14
  deviled pigs' feet 132, **145**
  dry-aging 107
  farming our own 16, 104, 105, 106

genetics/feed 104-6
habanero pigs' ears 64-5
hot rib tips 100-1, 148
House sausage 140-1, 143
pig pickin's 9
porger sausage 155
pork chop 152-3
pork fat 104, 105, 107-8
pork shoulder 150-1
pulled pig's head crubeens 132-3
pulled pork bun **136-7**, 138, 143
pulled pork shoulder **134-5**, 210
ribs 148-9
rub **118**, 132, 198
scratchings, fennel 62-3
slaughtering/eating 9, 10, 106
suckling pig 128-9
  see also bacon; meat
Pimm's mess 255
Pimm's sorbet 255, **280**
pineapple & chile ketchup 127
Pink Pig 50
Pitt Cue
  formation 10, 13
  popularity growth 13
  Soho restaurant 13, 112, 188, 244
  trailer 60, 112, 138, 164, 184
Pitt Pony 48
plums
  pickled 193
  in whipped custard mess 252
pomegranate, pickled 197
  with duck giblet sausages 182
  juice 27, 197
  red onion & baby gem salad 170, 171
popovers 164, **243**
pork *see* pig
port 31
potatoes
  duck & hominy hash 230-1
  mashed 226, 228
  potato rolls 129, 132, 135, 136, 138,
    141, 143, 159, 163, 180, **240**
  pumpkin home fries 232
  skins 226, 227
  sweet 231
prunes
  pickled 182
  sticky bourbon & cola pudding 276
  in toffee apple grunt 262
  and whiskey ice cream 260, **268**

pulled meat
  the Big Ode 142-3
  duck & caviar buns 180-1
  pig's head crubeens 132-3
  pork bun 136-7, 138, 143
  pork shoulder 134-5
  trailer trash 138-9
pumpkin home fries 160, **232**

Q / R

quail, smoked 184-5

radish 206
raspberry
  sorbet 270, 271
  whipped custard mess 252
recipes, researching/developing 13, 15
Red Rye 27
red wine 31
restaurant
  equipment 112, 188, 244
  opens in Soho 13
rhubarb
  and lemon tart 274-5
  syrup 50
  in whipped custard mess 252
ribs
  beef 168-9
  belly chops 146-7
  dry-aged 107
  hot mutton 175
  hot rib tips 100-1, 148
  lamb 170-1
  pork 148-9
robatayaki 10
rubs
  bacon 119, 148, 235
  beef 118, 160, 164
  dry cure 62, **119**, 144
  duck 77, **118**, 179, 182
  house 66, 72, 92, 93, 101, **119**,
    129, 135, 138, 148, 157,
    168, 176, 184, 224
  lamb **118**, 170, 172, 174
  penny bun **119**
  pork 118, 132, 198
rum 26
rye whiskey 21, 24, 26, 27, 34, 37

S

salad cream, anchovy 99, 176, **205**

salads
    apple, fennel, watercress & radish 206–7
    cucumber & pickled watermelon 212–13
    dressings 204–5, 206, 208, 210, 213
    grilled   170, 188
    kimchi   129, 132, **214**
    nasturtium & tomato   208
    pickled carrot   210
    see also lettuce; slaws
salt, dry cure   **119**, 144
salted caramel ice cream   269
saltine crackers   96–7
sauce
    anchovy hollandaise   **173**, 223
    barbecue   72, 101, **122**, 129, 136,
        140, 158, 168, 174, 175, 199, 239
    barbecue mayo **136**, 138, 141, 143, 159
    b****** hot   90, **125**
    bourbon caramel   248, 251, **276**
    cheese   235, 236
    chipotle ketchup   122, **125**, 130
    hot   66, 90, 92, 101, **124**, 132,
        136, 138, 141, 143, 159, 175, 199
    kimchi hot   92, 99, **124**, 199
    Mother   69, **120**, 135, 136, 141,
                148, 158, 159, 168, 170,
                180, 184, 228, 239
    Southern states   10
    Stilton   66
sausage
    bun   141
    duck giblet   182–3
    hot guts   154–5
    House sausage   140–1, 143
    meat   129, 155
    porger   155
scallops, pickled   82
scratchings, fennel-cured   62–3
seafood, pickled   80–3
shallots & tomatoes on toast   94–5
shandy, mean   45
sheep
    cuts   110
    cuts for grilling   113
    cuts for smoking   113–14
    husbandry   106
    see also lamb; mutton
shiitake, pickled   **88–9**, 163, 168
shortcakes   248
shrimp
    jarred salted   214
    pickled   82
side dishes   188–243
    bread/rolls   240–3

hot vegetable   217–39
pickles   192–7
salads   204–14
slaws   198–203
the Side Truck   38
slaws   188, 198–203
    chipotle & confit garlic slaw   198
    green   202
    green chile   141, **203**
    kimchi   199
    mustard   202
    red   199
    vinegar   136, 143, 159, **203**
    see also salads
sloe berries
    pickled   193
    in whipped custard mess   252
smoker, arrival   10, 13
smoking   112–17
    cooking time   15, 116, 117
    heat source   114
    history   9
    setting up   114–15
    suitable cuts   113–14
    temperature control   115, 117
snacks   60–101
"Snickers" mess   250–1
Soho sour   32
sorbet   255, 271, 280
sours   29–39
Spain, barbecues   9, 10, 112
spice mix   50, **57**, 122
sprout tops   220
Stilton   66, 235
strawberries   252, 255
suckling pig   128–9
sugar syrup 29, 31, 32, 34, 37, 38, 50, **56**
sweet potatoes   231
syrups   56, 278

toffee apple grunt   262–3
tomatoes
    and nasturtium salad   208
    sauce   239
    and shallots on toast   94–5
    tomato juice   50
trailer
    early days   60, 112
    menu   138, 164, 184
    opening   13
Trash cocktail   46
trencher, bone marrow   164, 166
trotters, deviled   132, **145**
Tuaca   55
turkey, butter confit wings   93
Turkish barbecues   10, 112, 170
Turner, Richard   13

U / V / W / Z

United States of America
    barbecue history   9
    history of bourbon   20–1
    Prohibition   21, 27
    South, the   9–10, 13, 20, 122, 157, 188

vegetables   217–39
    see also pickles; salads; slaws
vermouth
    red   26, 27
    sweet   24, 40
vinegar
    as drink   23, 26, 74
    pickle brine   78, 184, 190, 193
    slaw   136, 143, 159, **203**
vodka, bacon   50

walnuts, pickled   72
watercress   206
watermelon
    pickled, and cucumber salad   212–13
    pickled rind   **196**, 213
water trays   115, 117
whiskey   20–1
    and prune ice cream   260, **268**
    sour   29
    see also bourbon
White Dog Mash   20, 34
wieners, pickled   84–5
wood   114, 117

zucchini, grilled, with Tunworth   218–19

T

tails
    buffalo pigs'   66–7
    oxtail & ogleshield nuggets   68–9
Tamworth pigs   14, 105, 106
tart
    peanut butter & chocolate   272–3
    rhubarb & lemon   274–5
tea brine   178
temperature control   115, 117
toast
    burnt tomatoes & shallots   94–5
    smoked ox cheek   72–3

ACKNOWLEDGMENTS

As with anything that grows from nothing, Pitt Cue has relied on a lot of luck and a lot of help. We are incredibly fortunate to have amazing people involved in Pitt Cue and to have had so many people support us when we first started. The team in Soho have put up with one of the smallest restaurants known to man and played a huge part in creating the recipes in this book, especially Fran, Thea, Neil, Swanny, and Chris, all of whom have been integral in bringing it to fruition. Looking back from when we first decided to buy a trailer there are a ridiculous number of people who should take credit for where we are now:

The Adams clan in Pitt for absolute awesomeness on all fronts: Mother Adams for putting up with lots of hairy pigs at home. Georgie Adams, Pitt Cue's first employee and creator of beautiful illustrations. And to Augustus, Empress, Bacon Head, and Juno: Pitt's finest pigs.

Robbie Bargh for making the introductions to get us that first pitch on the South Bank.

Charlie, Frank, and Jackson Boxer for the idea, inspiration, and support, and for housing the trailer, the smoker, Tom, Georgie, and Jamie.

Sam Burge, one of the few people as white as Tom, for looking after the pigs in Pitt and babysitting the trailer all winter long.

Matt Chatfield for huge dedication to bringing Cornish produce and Warrens Butchers to London, and for being very Cornish: a food hero.

Jonathan Downey for making shit happen all summer long, and bringing the vibes.

David Ezrine for constant egg supply, showing us the importance of "no peeking" and more awesomeness. Hater of flan.

Hawksmoor for giving Richard freedom to pursue outside interests.

Peder Henriksson. There from before the start: the bearded Swede—scourge of the Baltic.

Anne Hynes for understanding barbecue and allowing us to be part of the Festival of Britain 60th Anniversary celebrations.

Nick Kelvin for bringing brilliant smokers to London.

Jeremy Lee for kisses and fondles.

Sean O'Neil at Keveral Farm for being an all-round legend and growing things we never knew existed. James George, for putting up with lots of shit, helping us all the way, and being a general geezer. Dermot, for putting up with even more shit than James on a daily basis.

Erica Page for her blackboard writing skills and for putting up with Simon.

Barry Skarin for whipping us all into shape, a fountain of knowledge and reassurance. We'd be going backward if it weren't for your bollockings.

Andy and Lee Stevens for their investment and support in getting Soho off the ground.

The team at Speciality—Raj, Nic & Adriano—for keeping us awash with bourbon from Day One.

The whole gang at Warrens Butchers in Launceston, Cornwall. Especially Phillip Warren, Ian Warren, and Rhea Warren, the collective "Meat Bible" of Cornwall, for putting up with some ridiculous requests and rearing some beautiful animals. You guys have taught us so much in such a short space of time and continue to set the precedent. We owe so much to you.

Zeren Wilson, the walking restaurant guide and bible of wine. There from the start, the catalyst.

Paul Winch-Furness for beautiful photos and questionable shirts.

Charlie Hart, Cornish Pig Lord.

Pitt Cue Co. Cookbook

By

Tom Adams, Simon Anderson, Jamie Berger, and Richard H. Turner

An Hachette UK Company
www.hachette.co.uk

First published in Great Britain in 2013 by Mitchell Beazley,
an imprint of Octopus Publishing Group Ltd,
Endeavour House, 189 Shaftesbury Avenue, London WC2H 8JY
www.octopusbooks.co.uk
www.octopusbooksusa.com

Distributed in the US by Hachette Book Group USA
237 Park Avenue, New York, NY 10017 USA

Distributed in Canada by Canadian Manda Group
165 Dufferin Street, Toronto, Ontario, Canada M6K 3H6

Publisher Stephanie Jackson

Deputy art director Yasia Williams-Leedham

Jacket and book design Samuel Muir

Photographer Paul Winch-Furness (except page 16 middle right and 17 center Thomas Bowles)

Illustrations Georgie Adams (except page 116 Samuel Muir)

Senior editor Sybella Stephens

Assistant production manager Lucy Carter

ISBN: 978 1 84533 907 4

Printed and bound in China

Simon

Tom

Richard

Jamie

Pitt
—Cue—
co.

1 Newburgh Street, Soho, London W1F 7RB

www.pittcue.co.uk

@PittCueCo